W. B. YEATS

English Literature

Editor
JOHN LAWLOR
*Professor of English Language and Literature
in the University of Keele*

W. B. YEATS

A CRITICAL INTRODUCTION

Balachandra Rajan

Senior Professor of English
at the University of Western Ontario

HUTCHINSON UNIVERSITY LIBRARY
LONDON

HUTCHINSON & CO (*Publishers*) LTD

3 Fitzroy Square, London W1

London Melbourne Sydney Auckland
Wellington Johannesburg Cape Town
and agencies throughout the world

First published 1965
Second edition 1969
Reprinted 1972

*The illustration on the cover and jacket shows
a portrait of Yeats by Augustus John. It is
reproduced by courtesy of the Trustees of the
National Portrait Gallery.*

*Printed in Great Britain by litho on smooth wove paper
by Anchor Press, and bound by Wm. Brendon,
both of Tiptree, Essex*

ISBN 0 09 075411 5 (cased)
0 09 075412 3 (paper)

Contents

ACKNOWLEDGEMENT

The author is most grateful to Mrs W. B. Yeats
and Messrs Macmillan & Co Ltd for permission
to quote from the work of W. B. Yeats.

Foreword

The volume of literature about Yeats has now reached mountainous proportions. This book adds little to the size of the mountain and does not greatly alter its shape. Its chief aim is to present a compact and reasonably comprehensive picture of Yeats' achievement and some of the means for an evaluation of that achievement. To this end both the poems and plays have been examined, some of Yeats' critical ideas have been briefly discussed and the System has been given such attention as it deserves.

In contrast to some recent studies of Yeats this book regards Yeats as a writer firmly and centrally in the tradition of English poetry whose concern is with the fundamental patterns of human experience, whatever may be his means of approach to these patterns. Yeats' achievement cannot but be diminished by attempts to regard him as primarily a metaphysical Irish nationalist, a neo-Platonic mystic, an occultist, a symbolist, a nostalgic aristocrat, an exponent of the magic world-view, or as anything less than a poet of the human condition. It is because of the depth and inescapable relevance of his concerns that he is successful in creating a language both eloquently public and authentically personal.

My debts to other Yeatsians are sometimes too fundamental to be stated, but I have tried to acknowledge them as far as is possible in a book of these dimensions and in the process to give some indication of the findings of current Yeats scholarship. Space has not permitted my disagreements to be fully reasoned but I hope the reasons are implied in the point of view I have attempted to develop. References to authors are to the works in the Reading List under the author's name; when the author is not listed the references are to Nos 43 and 95 in the Reading List.

7

Exchange restrictions limit severely the resources available for English scholarship in India. This book, written largely in India, is of course not the better for such restrictions.

B.R.

Madison, 1965

The Reality Within

The Two Trees, a poem in the second collection that Yeats published, begins as follows:

> Beloved, gaze in thine own heart,
> The holy tree is growing there;
> From joy the holy branches start,
> And all the trembling flowers they bear. (*CP*, p. 54)

Nearly fifty years later Yeats ends a very different poem, *The Circus Animals' Desertion*, as follows:

> I must lie down where all the ladders start,
> In the foul rag-and-bone shop of the heart. (*CP*, p. 392)

The lines, with their characteristic mixture of self-respect and self-contempt, define both the dramatic difference between Yeats' earlier and later poetry and the deep continuity which underlies the difference. The reader of Yeats must keep firmly in mind these two aspects of the poet's achievement. He must decline to see the later poetry as a disowning of the earlier and he must also be reluctant to see it as the mere reformation of what has already been said, the throwing away of an embroidered cloak. Thus, in *The Countess Cathleen*, the tree grows like the 'holy tree' from the heart, but it is fundamentally not a tree of joy but of protest, imagined in terms that approach the hyperbolical:

> I have sworn,
> By her whose heart the seven sorrows have pierced,
> To pray before this altar until my heart
> Has grown to Heaven like a tree, and there
> Rustled its leaves till Heaven has saved my people. (*CPl*, p. 27)

In *A Prayer for my Daughter* the tree is again seen in the interior landscape:

> May she become a flourishing hidden tree
> That all her thoughts may like the linnet be,
> And have no business but dispensing round
> Their magnanimities of sound. (*CP*, p. 213)

This particular tree, however, has also exterior and social roots:

> How but in custom and in ceremony
> Are innocence and beauty born?
> Ceremony's a name for the rich horn,
> And custom for the spreading laurel tree. (*CP*, p. 214)

In *Vacillation*, written when Yeats' mind had grown closer to its complete poetic definition, the tree of the heart embodies the heart's complexity, the organic interdependence of both life-giving and destructive elements:

> A tree there is that from its topmost bough
> Is half all glittering flame and half all green
> Abounding foliage moistened with the dew;
> And half is half and yet is all the scene;
> And half and half consume what they renew. (*CP*, pp. 282–3)

In *Among School Children* the tree remains the holy tree but it grows differently in a different landscape:

> O chestnut-tree, great-rooted blossomer,
> Are you the leaf, the blossom or the bole?
> O body swayed to music, O brightening glance,
> How can we know the dancer from the dance? (*CP*, p. 245)

Kermode is, of course, right in suggesting that 'this image summarises the traditional Romantic critical analogy of art as organism' and in tracing the two trees back (like so many of Yeats' poetic possessions) to an antithesis of Blake: 'Art is the tree of life— Science is the tree of Death.' Nevertheless the image is obviously more than the embodiment of a theory of the artistic process. The massive stresses of 'chestnut-tree, great-rooted' (where even the hyphenation assists the poetic effort) set against the scintillating

movement of 'Are you the leaf, the blossom or the bole?' create an
equilibrium of energy and rootedness that continues to be meaningful outside the immediate situation or the traditional symbol. It is
tempting to point to the conclusion of Hindu philosophy that the
roots both of reality and of creative power, of stillness and motion,
lie within the self; but it is better to recognise simply that we are
dealing with poetry written at the full stretch of Yeats' powers.
Both the immediacy and the range of validity are part of the poem's
way of life and the fusion is of a kind that no other poet has
achieved in our time. These qualities of Yeats' writing will receive
further exploration later; at the moment it is sufficient to say that
the tree, even if it was Blake's tree in the first place, need no longer
be framed in Blake's antithesis. It is also not quite the tree of
'trembling flowers'; its branches 'start' not from straightforward
'joy' but from 'Beauty born out of its own despair' and, in one of
Yeats' daring and characteristic juxtapositions, from the 'blear-
eyed wisdom' of the labouring scholar. The imagery is not simply
more complex; its ability to live through its own irony makes it
more confident and robust and the product of a different imaginative
climate. Finally, the tree is not talked about but presented; it
represents, in other words, the difference between gesture and
experience.

Yeats was a poet who seldom threw anything away, but by
exploring the same symbols in different contexts he not only re-
considered but to some extent transformed them. 'Hammer your
thoughts into unity' was a principle that came into his head without
his willing it, before he had published his first volume, and the ex-
hortation ought to remind us that the totality of his work is shaped
as carefully as any individual poem. It is true that Yeats' account of
his development reveals, among other things, his talents as a mythmaker—the evolution on which he looks back is slightly too
inexorable to be real—but the invitation to locate his work within
the larger legend of his life is both irresistible and, if done with
judgement, rewarding. How basic the continuity of his work is, is
shown by the unexpected forms in which it is revealed. Thus when
Yeats wrote *To Ireland in the Coming Times*, the concluding poem of
The Rose, he presented his work as taking shape in the lamplight of
eternity:

For round about my table go
The magical powers to and fro
In flood and fire and clay and wind,
They huddle from man's pondering mind. (Revised text, *CP*, p. 57)

This is the earlier text in which the emphasis is on Yeats' war with
the abstract. In the version familiar to most of us the last two lines
in particular have been altered to express the doctrine of the great
mind and the great memory. This is, however, a point of incidental
importance. The real purpose of the quotation is to connect the
picture with that of the same poet, some forty years later, sitting at
a strikingly different table (*My Table*):

Two heavy trestles, and a board
Where Sato's gift, a changeless sword,
By pen and paper lies,
That it may moralise
My days out of their aimlessness. (*CP*, p. 227)

Here, it is the contrasts, the matter-of-fact tone and the specificity
of the second poem which command attention. It becomes necessary
to remember that Sato's sword is 'emblematical of love and war' and
a crucial symbol in the *Dialogue between Self and Soul*. The elemental questions are still present, still engaged in the immediate reality
which lies no further away than the width of a table. The furniture
of Yeats' mind may have changed, but the preoccupations, if not
constant, remain at least vitally connected.

In the same vein we may recall an occasion (noted by Ure) when
Yeats attended a spiritualist séance organised by MacGregor
Mathers. He was given a cardboard symbol and closed his eyes:
'there rose before me mental images that I could not control: a
desert and black Titan raising himself by his two hands from the
middle of a heap of ancient ruins'. Mathers explained that Yeats
had seen a being of the Order of Salamanders but the explanation
fortunately did not exorcise the image. In *Wheels and Butterflies*
Yeats tells us that about the time he began *On Baile's Strand* he
imagined 'as always at my left side, just out of the range of the sight,
a brazen winged beast that I associated with laughing ecstatic
destruction'. The wild beast with iron teeth and brazen claws in
Where There is Nothing which stands for 'Laughter, the mightiest of

the enemies of God' is descended from this animal, as are 'The uncontrollable mystery on the bestial floor' in *The Magi* and the 'rough beast' in *The Second Coming*. Melchiori, among others, has traced the evolution of this image but has failed to bring out the fact that the apocalyptic monster of *The Second Coming* has little to do with either laughter or ecstasy. Indeed its grim impressiveness arises at least partially from the stony indifference it brings to its historical function. Most readers will also feel that their response to the poem is unduly restricted by the knowledge that they are contemplating a being of the Order of Salamanders. Once again, both the sense of continuity and the awareness of difference have to be present in the attention the reader gives the poem.

The sharp division between the earlier and later Yeats, with its assumption that we are really dealing with two poets connected by little more than the same name, is now decidedly out of fashion. Instead, we have the proposition that the later Yeats is inherent in the earlier and critics have been busy hammering his thoughts into unity with even more assiduity than the poet himself. These swings of the pendulum recall a saying that Yeats took over from Blake and made his own: without contraries there can be no progression. The reader, if he is to progress in his understanding of Yeats' poetry, must take an intelligent position between contraries. Extreme advocates of the unity of Yeats sometimes argue that he spent his whole life writing the same poem (which if it were true would make his poetry unreadable) or that all his poems are part of the same metaphor (the metaphor, of course, is never defined). But continuity and difference, the redefinition and transformation of the past, are part of the process of organic growth and to concentrate only on the change or the sameness is to slight both the complexity and vitality of the process. In any case the difference between the earlier and later Yeats is at least the difference between the nineteenth and twentieth centuries and could not very well be less without diminishing his achievement as a poet. Even statements that Yeats was first and last a symbolist poet have to be accepted with some degree of caution. Yeats did say 'I have no speech but symbol' but he also said some years later:

> Players and painted stage took all my love
> And not those things that they were emblems of. (*CP*, p. 392)

This remark is made in self-reproach, but the fact remains that without its engrossment in a physical world Yeats' later poetry would lack its characteristic solidity. Yeats may declare that:

> the abstract joy
> The half-read wisdom of daemonic images
> Suffice the aged man as once the growing boy. (*CP*, p. 232)

but he also did not forget Blake's maxim that 'it is in particulars that wisdom consists', or his own sense of a mythology married 'to rock and hill' and of 'familiar woods and rivers' fading into symbol. The best of his poetry rests on a firm reconciliation of the immediate and the ultimate. To call such a marriage symbolist may be convenient but it is not necessarily profitable. Yeats' rhymes may 'more than their rhyming tell' but this is true of any poetry worth the writing and the use of a common label can only confuse the quite dramatic differences between such poems as *Sailing to Byzantium* and *He bids his Beloved be at Peace*.

To go back to the quotations which begin this chapter, there is, of course, a special inclusiveness in poetry which can accommodate at its centre both the holy tree and the foul rag-and-bone shop. Apart from this, it can be argued that Yeats is not saying anything particularly original, however Yeatsian the manner of his saying it. Dryden made it Shakespeare's special merit that he looked inwards in order to see nature. 'Fool, said my muse to me, look in thy heart and write' carries the doctrine back as far as Sidney and a slight investigation would certainly carry it back much further. In our own times Mr Eliot, though warning us that poetry is designed as an escape from personality, has advised us to look not only into the heart but into the cerebral cortex and digestive system. Yeats, incidentally, has made more effective use of this counsel than Mr Eliot and that is perhaps because in telling us that the holy tree grows in the heart he is not recommending anything as simple as sincerity. The essential self, the noumenal as against the phenomenal personality, is for him the core of reality and of creative power; it stands in opposition to the abstract, impersonal, external, scientific world (the terms of reprobation are more or less interchangeable) which is normally taken as the basis of reality. The position is clearly stated in his essay on 'First Principles':

... in the end the creative energy of men depends on their believing that they have, within themselves, something immortal and imperishable, and that all else is but an image in a looking glass. So long as that belief is not a formal thing a man will create out of a joyful energy, seeking little for any external test of an impulse that may be sacred and looking for no foundation outside life itself. (*The Irish Dramatic Movement*)

'Life' is evidently the inner, creative life, as is made clearer later in the essay:

We, who are believers, cannot see reality anywhere but in the soul itself, and seeing it there we cannot do other than rejoice in every energy, whether of gesture, or of action, or of speech, coming out of the personality, the soul's image.

The mannered prose suggests a mannered argument, but that the conclusion is fundamental to Yeats is apparent from the solidity it gives to his other comments. Remarks such as the following gain in purposefulness and weight if we see them as rooted in the personal principle:

We lose our freedom more and more as we get away from ourselves— because we have turned the table of value upside down and believe that the root of reality is not in the centre but somewhere in that whirling circumference. (*The Irish Dramatic Movement*)

The death of language, the substitution of phrases as nearly impersonal as algebra for words and rhythms varying from man to man, is but a part of the tyranny of impersonal things. (*The Well of the Saints*)

I know that revelation is from the self, but from that age-long memoried self, that shapes the elaborate shell of the mollusc and the child in the womb, that teaches the birds to make their nest; and that genius is a crisis that joins that buried self for certain moments to our trivial daily mind. (*Hodos Chameliontos.*)

Synge, like all of the great kin, sought for the race, not through the eyes, or in history, or even in the future, but where those monks found God, in the depths of the mind. (*J. M. Synge and the Ireland of His Time*)

I am orthodox and pray for a resurrection of the body, and am certain that a man should find his holy land where he first crept on the floor, and that familiar woods and rivers should fade into symbol. (*Discoveries*)

Even Yeats' favourite concept of the right aesthetic distance is put in terms of his theory of personality:

An art may become impersonal because it has too much circumstance or too little, because the world is too little or too much with it, because it is too near the ground or too far up among the branches. (*Discoveries*)

In the same way the distinction which Yeats took over from his father—'We make out of the quarrel with others, rhetoric, but of the quarrel with ourselves, poetry'—provides a contrast which is basic as well as striking. Conflict, to Yeats, is always the condition of life and the quarrel with one's self is the most fundamental conflict that is possible. The 'anti-self or the antithetical self' which is, so to speak, man's antagonist in this deepest of conflicts, therefore comes only 'to those who are no longer deceived, whose passion is reality'. So when Yeats asks elsewhere—'Why should we honour only those who die upon the field of battle? A man may show as desperate courage in venturing into the abyss of himself'—the slightly 'posed' quality of the declaration underlines the element of truth in it. Man's mind is a battlefield also, and to face and define the 'desolation of reality' one needs an honesty that is not more frequent than courage.

In 1937 Yeats wrote a 'General Introduction' to his works. The first section is entitled 'The First Principle' and the opening sentence is as follows:

A poet writes always of his personal life, in his finest work out of his tragedy, whatever it be, remorse, lost love, or mere loneliness;

In keeping with Yeats' newly kindled interest in Indian philosophy, the remark is buttressed with quotations from the *Prashna* and *Chandogya* Upanishads, the aim of which is to suggest that personality is fundamentally the same thing as the Upanishadic self.

Some blurring of distinctions is involved here. Yeats does not always firmly separate the personality or self which lives and suffers in the world from the ultimate self which is reality manifested, and, even when he makes the separation, he is inclined to treat the former as a way of approaching the latter. In Indian philosophy on the other hand, the phenomenal self is a configuration of attachment which must be abandoned for the ultimate self to be reached. The ego is *shed* in the process of attaining selfhood; it is not retrieved or even regenerated. Yeats' position is sometimes close to this; at other times it seems closer to Jungian conceptions of the collective unconscious. These complications, however, exist mainly to harass

the critic and philosopher; they do not prevent Yeats, with his tire-
less capacity for unification, from proceeding to what is both a
declaration of faith and his most comprehensive synthesis.

I was born into this faith, have lived in it, and shall die in it; My Christ,
a legitimate deduction from the Creed of St Patrick as I think, is that Unity
of Being Dante compared to a perfectly proportioned human body,
Blake's 'Imagination', what the Upanishads have named 'Self'; nor is this
unity distant and therefore intellectually understandable, but imminent,
differing from man to man and age to age, taking upon itself pain and
ugliness, 'eye of newt and toe of frog'.

A scholar might hesitantly ask whether Dante, Blake and the
Upanishads say quite the same thing and whether what they say can
be so confidently identified with legitimate deductions from the
Creed of St Patrick. It is perhaps more fruitful to remember Vico's
comment (which Yeats quotes with approval) that one should reject
all philosophy that does not begin in myth. What matters in this
passage is not its factual accuracy (the identifications in any case
may be less forced than one supposes) but the deep creative importance which Yeats attaches to self and the firm linking of the individual to the ultimate, so that unities which are personal and therefore creative (the two requirements are bound together for Yeats)
become in an important sense impersonal, in that they reflect the
unity of reality. Any such unity should be inclusive enough to take
in pain and ugliness (Eternal Beauty is significantly absent from this
synthesis) and it should be apparent that Yeats' poetic development
is basically a movement towards this openness and honesty. The
views he enunciates may be open to question as aesthetic theories
but for Yeats they are true and also far more than aesthetic truth.

In the end the poetry is the test. It is unquestionable that Yeats'
poetry is, nearly all of it, about himself; it is also unquestionable
that it is about a great deal more. The best of his work bears most
strongly his individual stamp but it is also impersonal ('Objective'
would be a better though not an ideal word), because it is a whole,
creating its own *raison d'être* and logic. Yet the poems, while complete in themselves, are also parts of a world and gain in significance
by being located in this world. Eliot, as early as 1932, had abandoned the rigidities of impersonality sufficiently to suggest that a
great poet acquires his additional significance because one feels his

work to be united 'by one significant, consistent and developing personality'. Though it is preferable to speak of a world than of a personality, there need be no doubt that the total work of any major writer forms a whole which is greater than the sum of its parts and that Eliot is right in making this test a specific measure of Yeats' achievement. More recently, Kenner and Unterecker have persuasively demonstrated that Yeats' *Collected Poems* ought to be read as an entity and that each poem gains in richness and significance by being set among the poems that surround it. The *Collected Poems* form a consciously shaped universe in which every poem has its place and is illuminated by the place it occupies. Each work contributes to the whole work; but the converse of this recognition is surely that each work has to be seen in its own individuality, its own achieved and largely sufficient life, if we are to see it correctly as part of the community which it helps to create.

To say this is not to unconditionally endorse Yeats' theories; one must remember that T. S. Eliot reached a comparable objectivity and built up a world of comparable cohesiveness from a critical position which is radically dissimilar. Whether significance is achieved by escaping from personality or by sinking through personality to the essential self below are choices of creative procedure which it is obviously unreasonable to prescribe. The primary concern should be with the achievement. If the manner in which it is reached has been described in some detail that is because a knowledge of the method enables us to assess the product more responsibly. For example, D. S. Savage's thesis that Yeats' poetic development was essentially a betrayal of the personal principle flies, despite its incidental perceptiveness, in the face of both theory and fact. Yeats' growth, on the contrary, is basically the record of his discovery of himself, the stripping away of distractions, the withering (which is ironically blossoming) into the truth, the resolute determination to speak only with his own voice. His poetry moves in an area which is deliberately restricted; but it moves in it with a power that is only possible because of the fundamental forces which are made to choose that area as their battleground.

2

The Island and Lost Souls

I

'IN DREAMS begin responsibility' is the epigraph to Yeats' 1914 collection. The words indicate both a change of direction and an attempt to set the poet's literary past in order. There can be no doubt that the tension between the two concepts was fundamental in Yeats' creative life and that like all such fundamental contrasts it is connected to others which both reflect it and modify it—action and contemplation, the life and the work, time and eternity, Robartes and Aherne.

It is tempting to consider Yeats' early poetry as a straightforward commitment to the dream. He himself, writing in 1899 to Katherine Tynan, encourages this conclusion by describing a thicket near Howth in these revealing words:

That thicket gave me my first thought of what a long poem should be; I thought of it as a region into which one should wander from the cares of life. The characters were to be no more real than the shadows that people the Howth thicket. Their mission was to lessen the solitude without destroying its peace. (*Letters*, p. 106)

Mosada and the *Island of Statues* are two of the poems written in the thicket. The former, with its theatricalities of the Inquisition, death by poison and the infatuated priest, provides an appropriately lurid setting for the imagery of escape. In the *Island of Statues* a shepherd and shepherdess overcome an enchantress on an island and find the flower which will restore to life those whom she has turned into statues. Given their choice between the world and

19

Arcady, the erstwhile statues choose to remain Arcadians. The epilogue 'spoken by a Satyr carrying a sea-shell' informs us nostalgically that:

> Of old the world on dreaming fed
> Grey Truth is now her painted toy; (*CP*, 7)

In words that are evocative of *The Two Trees* the 'optic glass' of science is contrasted with the 'twisted echo-harbouring shell' of art, and 'dusty deeds' and the fierce hungering after external truth are contrasted with the real source of truth in man's own heart. The repeated conclusion that 'Words alone are certain good' is, of course, a consoling proposition for a young poet at the outset of his career.

Yeats' position, however, is not entirely simple, even among the apparent simplicities of his earliest verse. *The Two Titans*, published in March 1886, is boldly subtitled 'A Political Poem', a claim which obliges us to see the sybil and the youth, bound to each other 'with a coiling chain', as representing England and Ireland respectively. Ellmann has suggested, more speculatively, that the figures also stand for Yeats and his father. Neither political nor psychological interpretation can improve the poem greatly and Hopkins, while admitting that it contained 'fine lines and vivid imagery', rightly concluded that the allegory was 'strained and unworkable'. Nevertheless the poem shows Yeats moving, however awkwardly, towards the poetry of engagement. Significantly, the epilogue to the *Island of Statues*, when reprinted in the 1895 collection as *The Song of the Happy Shepherd*, is counter-poised by *The Song of the Sad Shepherd*, the theme of which seems to be the indifference of life and nature to the artist.

Before publishing his first volume Yeats had written *The Seeker* (1885), in which a knight, wandering in search of what could be Eternal Beauty, finds at the end of his search a hag called Infamy. The irony is not exploited and perhaps not even felt as an irony, but both this poem and *The Wanderings of Oisin* (1889) mark Yeats' abandonment of the security of the Howth thicket. His early work, he tells Katherine Tynan, was always 'harmonious, narrow, calm', the result of never thinking out of his depth. Now, his implicit metaphors suggest, he has embarked on an uncertain voyage of discovery:

Since I have left the 'Island' [Of Statues] I have been going about on shore-less seas. Nothing anywhere has clear outline. Everything is cloud and foam. *Oisin* and *The Seeker* are the only readable result. . . . The early poems I know to be quite coherent and at no time are there clouds in my details for I hate the soft modern manner. (*Letters*, p. 88)

Yeats overrates the coherence of his earliest poems here, and, later in his life, was able to see them differently.

I was but eighteen or nineteen and had already, under the influence of *The Faerie Queen* and *The Sad Shepherd*, written a pastoral play, and under that of Shelley's *Prometheus Unbound* two plays, one staged somewhere in the Caucasus, the other in a crater of the moon; and I knew myself to be confused and incoherent. (*A General Introduction to my Work*)

Oisin is thus not quite the plunge from solidity to turbulence that it is made out to be, but it does represent a considerable step forward imaginatively. It is not a step achieved without labour. Yeats spent three years writing it and the third part had to be rewritten completely. 'Never has any poem given me so much trouble', he wrote to Katherine Tynan, and added that 'a long poem is like a fever'.

In the poem, Oisin, when hunting with his fellow Fenians, is enticed away by 'pearl-pale' Niamh (later to become 'Man-picker Niamh'). He spends a hundred years on each of three islands which, according to Yeats, represent the 'three incompatible things which man is always seeking—infinite feeling, infinite battle, infinite repose'. In a much later poem Yeats describes the sequence slightly differently as,

> three enchanted islands, allegorical dreams,
> Vain gaiety, vain battle, vain repose,
> Themes of the embittered heart, or so it seems . . . (*CP*, p. 391)

and in *Oisin* itself the islands are described as the Islands of Living (later revised to Dancing), Victories and Forgetfulness.

None of the islands offers a permanent refuge. The staff of a warrior's lance, recalling battle, breaks the spell of the first island; a bell bough, suggesting sleep and forgetfulness, breaks that of the second; and the sheer fact of being human dissolves the enchantment of the third:

She murmured, 'O wandering Oisin, the strength of the bell-branch is
   naught,
For there moves alive in your fingers the fluttering sadness of earth. (*CP*,
   p. 440)

Oisin becomes an old man the moment he touches Irish soil. Time
demands its price which cannot be evaded. When Oisin asks at the
end of the second book which of the three islands is the Isle of
Youth, Niamh's response is significant:

> 'None know,' she said;
> And on my bosom laid her weeping head. (*CP*, p. 431)

In later versions Oisin is made to seek not the 'Isle of Youth' but the
'Island of Content'. The revision makes the implications plainer.
The dream haunts the world, and the world the dream; man, being
man, can make no lasting choice between them. This is a theme that
is germinal in Yeats' writing and its appearance so early in his work
is evidence of the extraordinary single-mindedness that makes his
growth seem not so much development as a process of pruning
away, the stripping down of the mind to its essential creativeness.

Oisin is a poem restlessly experimental. Many voices are heard in
it but they do not blend into a personal whole. The signs of poetic
power are more evident here than in any of the earlier verse, but it
is a power expressed in terms of craftsmanship rather than in terms
of the insight which makes craftsmanship its agent. Yeats was not
satisfied with the poem, as might be expected of a growing poet, and
vigorously expressed his reaction against its *décor*.

Years afterwards when I had finished *The Wanderings of Oisin*, dissatisfied
with its yellow and its dull green, with all that overcharged colour inherited
from the romantic movement, I deliberately reshaped my style, deliberately sought out an impression as of cold light and tumbling clouds. I cast
off traditional metaphor and loosened my rhythm, and recognising that
all the criticism of life known to me was alien and English, became as
emotional as possible but with an emotion which I described to myself as
cold. (*Reveries over Childhood and Youth*)

Yellow and dull green do not seem the predominant colours of
Yeats' first long poem, and cold light, tumbling clouds, the rejection
of traditional metaphors and the cultivation of an emotion both

intense and cold, hardly seem to define the quality of the poems which immediately follow. They do however define with revealing accuracy the specific qualities of a poem written many years later. In *The Fisherman* (February 1916) Yeats imagines a man in 'grey Connemara cloth' climbing up to a place of cold light and tumbling clouds 'Where stone is dark under froth' and cries out his hope of writing for this man a poem 'cold and passionate as the dawn'. The image recurs in *The Tower*, where it embodies the 'pride' which Yeats wills to posterity, and is evoked in the opening lyric of *At the Hawk's Well*. Its prefiguration soon after the completion of *Oisin* may merely reflect the fact that *Reveries* was written in 1914, but it also suggests the typical pattern of Yeats' growth, in which basic intentions are sensed from the beginning, though their poetic embodiment may not come till many years later.

Yeats may not have been certain of his direction stylistically, but he was better aware of the manner in which his mind had to grow at the deeper level which eventually finds its own style. It is startling to find him, as early as 1888, writing in these terms to Katherine Tynan:

I have much improved *Mosada* by polishing the verse here and there. I have noticed some things about my poetry I did not know before, in this process of correction; for instance that it is almost all a flight into fairyland ✓ from the real world and a summons to that flight. The chorus to *The Stolen Child* sums it up—that it is not the poetry of insight, but of longing and complaint—the cry of the heart against necessity. I hope some day to alter that and write poetry of insight and knowledge. (*Letters*, p. 63)

The 'cry of the heart against necessity' was later to become metamorphosed into 'the heroic cry in the midst of despair'; but in between these two forms of rejection (the second rejection is more formal than real) Yeats was to write a poetry of acceptance, and thereby of insight and knowledge, more open-eyed and comprehensive than any written in our time. Yeats is perhaps not wholly just here to his own work; *The Stolen Child* is considerably more than its chorus and the dream of fairyland involves not merely longing but (most specifically in the last stanza of the poem) an element of terror at the abandonment of the world. Despite its severity, the diagnosis is fundamentally correct, and though Yeats' poetic life, in running its course between contraries, is frequently too close to one extremity or the other, it does eventually succeed in creating imaginatively the middle ground of his characteristic greatness.

II

Yeats is perhaps the most dialectical of poets. Man's mind to him exists between oppositions; if it is to remain alive it must consent to be a battlefield. The 'contraries' which animate reality can either be felt in the living centre of a single poem, or confront each other in different works, formally posed as thesis and antithesis. *The Countess Cathleen* begun in 1884 and completed in 1892 is a kind of counterpoise to *The Wanderings of Oisin*. In his preface to the first published edition of the play Yeats describes it 'as an attempt to mingle personal thought and feeling with the beliefs and customs of Christian Ireland'. *Oisin*, on the other hand, represents 'the impress left on my imagination by the Pre-Christian cycle of legends'. The 'contending moods and moral motives' of the former call for dramatic treatment, while the 'vast and shadowy activities' and 'great impersonal emotions' of the latter express themselves naturally in 'epic and epic-lyric measures'. These are large claims which the texts do not focus. More pertinent is *The Circus Animals' Desertion* where *The Countess Cathleen* is explicitly presented as a counter-truth to *Oisin*.

> And then a counter-truth filled out its play,
> *The Countess Cathleen* was the name I gave it;
> She, pity-crazed, had given her soul away,
> But masterful Heaven had intervened to save it.
> I thought my dear must her own soul destroy,
> So did fanaticism and hate enslave it. . . .

Ure and others read this stanza as suggesting that the Countess and Maud Gonne are parallel cases, but the words permit and indeed encourage certain contrasts. In any event, as Ure himself emphasises, it is nearly impossible to think of the Countess as enslaved by fanaticism and hate. The Countess may resemble Maud Gonne in reckless generosity, just as Aleel may resemble Yeats in helpless love, but to push the comparisons further is merely to be exposed for no obvious aesthetic purpose to the hazards of bio-literary criticism.

The four stages of revision which the play underwent may show the increasing intrusion of the personal element, but even in its final form *The Countess Cathleen* is clearly a statement of responsibility, with Aleel representing the temptation of the dream. It is in this direct sense that it is a counter-truth to *Oisin*.

In a diary kept in 1909, Yeats declares that a play having 'psychological depth' begins in the first place as 'a bundle of ideas, something that can be stated in philosophical terms; my *Countess Cathleen* for instance was once the moral question, may a soul sacrifice itself for a good end? But gradually philosophy is eliminated until at last the only philosophy audible, if there is even that, is the mere expression of one character or another.' This is certainly the ideal to which a play dealing with moral questions should approximate but *The Countess Cathleen* does not have this effect, and is unsuccessful in defining the crisis of choice either in terms of character or values. Yeats speaks of it more realistically in *Dramatis Personae* as 'ill-constructed, the dialogue turning aside at the lure of word or metaphor, very different, I hope, from the play as it is today after many alterations, every alteration tested by performance'. Even this cautious endorsement is taken back in the very next sentence: 'It was not, nor is it now, more than a piece of tapestry.' Yeats then reaches the heart of the play's inadequacy. 'The Countess sells her soul but she is not transformed.' She is in fact not only unaffected by her choice but undergoes no struggle in making the choice. Poverty lights no questions in her heart, and when a peasant complains that 'God forsakes us' her answer is that God models the world in His image and that any failure in the modelling is due either to a slip of the hand or to deficiencies in the clay that is modelled. This is too easy an explanation of evil to be dramatic and, confronted with the sufferings of her people, Cathleen responds characteristically, not with doubt, but with more and more lavish outbursts of generosity, which culminate logically in the selling of her soul. Even this decision is made with a singular lack of hesitation. That 'starving men may take what's necessary/And yet be sinless' is a conclusion which Cathleen has reached much earlier and she has proceeded to couple the right to revolution with a declaration of the infinite forgiveness of God.

> God cannot help but pardon. There is no soul
> But it's unlike all others in the world,
> Not one but lifts a strangeness to God's love
> Till that's grown infinite, and therefore none
> Whose loss were less than irremediable
> Although it were the wickedest in the world. (*CPl*, p. 21)

A strikingly similar conviction came to Yeats in a 'dream' he had in 1897 or 1898. He tells us that he awoke near dawn to hear a voice saying:

The love of God is infinite for every human soul because every human soul is unique; no other can satisfy the same need in God. (*The Stirring of the Bones; Anima Mundi sec. V*)

Unfortunately, the infinite love of God is not felt as a force in the poem and the chief effect of Cathleen's words is that her redemption can be taken for granted, thus weakening the overall suspense. As for Aleel, his call to the dream (this 'love-scene' was added after the first performance in 1899) is less a temptation than a distraction, masterfully rejected. Indeed, as a counter to the counter-truth, Aleel is scarcely more effective than St Patrick in *Oisin*. These shortcomings indicate how, despite the potency of the fable, Yeats is unable to manipulate plot and character purposively within it. The verse, deliberately cadenced, can rise to an aloof and statuesque stateliness, but, to reiterate Yeats' own criticism, it tends to turn aside at the lure of word or metaphor. An image like

> The years like great black oxen tread the world,
> And God the herdsman goads them on behind,
> And I am broken by their passing feet. (*CPl*, p. 50)

is effective in its own right but not in very much more. There is of course an intended contrast between the trodden field of the world and the 'floor of peace' on which Cathleen now walks, between transfiguration and mortality; but the other undertones are not drawn or meant to be drawn into the dramatic pattern.

When we consider *The Countess Cathleen* it is easy to conclude that Yeats had a long way to travel, but that is partially because we are looking back along a road which he discovered and hewed out for himself. Despite minor excesses he is one of his best critics and, even when his criticism provides no specific or relevant judgement, his later work is almost infallible in placing and valuing his earlier. It is in the light of his own work that one can see how stylised *Oisin* and *The Countess* are in their opposition of truth and counter-truth and how the internal 'contraries' which should give each poem its balance are both subdued and aesthetically ineffective. In the later poems the antitheses are significantly recast. Byzantium, the world beyond nature, is associated with age, and youth is linked, not with the 'land of faery', but with the world of growth and change, the 'salmon falls, the mackerel crowded seas'. The dream has its price, responsibility blends into failure, and even partial fulfilment is undercut by irony. The emphasis is on completion rather than escape and instead of the selling of souls one faces the more complex task of discovering and learning to live with both soul and body. Between the earlier and the later poetry there is a difference of perception, not simply of tone and attack. The end consummates the beginning, but only in retrospect can it be predicted from it. Bridging the two is that radical and vital movement forward, which only poetic genius is capable of creating.

3

The Dream-burdened Will

I

IN THE years after 1887 Yeats was strenuously engaged in what seem to the spectator incompatible activities. In 1888 the spiritualist in him joined the esoteric section of the Theosophic Society. Disagreements with Madame Blavatsky led to his resignation in 1890, but on 7 March of the same year he joined the Hermetic students of the Golden Dawn and, in 1893, was admitted to the inner circle of the Order. Meanwhile the Irish poet in him had founded the Irish Literary Society with John O'Leary's aid, on 24 March 1892. The man of action joined the Irish Republican Brotherhood. The scholar was involved with Edwin Ellis in a three-volume edition of Blake's works. The dramatist wrote *The Land of Heart's Desire*. The lover met Maud Gonne on 30 January 1889, a meeting which he later said reverberated in his life like the sound of a Burmese gong in the middle of a tent. A strictly chronological account of his activities, Richard Ellmann comments, 'would give the impression of a man in frenzy, beating on every door in the hotel, in an attempt to find his own room'. It was not till many years later that Yeats found that every door he beat on led felicitously to the same room.

The poetry after 1889 reflects singularly little of this tumult. The collection now known as *The Rose* appeared in 1892 (with three exceptions and without the title) in *The Countess Cathleen and Various Legends and Lyrics*. The opening poem (*To the Rose upon the Rood of Time*) and the closing one (*To Ireland in the Coming Times*) enclose the rest of the series in a tight formal pattern of truth and

28

counter-truth. Yeats first takes two steps in the direction of eternity
inviting the Rose to

> Come near, that no more blinded by man's fate,
> I find under the boughs of love and hate,
> In all poor foolish things that live a day,
> Eternal beauty wandering on her way.

He then takes a measured step backwards.

>   . . . leave me still
> A little space for the rose-breath to fill!
> Lest I no more hear common things that crave;
> The weak worm hiding down in its small cave,
> The field-mouse running by me in the grass,
>
> .   .   .   .
>
> And learn to chaunt a tongue men do not know. (*CP*, p. 35)

To Ireland in the Coming Times faces in the opposite direction and
moves backwards to the same point of balance. Yeats asks to be
counted one 'With Davis, Mangan, Ferguson', with those who write
in the popular and national current, though his rhymes tell more
than his rhyming, though magical creatures go to and fro about
his table, and though

> The red-rose-bordered hem,
> Of her, whose history began
> Before God made the angelic clan,
> Trails all about the written page. (*CP*, p. 56)

Unfortunately, the poems themselves fail to make real this ideal of
co-existence. Weak worms and field mice are conspicuous by their
absence and the nearest approach to the poetry of the everyday is in
the embarrassing sentimentalities of *The Ballad of Father Gilligan*.
When Yeats notes several years afterwards that 'the quality symbolised as The Rose differs from the Intellectual Beauty of Shelley and
Spenser in that I have imagined it as suffering with man and not as
something pursued and seen from afar', he is merely following the
fashion of his critics by reading his later self too resolutely into his
earlier self. It is true that Eternal Beauty, which in *Anashuya and
Vijaya* was a phantom in a mist of tears 'ever pacing on the verge of
things', is now more decisively on stage and is to be found 'In all
poor foolish things that live a day'. Her progress through the world,

however, is a procession rather than an involvement. The moods of sorrow and loneliness in which she is painted place her at a certain reflective distance from the everyday, so that, while in this world, she is definitely not of it. At slightly more significant levels, sorrow and loneliness convey the frustration of the lover, the solitariness of the artist and the alienation of the ideal from the actual which, used in terms of political anger rather than literary convention, can result in a poem such as *No Second Troy*.

Yeats' craftsmanship in *The Rose* is more confident and more fully co-ordinated than in his earlier writing. A poem such as *The Rose of the World* invites appreciation by its merging of two traditions in the Helen-Deirdre image, by the manner in which the double use of 'dream' helps to give weight to the rhetoric of the first line, and by the manner in which the lingering stresses of the fourth line prolong the funeral gleam of burning Troy. Similarly, in *When You are Old* (based on Ronsard's sonnet *Quand Vous Serez Bien Vieille*) the heavily monosyllabic content of the first stanza (only three out of thirty-seven words are dissyllables), and the six-times-repeated use of 'and' (a device which elsewhere is a mannerism), gives the stanza its stiff, composed, deliberate movement that is both evocative of age and planned to contrast dramatically with the soaring cadence of the stanza which follows. Appreciation, however, is qualified by the knowledge that the craftsmanship, though expert, is applied; it manipulates the poem instead of growing out of its life. Sentimentality is never far enough from the language, and even if one ignores the third stanza of *The Rose of the World* (written because Maud Gonne was tired after a long walk), there is the significant loss of tension in the third line of the first stanza, where the betrayal of the heroic by the contemporary arouses no emotion beyond distant and abstract reproof. Similarly in *When You are Old*, the rhetorical pressure cannot sustain the third stanza and its absence obliges one to recognise the vulnerability of the poem's content. These failures of craftsmanship to bind the poems together completely suggest that the underlying orientations are too simplified to make the craftsmanship vital. It is only necessary to compare the attitude to age in the first version of *The Lamentation of the Old Pensioner* with that in *The Tower* or *Sailing to Byzantium* to realise both the difference and its creative consequences. It was a difference which became apparent to Yeats himself, and in the totally rewritten version which appears in *Collected Poems* both the ambiguous word 'transfigures' and the irony of the refrain bring into the work some of the characteristic tensions of the later poetry.

The differences between the earlier and later Yeats are shown (not wholly satisfactorily) by his rewriting of *The Sorrow of Love*. In the earlier version 'earth's old and weary cry', which has been 'hid away', is restored by a girl with 'red mournful lips', who brings with her 'the whole of the World's tears' and 'all the sorrow of her labouring ships'. Yeats confessed in 1901 that he was 'not very proud' of the poem and in subsequently remodelling it he drastically changed its basis. The girl is now seen in more tragic perspectives:

> Doomed like Odysseus and the labouring ships
> And proud as Priam murdered with his peers; (*CP*, p. 46)

and what is restored is not the weary cry of the earth, but, more heroically, man's image and his cry. Macneice considers that these changes are for the worse. Ellmann and Stallworthy are among those who disagree. To some extent these differences are unavoidable because neither poem is adequately realised. Nevertheless it should be clear that what matters in the rewriting is not simply the change of tone brought about by the louder, harder and more resolute speaking voice; it is also the shift from nature to man as the centre of significance, and the supporting change in vision from the languid to the tragic. The central image which now adds pride to mournfulness and couples the 'greatness' of the world to its 'tears' helps to define this difference, though its cluster of qualities, evocative of Niamh and Eternal Beauty, was not one which Yeats was able to objectify. The basic theme that nature may seem a distraction from man's fate, but on further exploration becomes inexorably an expression of man's fate, is charged with potency, though it remains for other poems to make that potency actual.

The contours of Yeats' mind in this particular phase are drawn with some justice in *The White Birds*:

I am haunted by numberless islands, and many a Danaan shore,
Where Time would surely forget us, and Sorrow come near us no more;
Soon far from the rose and the lily and fret of the flames would we be,
Were we only white birds, my beloved, buoyed out on the foam of the sea!

(*CP*, p. 47)

Jeffares tells us that the poem originated when Yeats and Maud Gonne were resting after a walk on the cliffs at Howth. Two seagulls flew over their heads and out to sea and Maud Gonne observed (not very originally) that if she were to have the choice of being any bird she would choose to be a seagull. Three days later Yeats sent her the poem. The account takes its place with that of the origin of the last stanza of *The Rose of the World* and the disclosure that *The Lake Isle of Innisfree* was inspired by the sight of a shop window in the Strand where a wooden ball was balanced on top of a water jet. It is not clear what these 'explanations' contribute to the poems, apart from the excitement of a biographical connection, and the reminder that even lesser works of art are greater than, and significantly different from, their causes. The story of *Innisfree* in particular seems unlikely to decrease the generally fashionable dislike of the poem. Yeats' note that the Danaan shore is *Tier-nan-oge* or fairyland, and that the birds of fairyland are said to be white as snow, adds a literary reverberation to the poem, but also seems to limit its central movement, which is an uncomplicated and comprehensive longing for escape. The lighting of the poem is typically low-key. Passion, anger and bitterness do not enter its graceful gestures of rejection. The rim of the sky, the twilight, the dew-dabbled dreamers, are blurred and dim at the periphery of reality. The flames are the remote flames of star and meteor. They do nothing more drastic than to fret while the lily and rose exhale a languid weariness. The longing for a world beyond the shadowy waters, forgotten by time and unapproached by sorrow, suggests not so much fulfilment as oblivion. Across the sea is not Byzantium, or the higher or counter-reality, but the simple erasure or correction of those facts which are unpleasant in the reality we know.

Many years later, in *A Woman Young and Old*, Yeats saw the same image in more potent perspectives:

> And now we stare astonished at the sea,
> And a miraculous strange bird shrieks at us. (*CP*, p. 310)

Here the thrust of the poem is into, and not away from, life. The world of convention (if the simplification may be used as a way of approach) is identified with the 'dragon's will'. But imprisonment is also a protection. It is a refuge from responsibility, the confrontation of the Medusa face of freedom. The chain of social ritual binds man merely by the ankles and though it subjugates his inner nature it is accepted precisely because it protects that nature from the tormenting questions of how to live at a depth beyond casual existence. Break it and the compromises of daily life are broken; he faces the sea both in its promise and its elemental challenges. The astonishment and the fear of freedom, the awakening into miraculous, desolate life are conveyed with the kind of sensitive balance of tensions that makes Yeats' best poetry less argument than embodiment. A reader of the poem could reward himself by exploring what an eighteenth-century critic would call its beauties: how the overflow from the second to the third line underlines 'casual improvisation', while the endstopping underlines 'settled game'; how the contrived elegance of the fifth and sixth lines expresses and yet judges the life from which it issues; how the liberator is not welcomed but 'mocked' in an echo of the wit which is 'heavenly music' in the world of the dragon; how the Perseus image and the finely judged use of 'stare' make the sea of freedom suggest the Gorgon's mirror, binding both liberation and captivity in a common language of struggle; and how the 'miraculous strange bird' re-creates in terms of personal rebirth the 'indignant desert birds' of *The Second Coming*. Exploring these subtleties, the reader is increasingly brought to recognise how inescapably they bind the poem together and how deeply they are expressive of its life. More difficult is the recognition that the vigour of this life is based upon the clear-eyed acceptance of conflict. Rejection and escape are out of place here; and if the poem succeeds, it is because, unlike some of Yeats' poetry of the nineties, it is not prepared to do the dragon's will.

Because Yeats was a poet who abhorred generalisations he wrote poetry about which it is dangerous to generalise. *The Rose* represents one line of development which *The Wind Among the Reeds* carries to its extreme. At the same time, however, Yeats was writing *The Land of Heart's Desire*, a play which was later to become the focus for his vigorous denunciation of his own past. 'I had grown to dislike it without knowing what I disliked in it', he observed in a 1912 note, but eight years earlier the grounds for dislike had been specific enough:

B

In my *Land of Heart's Desire* and in some of my lyric verse of that time, there is an exaggeration of sentiment and sentimental beauty which I have come to think unmanly. The popularity of *The Land of Heart's Desire* seems to me to come not from its merits but because of this weakness. I have been fighting the prevailing decadence for years and have just got it under foot in my own heart . . . it is sentiment and sentimental sadness, a womanish introspection . . . this region of shadows is full of false images of the spirit and of the body. . . . I cannot probably be quite just to any poetry that speaks to me in the sweet insinuating feminine voice of the dwellers in that country of shadows and hollow images. I have dwelt there too long not to dread all that comes out of it. (*Letters*, p. 434)

These strictures can be made to apply to the language of *The Land of Heart's Desire*, but not without some injustice to its content. This drama of a fairy child who is brought into a house on May Night, gains power over it step by step and finally takes possession of the soul of a newly married bride, makes no steadfast commitment between opposing principles. The house is seen in terms of seclusion from the elemental forces outside it:

> By love alone
> God binds us to Himself and to the hearth,
> That shuts us from the waste beyond His peace,
> From maddening freedom and bewildering light. (*CPl*, p. 62)

But the very use of the words 'freedom' and 'light', however quali-fied, undermines not simply the security but the validity of life within the house. On the other hand the world of faery is seen in terms of fulfilment.

> Where beauty has no ebb, decay no flood
> But joy is wisdom, time an endless song. (*CPl*, p. 69)

But the price of fulfilment is death, and when 'the wind has laughed and murmured and sung, The lonely of heart is withered away'. The word 'withered' needs to be marked for its importation of change into the changeless. The play develops the mood of *The Stolen Child*, and in setting love, piety and discipline against 'maddening freedom' it creates a dream both beckoning and disquieting. The 'white bird' of Mary Bruin's soul that is reluctantly made to leave the house cannot be easily identified with the seagulls flying over the Howth cliffs. A different disposition of forces is at work and though the play only touches on instead of reaching into what could have been its central and creative conflict, the latent content is clearly not directed to an unequivocal acceptance of the dream.

II

The Wind Among the Reeds was published in 1899. Several influences contribute to its characteristic quality: unrequited love in Yeats' personal life, the influence of symbolism on his literary mind, his deepening interest in esoteric wisdom, and his consequent conviction that the 'invisible gates' were about to open, that a 'crowning crisis of the world' was imminent which would renew belief in a supersensual reality. The result is a poetry of the twilight, solemn, ceremonious and remote, and yet at the same time intensely and evocatively personal, a poetry which represents the farthest advance of Yeats' movement in the direction of the dream.

Yeats regarded symbolism as the only movement that was 'saying new things', and Bowra suggests that his absorption in the movement was so complete that 'he wrote almost deliberately on a theory'. Fortunately, the poems are much more alive than this procedure suggests and, in any case, Yeats, as Bowra himself recognises, was by no means a conventional symbolist. When he tells us that all sounds, colours and forms 'call down among us certain disembodied powers whose footsteps over our hearts we call emotions', magic as well as symbolism enters the aesthetic mixture, and when it is argued that because an emotion does not exist until it has found its expression, poets, painters and musicians 'are continually making and unmaking mankind', a public function is being claimed for poetry that is not normally associated with the symbolists. Yeats believes in fact that poetry is not an end in itself but concentrates a reality beyond itself. The 'little ritual' of verse resembles the 'great ritual' of nature. If Yeats denies that poetry is a criticism of life, it is to insist that it is 'a revelation of a hidden life' and, having disagreed with Arnold in one way, he approaches him in another: 'The arts are, I believe, about to take upon their shoulders the burdens that have fallen from the shoulders of priests'.

In one form or another, these doctrines retained their hold on Yeats' mind; fortunately they are ample enough to accommodate more than one approach to the actual writing of poetry. In the nineties Yeats saw them as a mandate to cast out of poetry 'those energetic rhythms, as of a man running' and to seek instead 'those wavering, meditative, organic rhythms, which are the embodiment of the imagination, that neither desires nor hates, because it has done with time'. To be done with time is indeed the predominant impulse of *The Wind Among the Reeds* and one expressed specifically in poem after poem:

> Time drops in decay . . . (*CP*, p. 62)
> . . . bid them wander obeying your will,
> Flame under flame, till Time be no more. . . . (*CP*, p. 61)
> . . . time and the world are ever in flight; (*CP*, p. 66)
> And therefore my heart will bow, when dew
> Is dropping sleep, until God burn time,
> Before the unlabouring stars and you. (*CP*, p. 75)
> . . . time and the world are ebbing away
> In twilights of dew and of fire. (*CP*, p. 77)

In an earlier volume, Yeats, in invoking the Rose, had wanted to preserve his concern in 'common things' and 'heavy mortal hopes that toil and pass'. The common things are now viewed in a less sympathetic light.

The cry of a child by the roadway, the creak of a lumbering cart,
The heavy steps of the ploughman, splashing the wintry mould.
Are wronging your image that blossoms a rose in the deeps of my heart.
(*CP*, p. 62)

The world beyond time is consequently seen as one of personal and natural fulfilment:

The wrong of unshapely things is a wrong too great to be told;
I hunger to build them anew and sit on a green knoll apart,
With the earth and the sky and the water, re-made, like a casket of gold.
(*ibid.*)

> Come, heart, where hill is heaped upon hill:
> For there the mystical brotherhood
> Of sun and moon and hollow and wood
> And river and stream work out their will; (*CP*, p. 66.)

Alternatively, the fulfilment can be apocalyptic:

> We who still labour by the cromlech on the shore,
> The grey cairn on the hill, when day sinks drowned in dew,
> Being weary of the world's empires, bow down to you,
> Master of the still stars and of the flaming door. (*CP*, p. 73)

> Surely thine hour has come, thy great wind blows,
> Far-off, most secret, and inviolate Rose? (*CP*, p. 78)

Finally, to the disappointed lover, the world beyond time represents not so much consummation as an end to frustration.

> *. . . they will find no other face fair*
> *Till all the valleys of the world have been withered away.* (*CP*, p. 74)

> *Until the axle break*
>
> .　　.　　.　　.　　.　　.　　.　　.　　.　　.
>
> *And the girdle of light is unbound,*
> *Your breast will not lie by the breast*
> *Of your beloved in sleep.* (*CP*, p. 75)

> I became a man, a hater of the wind,
> Knowing one, out of all things, alone, that his head
> May not lie on the breast nor his lips on the hair
> Of the woman that he loves, until he dies. (*CP*, pp. 81–2)

The Wind Among the Reeds is a more variegated collection than the remarks of some of its critics suggest. The incantatory lyrics are those strongly associated with the volume and their rhythms can sometimes be aggressively narcotic. But there are several poems which are more direct and in which the symbolic pretensions are subdued, such as *Into the Twilight, The Lover pleads with his Friend for Old Friends* and, in particular, *The Lover mourns for the Loss of Love*, which, after an all too characteristic opening, moves unexpectedly into an area of ordinary speech and immediate feeling. The impact which the poems still make is not because of their often ornate craftsmanship, but because of the corrective force of the personal element in them which humanises the otherwise sedative mixture of the Celtic Twilight and the Golden Dawn. The symbolic structure, when it is working correctly, magnifies and generalises the personal emotion; at the same time the emotion ensures that the structure is safeguarded by being constantly related to a core of

reality. A poem such as *He bids his Beloved be at Peace* indicates
both the balance achieved and the dangers skirted.

Yeats' love poetry at this stage has not yet achieved the richness
and range of attack, the differentiation, fusion and controlled juxtaposition of moods that give it its secure and singular place in the
language. Some differentiation is sought in *The Wind Among the
Reeds*, where the early editions divide the love poems among various
personae such as Aedh, Hanrahan, Robartes and Aherne. In one of
his notes Yeats tells us that Hanrahan is the 'simplicity of an
imagination too changeable to gather permanent possessions', while
Robartes is 'the pride of the imagination brooding upon the greatness of its possessions' and Aedh is the 'myrrh and frankincense that
the imagination offers continually before all that it loves'. These distinctions are not decisively maintained in the text and a reader without the Variorum might find it difficult to allot the poems correctly.
Yet more than one inflection can be discerned in the supplicating,
aspiring or reproaching voice. Scorn, anger, and self-contempt are
foreign to its manners at present, and the flare of bitterness which
surprises the reader in *He thinks of his Past Greatness* does not
appear until the 1922 text. Moreover, the mood once set is incapable
of being radically altered or ironically qualified. Nevertheless the
range of difference between *The Poet Pleads with the Elemental
Powers* and *He wishes his Beloved were Dead* (which occur next to
each other in the collection) should be a caution to those who consider the entire series to be contrived essentially in the same mono-
tone.

The general view of critics is that *The Wind Among the Reeds*,
together with *The Shadowy Waters*, represents Yeats' most extreme
commitment to the poetry of the dream. Yeats himself in 1904
vehemently recorded his conviction that he had dwelt too long in
'that country of shadows and hollow images', and in *In the Seven
Woods* (1903) he spoke of 'a change that may bring a less dream-
burdened will into my verses'. Jeffares is representative in describing
The Wind Among the Reeds as Yeats' 'final poetry written for
poetry's sake, for beauty's sake, and the swan song of his *fin de siècle*
composition'. Virginia Moore considers that the collection 'said
goodbye to overelaboration, however beautiful'. Leavis' position is
stimulatingly different and, not surprisingly, more complex. In dis-

cussing *He remembers Forgotten Beauty*, he finds in it 'a fresh un-
literary spontaneity comparable to that of Shelley' (a surprising
description even of this poem), and then suggests that Yeats' acceptance of the dream is significantly qualified:

Yet everywhere there is a recognition, implicit in the shifting, cloudy unseizableness of the imagery, that this 'reality' must be illusory, and that
even if it could be reached it would leave human longing unslaked. And
this recognition is subtly turned into a strength: it validates, as it were, the
dealising fanaticism of the poetry and counterpoises the obsession with
the transcendental. . . . The poetry of *The Wind Among the Reeds*, then, is
a very remarkable achievement; it is, though a poetry of withdrawal, both
more subtle and more vital than any pure product of Victorian romanti-
cism. (*New Bearings in English Poetry*)

One would like to endorse Leavis' argument, particularly as this
book itself endeavours to show how Yeats' best poetry grows out of
the tension between opposites, rather than out of commitment to
either opposite. The truth however is that 'shifting, cloudy unseizableness' is in its nature not evidence of anything. Moreover, even if
this 'unseizableness' were capable of establishing an implicit recognition, such a recognition might reveal nothing more than the uncertainty of the artist, his inability to make what he half sees live,
or his unfocussed awareness that something might possibly be said
in the other direction. It is simply not the same thing as a counter-
force active in the field of the poetry, and there is no indication that
the poetry of *The Wind Among the Reeds* is able to organise such a
counter-force. Parkinson is probably nearer the facts when he
observes that the 'potential conflict between time and eternity,
personal and impersonal, *anima hominis* and *anima mundi* . . .
cannot be explored because Yeats' poetic language is the language of
only the *anima mundi*'. It remains to add that the retreat into the
twilight had to be undergone, that the extreme had to be reached,
for Yeats to discover its barrenness, and so prepare his mind for
that new alignment of forces that was to make possible the poetry of
the whole man.

III

Although Yeats first mentions *The Shadowy Waters* in a letter of 5 November 1894 to his father, the conception seems to have fascinated him from his boyhood. Hone tells us that Yeats had outlined the plot of the play to George Russell when Russell and he were still students at the Arts School. Themes which brood over the mind are, perhaps for that reason, not always fully controlled by it; *The Shadowy Waters* was long in the shaping and this was not in the end satisfactorily shaped. Its first publication did not take place till 1900 when it was printed by the *North American Review* and issued in book form by Hodder and Stoughton. Yeats at this stage seemed satisfied with the work, describing it as 'magical and mystical beyond anything I have done' and as containing 'probably the best verse I have written'. However, after seeing it performed at the Court Theatre in London on 8 July 1905 (it had previously been staged at Dublin on 14 January 1904 when he was away in America), he confessed that he was surprised 'at the badness of a great deal of it in its present form'. By August he was prepared to describe it as 'the worst thing I ever did dramatically'.

A bout of almost violent revision followed and a new version of the play incorporating only forty-four lines of the original appeared in *Poems, 1899–1905*, published in 1906. It was succeeded by an acting version staged at the Abbey Theatre on 8 December 1906 and published in 1907. In his revision, Yeats claims that he was 'getting rid of needless symbols' and (the candour points to a decisive weakness in the original) 'making the people answer each other'. He thought that the play was now 'strong, simple drama' and that it had 'a simple passionate story for the common sightseer, though it keep back something for instructed eyes'.

The 1905 performance was indeed charged with symbolism and even the sail of Forgael's galley had a pattern of three rows of hounds which, among other things, were alleged to stand for *Tamas, Rajas* and *Sattva*. Ellmann suggests that, in terms of the play, the hounds stand for 'Forgael's death-wish, Dectora's life wish, and their fusion in "some mysterious transformation of the flesh" '. Again, Forgael wore a lily on his breast and Dectora a rose. 'Lilies of death-pale hope, roses of passionate dream' is how Yeats explains the implications in a poem entitled *The Travail of Passion*. The revision eliminates several of these Golden Dawn excesses. Parkinson shows also how in the rewriting the dramatic pattern is clarified, the characters humanised and their voices differentiated.

Unfortunately, even after these drastic alterations, certain stubborn and far-reaching deficiencies remain. The play is by no means 'strong simple drama' and it is legitimate to doubt if it is drama at all. Aibric's jealousy of Forgael's 'absorption in the dream' and his later jealousy of Dectora (who ironically is the only person capable of dissipating the dream) are emphasised in Yeats' letters, but the jealousy of Dectora scarcely emerges from the text and Aibric's protests against the dream remain minor objections, instead of an alternative view against which Forgael's stand can be tested. As for the sailors, what Yeats supposes to be their rough realism is less at sea in prose than in the verse of the original; but the use of prose only serves to emphasise a segregation that had always existed. There is no conflict and indeed no meeting between the point of view of Forgael and the sailors; indeed, their philosophy of wine, women and loot seems designed chiefly as a background of debasement against which Forgael can sail on his transcendental journey. With these lesser possibilities of dramatic interplay eliminated, there remains the primary conflict between Forgael and Dectora. Here it is relevant to consult a programme note for the 1905 performance (which Ellmann tells us is 'certainly' by Yeats) where we are informed that the union of Dectora's life-seeking 'vivid force' with Forgael's 'abyss-seeking desire for the waters of Death' makes 'a perfect humanity'. Unfortunately, this union is not imaginatively realised. Dectora's love for Forgael is secured by deceit (even though it survives the confession of deceit), and throughout the play there is no recognition, poetic or dramatic, that either needs the other to achieve a 'perfect humanity'. It is true up to a point that the *personae* of the revised version answer each other instead of answering Yeats; but they fail singularly to make any impact on each other with their answers.

In a letter to Arthur Symons on 10 September 1905 Yeats analysed the weakness of *The Shadowy Waters*.

. . . One thing I am now quite sure of is that all the finest poetry comes logically out of the fundamental action, and that the error of late periods like this is to believe that some things are inherently poetical, and to try and pull them on to the scene at every moment, it is just these seemingly inherently poetical things that wear out. My *Shadowy Waters* was full of them, and the fundamental thinking was nothing, and that gave the whole poem an impression of weakness. There was no internal life pressing for expression through the characters. (*Letters*, p. 460)

The inherent poetry of *The Shadowy Waters* suffers not only because it is not integrated into the fundamental action; it also suffers from the basic difficulty of giving poetic expression to a world-denying will. Some of Forgael's remarks can only be described as extraordinarily unmystical.

> You are not the world's core. O no, no, no!
> That cannot be the meaning of the birds.
> You are not its core. My teeth are in the world,
> But have not bitten yet. (*CPl*, p. 154. *CP*, p. 84)

At one point, the world beyond time is seen in terms of time:

> . . . for it is dreams
> That lift us to the flowing, changing world
> That the heart longs for. (*CP*, pp. 480–1)

At another point, the search is less for a reality beyond the world than for the world's quintessence.

> Where the world ends
> The mind is made unchanging, for it finds
> Miracle, ecstasy, the impossible hope,
> The flagstone under all, the fire of fires,
> The roots of the world. (*CP*, p. 477)

In the dramatic version, the objective of the quest is seen in terms of synthesis:

> . . . when the light is gone
> I have but images, analogies,
> The mystic bread, the sacramental wine,
> The red rose where the two shafts of the cross,
> Body and soul, waking and sleep, death, life,
> Whatever meaning ancient allegorists
> Have settled on, are mixed into one joy. (*CPl*, p. 152)

Poetry and Tradition (1907) elaborates this ideal in relation to the artist:

. . . the nobleness of the arts is in the mingling of contraries, the extremity of sorrow, the extremity of joy, perfection of personality, the perfection of its surrender, overflowing turbulent energy and marmorean stillness; and its red rose opens at the meeting of the two beams of the cross, and at the trysting place of mortal and immortal, time and eternity.

These quotations to some extent substantiate Ellis-Fermors' view (which is disputed by Donoghue) that the central theme of *The Shadowy Waters* is 'realisation of ideal love in terms of, not by the superseding of, natural love'; but the varied approaches also point to some irresolution in Yeats' grasp of his objective. This uncertainty becomes more explicit in a poem to Lady Gregory which Yeats puts at the beginning of the lyric version:

> Is Eden far away, or do you hide
> From human thought, as hares and mice and coneys
> That run before the reaping-hook and lie
> In the last ridge of the barley? Do our woods
> And winds and ponds cover more quiet woods,
> More shining winds, more star-glimmering ponds?
> Is Eden out of time and out of space? (*CP*, pp. 469–70)

In this passage (evocative of a very different poet, Wallace Stevens), the imaginative weight is almost entirely behind the suggestion that Eden is in this world and is indeed its heart. The alternative is no more than an abstract question. In *The Shadowy Waters*, however, the fundamental action drives towards an Eden out of time and out of space, and the counterpoising forces in the poetry are not able to achieve their intended effect. Were it not for this disjointedness it would not be possible to overlook the manner in which Dectora sees the 'unimaginable happiness' which Forgael has promised her.

> . . . in some island where the life of the world
> Leaps upward, as if all the streams o' the world
> Had run into one fountain. (*CP*, p. 497)

Here the thrust of the poetry unmistakably suggests that the higher reality is continuous with the lower; the leap upward suggests both the vitality of nature and the aspiration to something above, which completes nature rather than denies it. In the same way, Dectora's climactic words are an affirmation of life in the very act of severance from life.

O flower of the branch, O bird among the leaves,
O silver fish that my two hands have taken
Out of the running stream, O morning star,
Trembling in the blue heavens like a white fawn
Upon the misty border of the wood,
Bend lower, that I may cover you with my hair,
For we will gaze upon this world no longer.
(*CPl*, p. 167; *CP*, pp. 499–500)

The progression in the imagery ought not to be evaded. The flower suggests natural life in its abundance and consummation. The bird which adds the idea of movement and migration to that of growth is significantly among the leaves, unlike the grey birds that haunt Forgael's vision. The fish is silver because it is so in reality but also because it suggests the lunar principle with which Forgael is identified. This may seem an esoteric overtone but it is not necessary to be an initiate of the Golden Dawn to recognise the fish as a fertility symbol, a current of implication which is strengthened by 'running stream'. The morning star has traditional associations of rebirth which are particularised by 'white fawn' with its evocations of newly seen innocence and by the blend of fear and excitement which 'trembling' conveys. The whole passage has thus an animation and a poetic logic which is very far from Donoghue's description of it as 'tossing mere wool-balls of Pre-Raphaelite lyricism'. Yet such misunderstandings are possible and even plausible, because the poetry is at variance with the dramatic structure, and because both are only fitful embodiments of conceptions which remain evasively defined.

The common criticism that *The Shadowy Waters* is too shadowy is thus not as obtuse as it sounds. Language in its particularity is a product of the world and attitudes which are world-denying tend also to be language-denying. The higher dream can be a subject of poetry but it must be seen as reflected in and irradiating the lower. The way of the poet and that of the mystic are at best tangential and, while imaginative statement can sometimes work against the grain of language, it has to return to work in its normal direction. Both *The Shadowy Waters* and *The Wind Among the Reeds* represent an extreme in Yeats' zig-zag course between extremities. He had to reach the extreme and to write it out of his blood; in doing so, he made it obvious to himself as well as to others that the laws of his development pointed emphatically in a different direction.

4

In the Theatre

———

I

YEATS' next volume of verse, *In the Seven Woods*, was published in 1903. He tells us, in a note, that he wrote some of the poems in it 'before the big wind of nineteen hundred and three blew down so many trees and troubled the wild creatures, and changed the look of things; and I thought out there a good part of the play [*On Baile's Strand*] which follows. The first shape came to me in a dream, but it changed much in the making, foreshadowing, it may be, a change that may bring a less dream-burdened will into my verses.' These remarks are not as direct as they sound and Ellmann has shown that there was also a storm in Yeats' mind which blew down a great deal in it and drastically changed 'the look of things'. The event which so powerfully altered Yeats' life was Maud Gonne's marriage to Major John MacBride in February 1903. It is tempting to treat this event as an artistic as well as a personal watershed and there can be no doubt that it fundamentally reshaped the attitudes at work in Yeats' poetry. But the remaking of the poet had begun slightly earlier. In his introduction to the *Oxford Book of Modern Verse*, Yeats tells us that 'in 1900 everybody got down off his stilts' and ·
while this remark is not true of English poetry as a whole it is reasonably accurate in relation to Yeats himself. A letter to George Russell about May of this year gives a fuller indication of the direction which Yeats' mind was taking:

. . . vague forms, pictures, scenes, etc. are rather a modern idea of the poetic and I would not want to call up a modern kind of picture. I avoid every kind of word that seems to me either 'poetical' or 'modern' and above

45

all I avoid suggesting the ghostly (the vague) idea about a god, for it is a modern conception. All ancient vision was definite and precise. (*Letters*, p.343)

Yeats' critical comments are full of premonitions of later writers who are better known as critics; in this case, 'definite and precise' looks forward to Hulme's observation that 'the great aim of poetry is accurate, precise and definite description'. Clarity of outline is not compulsory for movement out of the twilight, but the point is that Yeats' approach, besides being valid for himself, makes him a pioneer of the modern temper. A letter to Fiona Macleod, written about November 1901, carries this development further and suggests other implications of the new simplicity:

You, as I think, should seek the delights of style in utter simplicity, in a self-effacing rhythm and language; in an expression that is like a tumbler of water rather than like a cup of wine. (*Letters*, p. 358)

This time the anticipation is of Eliot who in 1933 called for a poetry 'so transparent that in reading it we are intent on what the poem points at and not on the poetry', and who said in 1941 that the great poet in his greatest moments is 'writing transparently so that our attention is directed to the object and not to the medium'. Neither Eliot nor Yeats is wholly in the right here and for Yeats in particular the 'self-effacing rhythm' which he recommends is no great improvement on those 'wavering, meditative organic rhythms' which he is in the process of disowning. As frequently happens, the correct position is the one enunciated by Coleridge.

The words in prose ought to express the intended meaning and no more; if they attract attention to themselves, it is, in general, a fault. . . . But in verse you must do more: there the words, the media, must be beautiful and ought to attract your notice . . . yet not so much and so perpetually as to destroy the unity which ought to result from the whole poem. (*Table Talk*.)

Yeats' own work is fully illustrative of these remarks. When he is at his best his rhythms are the reverse of self-effacing. His words call attention vigorously to themselves and by doing so create a whole which is the poem itself and not what the poem points at. His works, to quote Coleridge again, exhibit not merely 'the balance or reconciliation of opposite or discordant qualities' but, more than that, of opposite and discordant principles; and if oppositions did not exist to be reconciled, Yeats, one imagines, would be eager to invent them.

The most emphatic statement of Yeats' new position is contained in a letter to George Russell in 1904, extracts from which have already been quoted. Here the contrasts with Yeats' views in *The Symbolism of Poetry* are so striking that it is tempting to conclude that a deliberate disowning is taking place. In the earlier essay Yeats had characterised as an invention of the will 'those energetic rhythms, as of a man running' and had committed himself to 'those wavering, meditative, organic rhythms that are the embodiment of the imagination'. In 1904 the commitments are studiously reversed: 'We possess nothing but the will and we must never let the children of vague desires breathe upon it nor the waters of sentiment rust the terrible mirror of its blade'. The man running is also brought back into favour. 'Let us have no emotions, however abstract, in which there is not an athletic joy.'

Yeats is more than a trifle ninetyish in his rejection of the nineties and it is unnecessary to press everything he says beyond its evident declamation-value. The man who wrote *The King's Threshold* is fully conscious of the rights of the imagination, and the poet engaged in his marathon struggle with *The Shadowy Waters* breathes more than a little upon the 'terrible mirror' of the will. Yeats' criticism has always its core of significance but it should also be regarded as tactical manœuvring in the struggle with himself. He once defined style as 'the self-conquest of a writer' and the plan of conquest must naturally depend on whatever demon has immediately to be exorcised.

It is with these precautions that the reader should approach Yeats' preface to *Poems, 1899–1905*, in which he says that drama for him 'has been the search for more of manful energy, more of cheerful acceptance of whatever arises out of the logic of events, and for clean outline, instead of those outlines of lyric poetry that are blurred with desire and vague regret'. 'Manful energy' and 'cheerful acceptance' suggest a public school rather than a poetic ethos and are very distant from the mood of *Deirdre* upon which Yeats was then engaged. But he is still involved in demolishing his past self and the necessity of that demolition is evident from the very next sentence: 'All art is in the last analysis an endeavour to condense as out of the flying vapour of the world an image of human perfection and for its own and not for the art's sake, and that is why the labour of the alchemists, who were called artists in their day, is a befitting comparison for all deliberate change of style.' Here even the disowning of art for art's sake is verbal rather than critical, and it would be difficult to find a passage in which 'manful energy' is less in evidence.

Nevertheless when allowance has been made for the strategies of self-conquest the main objectives of vigour, firmness of outline, avoidance of the 'poetical', and of commitment to the everyday rather than to the transcendental ('What moves natural men in the arts is what moves them in life') are clearly and consistently emphasised. Added to these is the doctrine of poetry as the expression of the whole man, which is the logical outcome of those theories of unity of being that played so dominant a part in Yeats' development. In *Discoveries* (1906) these views find their full and mature expression. Yeats begins by facing the literature of the immediate past but no longer as the victim of an 'uncontrollable shrinking from the shadows'. He is able to see both gain and loss in the nineties:

In literature, partly from that spoken word which knits us to normal man, we have lost in personality, in our delight in the whole man—blood imagination, intellect running together—but have found a new delight, in essences, in states of mind, in pure imagination, in all that comes to us most easily in elaborate music.

One pauses first to note the audacious rightness of that phrase— 'blood, imagination, intellect running together'—not simply as a critical proposition but as a description of the poetry Yeats was to write, of its controlled force and almost physical vigour. Put the formulation next to Eliot's—'Tennyson and Browning are poets and they think; but they do not feel their thought as immediately as the odour of a rose'—and the differences of temperament and attack should be evident. Despite Eliot's unacademic references to Spinoza and the smell of cooking it is difficult to think of him using the word 'blood', still less putting blood before imagination in the creative process.

Yeats' reference to essences and states of mind lacks the authenticity of his interest in the whole man, but it completes the theoretical map and enables him to argue that there are two choices for the writer:

There are two ways before literature—upward into ever-growing subtlety with Verhaeren, with Mallarmé, with Maeterlinck, until at least it may be, a new agreement among refined and studious men gives birth to a new passion, and what seems literature becomes religion; or downward taking the soul with us until all is simplified and solidified again.

Yeats' choice, as might be expected, is not a choice but a reconciliation:

... We should ascend out of common interests, the thoughts of the newspapers, of the market place, of men of science, but only so far as we can carry the normal, passionate, reasoning self, the personality as a whole ... An art may become impersonal because it has too much circumstance or too little, because the world is too little or too much with it, because it is too near the ground or too far up among the branches.

The balance must be kept, the right aesthetic distance maintained. But the undertow of the language, the instinctive preference which places 'blood' before 'imagination' and 'passionate' before 'reasoning', the recognition that it is the spoken word which makes literature expressive of the whole man, all point to immediacy, the seizure of the actual, as the ground from which unity of being grows and branches. At the end of *Discoveries* this conviction becomes eloquently explicit.

There are two pictures of Venice side by side in the house where I am writing this, a Canaletto ... and a Frans Francken. ... Neither painting could move us at all, if our thought did not rush out to the edges of our flesh, and it is so with all good art. ... Art bids us touch and taste and hear and see the world, and shrinks from what Blake calls mathematic form, from every abstract thing, from all that is of the brain only, from all that is not a fountain jetting from the entire hopes, memories and sensations of the body.

Again the comparison with Eliot is invited and the positive energy, the outflowing response, of 'if our thought did not rush out to the edges of our flesh' should be contrasted with Eliot's more fastidious conclusion that in Donne the intellect is at the tips of the senses. Again the difference exposes a difference in temperament reminding us that Yeats' poetry has a sheer power of impact which Eliot's poetry is unable, or perhaps does not seek, to attain, despite other and formidable virtues. The thought put forward is not original to either poet and it is not a question of influence, even though the phrasing is sharply similar; Kermode, for example, has shown us how the idea of unified sensibility goes considerably further back in literary history. But Yeats' formulation remains strikingly his own, in its delight in immediacy and in the buoyant pressure of the language that finds its consummation in the 'fountain jetting'. The whole man speaks when he speaks about the whole man and does so in accents firmly individual, yet unmistakably of the twentieth century.

II

Yeats tells us that the theatre for which his plays were written 'was the creation of seven people: four players, Sara Allgood, her sister Maire O'Neill, girls in a blind factory who joined a patriotic society; William Fay, Frank Fay, an electric light fitter and an accountant's clerk who got up plays at a coffee-house; three writers, Lady Gregory, John Synge and I'. This account does not mention Edward Martyn and George Moore, 'cousins and inseparable friends, bound one to the other by mutual contempt'. Martyn was a member of the Committee that founded the Irish Literary Theatre and Moore took a prominent part in its early counsels.

Performances began with *The Countess Cathleen* and two plays by Martyn, *The Heather Field* and *Maeve*. Both were well received, but Martyn's third effort, *The Tale of a Town*, was so much of an anticlimax that it had to be rewritten by Moore and Yeats. The experience drove Martyn out of collaboration with the theatre and Moore followed him not long afterwards when Yeats decided to throw in his fortunes with William and Frank Fay. The Irish Literary Theatre was reborn as the Irish National Theatre Society. AE joined the sponsors and the first plays produced were his *Deirdre* and Yeats' *Cathleen ni Houlihan*.

One other play by Yeats, his inconsequential *The Pot of Broth*, was produced in 1902. *Where There is Nothing* was written hurriedly in the same year to anticipate Moore who was threatening to write a novel on the same theme and to obtain an injunction if Yeats used the plot in a play. 1903 saw the staging of *The King's Threshold*. In the same year the company made its first visit to London, a visit undertaken under taxing conditions, but one which resulted in Miss Horniman agreeing to build the Abbey Theatre and to give the company the free use of it until it was financially secure. Lady Gregory showed her customary resourcefulness in securing a patent from the Crown against vigorous opposition from the other three Dublin theatres and in having the building ready for rehearsals a month after the patent was granted. The first performances took place on 27 December 1904, the plays being Yeats' *On Baile's Strand* and *Spreading the News* by Lady Gregory. In 1905 the last of many changes of title took place and the company became the Irish National Theatre Society Limited, better and more simply known as 'the Abbey'. The Irish dramatic movement was now on a secure financial and artistic foundation and the theatre continued to produce Yeats' plays down to *The Death of Cuchulain* in 1949.

In *The Fascination of What's Difficult* (dated 1909–10 by Ellmann) Yeats complains that his Pegasus has to 'Shiver under the lash, strain, sweat and jolt/As though it dragged road-metal' and bestows his curse

<blockquote>
on plays
That have to be set up in fifty ways,
On the day's war with every knave and dolt. . . . (*CP*, p. 104)
</blockquote>

Nevertheless 'Theatre business, management of men' taught him lessons that are evident in the poem itself. The experience strengthened his recognition that 'the element of strength in poetic construction is common passion'. It taught him the virtues of dramatic coherence; a notice called *Advice to Playwrights* issued by the Abbey Theatre in which Yeats' hand seems discernible is almost Aristotelian in its emphasis on the unity of action:

. . . any knot of events where there is passionate emotion and the clash of will, can be made the subject matter of a play, and the less like a play it is at the first sight, the better play may come of it in the end. Young writers should remember that they must get all their effects from the logical expression of their subject, and not by the addition of extraneous incidents; and that a work of art can have but one subject. A work of art, though it must have the effect of nature, is art because it is not nature, as Goethe said; and it must possess a unity unlike the accidental profusion of nature.

Cathleen ni Houlihan, though one of the most popular plays in the theatre's repertoire, is too slight to illustrate these theories. Cathleen, an old woman who symbolises Ireland, visits a cottage where a young man is about to marry security. She offers him nothing but blood, sweat and tears, but when she leaves the cottage he is committed to her. The younger son runs in, shouting that the French are landing at Killala. The elder son follows the old woman. When asked if he had met an old woman outside the cottage, the younger son replies:

> I did not, but I saw a young girl, and she had the
> walk of a queen. (*CPl*, p. 88)

The play is full of political overtones and perhaps consists of nothing but the overtones. Jeffares observes that the impact of the symbolism depends 'on the audience's knowledge of a popular street ballad called the "Shan Van Vocht" (Poor Old Woman) which preserved the tradition of French aid for Irish rebellions'. But a contemporary reference was also involved. In *Dramatis Personae* Yeats tells us that:

Maud Gonne had persuaded that Office [the French War Office] to take from a pigeon-hole a scheme for an invasion of Ireland—'What will you do', somebody asked the Express Editor, 'if the French land at Killala?' 'I will write the best article of my life' was the answer.

Maud Gonne played Cathleen 'magnificently and with weird power' and Stephen Gwynne reveals that the effect on him was such 'that I went home asking myself if such plays should be produced unless one was prepared for people to go out to shoot and be shot'. It was a question which Yeats also asked at the close of his career.

> Did that play of mine send out
> Certain men the English shot? (*CP*, p. 393)

Even if the answer is 'no', the mere asking of the question implies the power and responsibility of the poet's office. It is with the rights of poetry that Yeats is concerned in *The King's Threshold*.

The 'clash of will' in *The King's Threshold* is between Seanchan, Chief Poet and pioneer in civil disobedience, and King Guaire of Gort who has dismissed him from his place at the Council table on the ground that:

. . . it was the men who ruled the world
And not the men who sang to it, who should sit
Where there was the most honour. (*CPl*, p. 109)

Seanchan's retort is a fast unto death on the King's threshold. Various people attempt to dissuade him, including his pupils, an old servant, Brian, a pompous and time-serving Mayor, a soldier, the Lord Chamberlain, the King's daughters, Seanchan's wife, Fedelm, and, finally, the King himself. None of them is able to deflect Seanchan from his purpose. In the earlier versions the King capitulated, kneeling before Seanchan who accepted the crown from his hands. It was not until 1922 that Yeats became convinced of the falsity of this climax and substituted the present ending in which the King's position forbids him to withdraw, Seanchan's absolute faith in poetry forbids him to compromise and the death of the poet expresses bleakly and validly the fate of poetry in a practical world.

Though Yeats considered *The King's Threshold* to be 'constructed rather like a Greek play', there can be no deep dramatic interest in the clash of irreconcilable positions which it is impossible to modify. *Prometheus Bound* is not the analogy which it superficially seems to be, and perhaps the main impact of *Prometheus* is in areas other than the dramatic. The pleasure one derives from *The King's Threshold* is largely the result of the ironies that emerge out of the conflict between poetic faith and philistine attitudes. But Yeats is not wholly prepared even in 1922 for the bitterness of trailing poetry in the world's dust and Seanchan's death is surrounded by romantic heroics.

O Silver trumpets, be you lifted up
And cry to the great race that is to come.
Long-throated swans upon the waves of time,
Sing loudly, for beyond the wall of the world
That race may hear our music and awake. (*CPl*, p. 143)

The King's Threshold has the ambiguous distinction of being remembered almost entirely by five lines:

And I would have all know that when all falls
In ruin, poetry calls out in joy,
Being the scattering hand, the bursting pod,
The victim's joy among the holy flame,
God's laughter at the shattering of the world. (*CPl*, p. 114)

This apocalyptic vision of the nature of poetry is blazingly eloquent and, apart from being the core of Seanchan's faith, it is the first statement of the theme of tragic joy which was to occupy so important a position in Yeats' thought. But it is ecstatic rather than dramatic verse; it seems almost more effective out of its context than in it. There are other passages where the voice is more individuated and the speech movement follows more closely the movement of the body of the thought:

> You have rightly named me.
> I lie rolled up under the ragged thorns
> That are upon the edge of those great waters
> Where all things vanish away, and I have heard
> Murmurs that are the ending of all sound.
> I am out of life; I am rolled up, and yet,
> Hedgehog although I am, I'll not unroll
> For you, King's dog! Go to the King, your master. (*CPl*, pp. 125–6)

The King's Threshold is a play with fine moments and a variety of incidents that should make it effective in the theatre. But it evades romantically, instead of confronting fully, the harsh consequences of the oppositions it erects.

On Baile's Strand was performed later than *The King's Threshold* but was begun earlier, in 1901. Yeats described it, as usual, as the best play he had done and, as usual, he announced ten months later that it had been substantially rewritten. A letter to Frank Fay early in 1904 shows the kind of interest in Cuchulain's character for which Bradley is chided by the new critics:

He is probably about 40, not less than 35 or 36 and not more than 45 or 46, certainly not an old man, and one understands from his talk about women that he does not love like a young man. (*Letters*, p. 425)

The letter then goes on to make an important point about the play's structure:

The touch of something hard, repellent yet alluring, self assertive yet self immolating, is not all but it must be there. He is the fool—wandering passive, houseless and almost loveless. Concobhar is reason that is blind because it can only reason, because it is cold. Are they not the cold moon and the hot sun?

The relationship is central and dramatically potent. The Fool and the Blind Man reflect Cuchulain and Conchubar in the manner of the Elizabethan sub-plot and unlike Cuchulain and Conchubar (the irony is not casual) they are able, at their sordid level, to establish a working partnership. The fool makes clear the terms of the alliance.

You take the fowl out of my hands after I have stolen it and plucked it, and you put it into the big pot at the fire there, and I can go out and run races with the witches at the edge of the waves and get an appetite, and when I've got it, there's the hen waiting inside for me, done to the turn. (*CPl*, pp. 247–8)

It should be evident how tellingly 'the witches at the edge of the waves' foreshadow the manner of Cuchulain's death. The need of the Fool for the Blind Man, stated thus in terms of the kitchen, is stated by Conchubar in terms of the palace:

> You are but half a king and I but half;
> I need your might of hand and burning heart,
> And you my wisdom. (*CPl*, p. 260.)

When Cuchulain takes the oath of allegiance the unity supposed to have been achieved is asserted:

> We are one being, as these flames are one:
> I give my wisdom, and I take your strength. (*CPl*, p. 263.)

And as Cuchulain goes out to kill his son, the breakdown of the synthesis is recognised:

> Life drifts between a fool and a blind man
> To the end, and nobody can know his end. (*CPl*, p. 271.)

Thus, the sub-plot envelops the main core of the action, extending its significance and putting heroic and low life into a juxtaposition in which each underwrites the validity of the other. The two elements drive to a common climax as the Fool strips bare the Blind Man's hidden and terrifying knowledge revealing to Cuchulain the truth that is to destroy him. The moment of disclosure is masterfully shaped. At the point of crisis Cuchulain does not speak. It is the Fool and the Blind Man who speak for him.

Blind Man. Somebody is trembling, Fool! The bench is shaking. Why are you trembling? Is Cuchulain going to hurt us? It was not I who told you, Cuchulain.
Fool. It is Cuchulain who is trembling. It is Cuchulain who is shaking the bench.
Blind Man. It is his own son he has slain. (*CPl*, p. 276)

When Cuchulain does speak, his chaotic, almost delirious, language makes it clear that his mind as well as his body is trembling. Death is on him before he rushes out to fight the waves.

In the original version the first part of the play was taken up by a discussion of Conchubar's plan for building his city. Yeats later replaced this discussion by the long debate between Cuchulain and Conchubar which is now in the text and which ends in Cuchulain taking his oath of allegiance. As a result, Cuchulain's son does not make his entrance until half the play is over, but the structural disproportion only exists in the abstract. The point of the debate is to establish Cuchulain's desire for a son and his ideal of a son who would reproduce his image, who would be 'No pallid ghost or mockery of a man', but one able to face 'Even myself in battle'. The pattern of irony is grimly drawn here and is strengthened when Conchubar protests:

> Now as ever
> You mock at every reasonable hope,
> And would have nothing, or impossible things.
> What eye has ever looked upon the child
> Would satisfy a mind like that? (*CPl*, p. 257)

Then, as Cuchulain vividly describes Aoife's beauty, the knot of irony is pulled even tighter:

> None other had all beauty, queen or lover,
> Or was so fitted to give birth to kings. (*CPl*, p. 259)

When Aoife's son enters to challenge Cuchulain, and is asked to prove that he is of noble birth, his answer is one made in Cuchulain's language.

> I will give no other proof than the hawk gives
> That it's no sparrow! (*CPl*, p. 265)

To this, one should link Cuchulain's earlier remark:

> For I would need a weightier argument
> Than one that marred me in the copying,
> As I have that clean hawk out of the air
> That, as men say, begot this body of mine
> Upon a mortal woman. (*CPl*, p. 257)

The relationship which the imagery establishes is half recognised by Cuchulain. He sees in the young man Aoife's 'fierceness' and her 'stone-pale cheek'. He offers him his friendship and when the young man protests that Aoife might think him a coward he offers him his cloak in a further gesture of conciliation:

> My father gave me this.
> He came to try me, rising up at dawn
> Out of the cold dark of the rich sea.
> He challenged me to battle, but before
> My sword had touched his sword, told me his name,
> Gave me this cloak, and vanished. (*CPl*, p. 268)

This is perhaps the key image of the play. Not only does it reflect the immediate reality—the father recognising the son's courage and bestowing the cloak of peace—but the mention of the sea leaps forward to the play's climax and locks the whole action in a rhythm of recurrence that seems larger than any individual fate; the father kills the son and the father must kill the son again.

Murmurs of witchcraft are heard as Cuchulain's fondness for his unknown son deepens. The other kings offer to do battle with the young man and Cuchulain stands by him, drawing his sword.

> This mutterer, this old whistler, this sand-piper,
> This edge that's greyer than the tide, this mouse
> That's gnawing at the timbers of the world,
> This, this—Boy I would meet them all in arms
> If I'd a son like you. (*CPl*, p. 269)

The verse is arresting in its own right, the language sharpening the heroic against the familiar, but, heard in the dramatic context, it is possible to feel the tide sweeping in and the timbers of Cuchulain's world being gnawed at. The last lines surely make their own comment as they fall into the tragic and by now implacable pattern.

Allied with Cuchulain against a common enemy, the young man at last accepts his father's friendship. Cuchulain symbolically spreads

the cloak before him. Then when Conchubar reminds him of his
duty he lays hands on the High King himself. At this point the
conflict between appearance and reality is at its sharpest. The civic
code is sanity and rebellion against it is witchcraft. So Cuchulain
who has sworn allegiance to 'the threshold and the hearth stone' is
derelict in his duty for desiring precisely that. The son who has
drawn him into the instinctive alliance of blood is presented as
having bewitched him. Both as warrior and as the King's servant
Cuchulain is compelled to strike at the roots of his own being;
significantly his roof-tree leaps into fire and the walls of his house
blacken not when he dies but when he kills his son. When the
second woman laments:

> Who could have thought that one so great as he
> Should meet his end at this unnoted sword! (*CPl*, p. 271)

she is displaying the kind of local ignorance that dramatically un-
covers a deeper truth.

The bitter climax of the play comes when all eyes are watching
Cuchulain's fight with the sea and the Blind Man tells the Fool that
now is the time to put their hands in the ovens. The death of the
hero is quixotic to the spectator and a heaven-sent occasion to the
opportunist. It can have meaning only to the hero himself.

On Baile's Strand is described by Parkinson as 'among the best
poetic plays of the century' and as resolving 'almost perfectly what
Yeats saw as the dramatist's general problem'. It deserves the tribute
because of its fully unified complexity, the archetypal power of its
theme and the manner in which language and situation are made
responsible to an almost Sophoclean power of structural irony.

III

Yeats was a professional mask-maker well before he invented the
theory of the mask. A truth completes itself, or, more precisely,
enables itself to be lived, only by calling its counter-truth into being.
In the same way, a given literary situation calls for its over-com-
pensated opposite if a creative mean is to be established between
them. The immediate poetic tradition from which Yeats swung away

after 1900 was that of aestheticism, and his criticism, buttressed with references to the drama, is preoccupied with manful energy, athletic joy, the thinking of the body and the poetry of the whole man. But the dramatic tradition he inherited was that of naturalism (middle Ibsen being the typical influence), and the movement of protest was therefore in another direction.

In 1899 Yeats declared that the 'theatre began in ritual, and it cannot come to its greatness again without recalling words to their ancient sovereignty'. The objective would be beyond dispute, were it not for the betraying use of 'ritual' which conjures up echoes that Yeats' poetry was already beginning to forget. In *Samhain: 1903*, perhaps under the pressure of his own dramatic practice, he takes a more balanced position which recognises the importance of dramatic construction as well as of the 'sovereignty of words'.

If we do not know how to construct, if we cannot arrange much complicated life into a single action, our work will not hold the attention or linger in the memory, but if we are not in love with words it will lack the delicate movement of living speech that is the chief garment of life.

In *Samhain*, of the following year, language is still the source of particularity.

What the ever-moving, delicately moulded flesh is to human beauty vivid musical words are to passion. Somebody has said that every nation begins with poetry and ends with algebra, and passion has always refused to express itself in algebraical terms.

But a different element is beginning to enter:

What is there left for us . . . but to labour with a high heart, though it may be with weak hands, to rediscover an art of the theatre that shall be joyful, fantastic, extravagant, whimsical, beautiful, resonant and altogether reckless. The arts are at their greatest when they seek for a life growing ever more scornful of everything that is not itself and passing into its own fullness . . . and attaining that fullness, perfectly it may be . . . and from this is tragic joy and the perfectness of tragedy . . . when the world itself has slipped away in death.

The germ of much of the later Yeats is here. The conflict of the heroic and the actual, the fate which man cannot alter but which cannot alter man, the recklessness of those who come 'Proud, open-eyed and laughing to the tomb', the tragic joy of self-realisation, and the discovering of identity in death, are themes that loom large, particularly in his last poems. One could also agree that Seanchan (though not tragic until 1922) fits the ideal of extravagance and recklessness, though the Cuchulain of *On Baile's Strand* calls for a different framework of understanding. But *Deirdre* was at the forefront of Yeats' mind when he wrote this: 'I hope to have ready for the spring a play on the subject of *Deirdre*, with choruses somewhat in the Greek manner.' It is again *Deirdre* which one is expected to relate to Yeats' essay on *The Tragic Theatre* and not only because the essay begins with a reference to Synge's *Deirdre of the Sorrows*.

Yeats first takes issue with the proposition that 'the dramatic moment is always the contest of character with character'. As one enters the great periods of drama 'character grows less and sometimes disappears' and one suddenly realises that 'character is continuously present in comedy alone'. The tragedy of Corneille, Racine, Greece and Rome is a tragedy of 'passions and motives'. Shakespeare, who refuses to fit into these definitions, is 'always a writer of tragi-comedy'. Tragedy, Yeats proceeds, using a startling and expressive image, 'must always be a drowning and breaking of the dykes that separate man from man and . . . it is upon these dykes that comedy keeps house'. The technique of tragic art is therefore distinguished by 'devices to exclude or lessen character'.

If the real world is not altogether rejected, it is but touched here and there and into the places we have left empty we summon rhythm, balance, pattern, images that remind us of vast passions, the vagueness of past times, all the chimeras that haunt the edge of trance.

The essay proceeds to its climax with the image of collapsing dykes letting in the flood of *anima mundi*:

Tragic art, passionate art, the drowner of dykes, the confounder of understanding, moves us by setting us to reverie, by alluring us almost to the intensity of trance. The persons upon the stage, let us say, greaten till they are humanity itself. We feel our minds expand convulsively or spread out slowly like some moon-brightened image-crowded sea.

Leavis has rightly reminded us that reverie and trance are 'dangerous words' but it should also be remembered that the specific examples Yeats quotes in support of his theories are the Greek and Roman dramatists, Corneille and Racine, none of whom lulls one into a state of hypnosis. Devices to 'lessen character' can be found in classical drama and the idea that tragedy is concerned with 'passions and motives' is not unknown in Restoration criticism. The persons in *King Lear* do 'greaten until they are humanity itself', though the state in which one contemplates them is not one of stupefaction but of aroused intelligence, a response in which the whole mind is intensely and alertly engaged. The excesses of Yeats' position should not prevent us from seeing that he is concerned to achieve the universal in the particular, to find and hold the right distance against the 'pushing world' of the naturalistic theatre. Though the distance here is judged extremely badly, that does not mean that it ought not to exist.

Deirdre is a better play than Yeats' theories suggest and is better partly because it is not unduly deferential to those theories. It is interesting to note that Yeats preferred Miss Daragh in the main part because she had 'more intellectual tragedy in her' and because the new school to which she belonged was interested 'in building up character bit by bit'. The truth is that however hard Deirdre may try to haunt the edge of trance, she is more individualised than Cuchulain or Seanchan. But the pattern in which she moves exists without her; the story has been told before and will be told again; as Ure perceives, the effect of the play depends on Deirdre's attempt to alter the story from the inside.

Everyone in the play has some awareness of the nature of its end, though the style of the end has still to be determined. The musicians three times tell Fergus that old men are jealous and ask if Deirdre and her lover are tired of life. Fergus, who upbraids them, and who on three occasions insists that he knows the King's mind as if it were his own, nevertheless slips into the truth in a betraying reference to Lugaidh Redstripe. Deirdre throughout knows what is to come; her effort is to change the pattern's shape and, if she is unable to do so, to die well and to have her story sung rightly. Naoise, whose uncompromising commitment to the King's word is read by some as heroic 'recklessness' akin to that of Seanchan and Cuchulain, also knows where the King's word will lead him. When Deirdre says:

> When first we came into this empty house
> You had foreknowledge of our death, and even
> When speaking of the paleness of my cheek
> Your own cheek blanched. (*CPl*, pp. 184–5)

Naoise does not answer her but refers her to Fergus for an answer.

The chessboard where Lugaidh Redstripe and his wife played chess before they were put to death provides both a reminder of fate and a design for dying:

> When it was plain that they had been betrayed,
> They moved the men and waited for the end
> As it were bedtime, and had so quiet minds
> They hardly winked their eyes when the sword flashed.
>
> (*CPl*, pp. 179–80)

But the old story does not quite fit the new lovers; Naoise, whose first impulse is to a fighting finish, chooses on reflection to die more impassively:

> I never heard a death so out of reach
> Of common hearts, a high and comely end.
> What need have I, that gave up all for love,
> To die like an old king out of a fable,
> Fighting and passionate? (*CPl*, p. 190)

But it is Conchubar, not Naoise, who is master of the chessboard, When Conchubar shows himself at the door, and then disappears. Naoise rushes out imagining he is the hunter, is hunted instead, and is caught symbolically and actually in a net.

Deirdre too accepts the chess game, the enactment of the past, but she, like Naoise, requires a different style of dying. 'A good end to the long cloudy day' is what she seeks, but she has to seek it in another fashion:

> I cannot go on playing like that woman
> That had but the cold blood of the sea in her veins.
>
> (*CPl*, pp. 191–2)

The difference between Deirdre and Naoise is that Deirdre is able to create her style. Naoise may die with dignity but he dies trapped and silent. Deirdre fights for her death and makes her death reflect her. Her last scene with Conchubar in which she first displays resignation, then pretends to be attracted to the man of power, demands to pay her last debts to the old lover so that she can make a better start with the new one, beats down Conchubar's suspicions

and, in a final decisive flare of disdain, challenges him to search her
for the knife which is concealed on her, not only imposes her personality on the man at the centre of the spider's web but also obliges
the fate she cannot change, to respond to and to fulfil her nature.
Her death is her triumph because it is the only triumph which the
story can offer. At the beginning of the play the musicians observe
that the tale of Naoise and Deirdre 'were well enough/Had it a
finish'. It now has an end that is in order aesthetically as well as
tragically.

Critical opinion on *Deirdre* covers a fairly wide spectrum, the
most piquant contrast being between Henn's view that it is 'pseudo-
Elizabethan' and Ellis-Fermor's conclusion that the play has 'an
immediacy as terrible as that of Middleton, severest of Jacobean
dramatists'. The valuation suggested here is not just between these
but also to one side of them. *Deirdre* lacks the richness of *On Baile's
Strand*, the interplay between two levels of reality. Its dramatic
organisation is such that it is obliged to relinquish irony. It moves on
one plane, and almost entirely within one tone, and even the verse
runs largely at one tempo. The losses involved in these dramatic
choices do not need to be emphasised; the gains are stateliness, a
sense of ritual in the play's movement and at best the kind of 'grave
ecstasy' in the language which Yeats tried to get into *The Shadowy
Waters*. If, notwithstanding its studied remoteness, the play invites
comparison with Elizabethan drama, it is largely because of Deirdre
herself and her struggle to ensure that the events which form her
fate do not overwhelm her nature. Equally, if in reading the play
there is a certain implausibility in Deirdre's attempts to arouse
Naoise's jealousy and in her lightning changes of posture in her
dealings with Conchubar, it is only because Deirdre as a dramatic
creation is sufficiently real to allow this kind of response. Far from
being a personage on the edge of trance, she is a woman fighting to
preserve her dignity. The real world instead of being merely 'touched
here and there' is always present in her struggle to die well. Yet, to
the extent that the play escapes from ritual, it becomes clear that it is
not the kind of Elizabethan play in which it is possible to reach
through living *dramatis personae* to the larger issues that achieve
expression through them. Here the larger issues, whatever they may
be, are chimerically defined; the *dramatis personae* are insufficiently

fleshed for the particular distance from reality which they establish. The play is a mixture and succeeds and fails because of it; but the mere fact that a mixture was found unavoidable seems to expose certain weaknesses in Yeats' conception of a tragic theatre.

5

Towards Responsibilities

I

BEFORE the wind of change blew out of the Seven Woods and into
Yeats' poetry he had written two poems, *Adam's Curse* and *The
Folly of Being Comforted*, which are particularly representative of
the new spirit. Eliot comments that in these poems 'Something is
coming through' and that Yeats 'in beginning to speak as a particular man . . . is beginning to speak for man'.

The Folly of Being Comforted begins with a surprising recognition:

> One that is ever kind said yesterday:
> 'Your well-belovèd's hair has threads of grey,
> And little shadows come about her eyes;
> Time can but make it easier to be wise. . . . '

The matter-of-factness balances and validates the romantic
assertion when it returns with its old intensity:

> Time can but make her beauty over again:
> Because of that great nobleness of hers
> The fire that stirs about her, when she stirs,
> Burns but more clearly. (*CP*, p. 86)

It is an image which looks forward to *No Second Troy*:

> What could have made her peaceful with a mind
> That nobleness made simple as a fire. . . . (*CP*, p. 101)

And, looking backwards, there is a significant change in the quality
of the tribute:

C   65

But let a gentle silence wrought with music flow
Whither her footsteps go. (*CP*, p. 80)

It is not simply the replacement of music by fire (suggesting both destructiveness and purification) which is material, but the double use of 'stirs' and the knot in the movement of the verse that is almost a lump in the speaker's throat. These are the signs of a language that is beginning to be shaped less by the pattern of convention than by the pressure of feeling.

Adam's Curse includes a revealing aside on how Yeats wrote his poetry.

I said, 'A line will take us hours maybe;
Yet if it does not seem a moment's thought,
Our stitching and unstitching has been naught. . . .' (*CP*, p. 88)

There is a sense in which poetry did come to Yeats 'as naturally as the leaves to a tree' but if it came naturally it certainly did not come easily. In an 1897 letter to Bridges he refers to his desperation about 'a dramatic poem which refused to go faster than my average of some eight or nine lines a day' and in *Dramatis Personae* his output is set even lower: 'When I wrote verse, five or six lines in two or three laborious hours were a day's work, and I longed for somebody to interrupt me.' Apart from composing slowly, Yeats revised incessantly. The variorum edition displays only a small part of his stitching and unstitching. Ellmann, Jeffares and Stallworthy are among those who have shown the many and radical changes which his poems went through before they reached the threshold of publication. There are even occasions when, to judge from his diaries, Yeats follows Ben Jonson, who wrote his poems first in prose because his master Camden learned him so. Yet the effect of these revisions, particularly in the later work (when revision did not mean a disowning of the past), is nearly always in the direction of greater immediacy. It is one of the paradoxes of the creative process that a writer whose methods of composition were so painfully deliberate should have a force of impact that is unapproached by any writer of the twentieth century.

Adam's Curse is a breakaway in the direction of common speech but remains self-conscious in the manner of its breakaway.

Better go down upon your marrow-bones
And scrub a kitchen pavement, or break stones
Like an old pauper, in all kinds of weather;
For to articulate sweet sounds together
Is to work harder than all these, and yet
Be thought an idler by the noisy set
Of Bankers, Schoolmasters, and Clergymen
The martyrs call the world. (*CP*, p. 89)

Note the element of self-pity in 'martyrs', the highly simplified conception of the 'world' and the limited view of poetry as the articulation of 'sweet sounds'. The language moves in what we must accept as the right direction but in its studied avoidance of artificiality it is not immune from an artificiality of its own. The decorum is still provisional and unsettled and, towards the end of the poem, lapses back into something like the old manner.

The Green Helmet which occupies twelve pages of *Collected Poems* comprises, with *In the Seven Woods*, the total of Yeats' poetry for over a decade. The collection is distinguished by a new note of political bitterness, and though 'Romantic Ireland' has still to be buried in poetry it has already become a 'blind, bitter' and a 'fool-driven' land. The 'levelling, rancorous' mind is at its work:

The weak lay hands on what the strong has done,
Till that be tumbled that was lifted high
And discord follow upon unison,
And all things at one common level lie. (*CP*, pp. 107–8)

The Abbey audience which rioted over Synge's *Playboy of the Western World* and in which MacBride's partisans hissed Maud Gonne (she had been seeking and later secured a separation) is dismissed as a collection of 'knaves and dolts'. Both the aesthetic ideal and the political are dragged in the same ingratitude and art becomes a process of contemptuous withdrawal.

A secret between you two,
Between the proud and the proud. (*CP*, p. 103)

Yeats is more confident now about his accomplishment as a poet. He has come into his strength and words obey his call. Many things have tempted him from the craft of verse but, in the end, the craft has triumphed:

> Now nothing but comes readier to the hand
> Than this accustomed toil. (*CP*, p. 109)

But the real value of the triumph is disputable. As Helen-Maud passes across the stage of Yeats' judgement

> . . . life and letters seem
> But an heroic dream. (*CP*, p. 100)

Language is always worth less than what it expresses.

> I might have thrown poor words away
> And been content to live. (*CP*, p. 101)

The latent paradoxes are drawn together in a brief, shapely poem entitled *The Coming of Wisdom with Time*.

> Though leaves are many, the root is one;
> Through all the lying days of my youth
> I swayed my leaves and flowers in the sun;
> Now I may wither into the truth. (*CP*, p. 105)

The association of art with age and withering, and of youth with vitality, abundance and natural beauty, are, of course, characteristic lines of force in Yeats' later poetry. They undercut the antithesis between truth and lying, making 'lying' suggest not only falsity and the indolence of youth but also experience lying dormant until it is awakened into art. At the other extreme of the contrast, age is a stripping away, a simplification, a concentration upon the one root instead of the many flowers. Yet it is the root from which the flowers and leaves grow. The price of wisdom may be bleakness and the price of life avoidance of the deeper reality. But the exclusions are not final; they recover what is excluded in the total life of the image.

Political and personal passion combine in *No Second Troy*, the most celebrated poem in the collection. It starts with an explosive question:

> Why should I blame her that she filled my days
> With misery . . . (*CP*, p. 101)

and the manner in which the overflow completes and alters something which had seemed already complete in the first line is typical of the kind of suspense achieved in the poem's rhetorical management. Until the last line it is uncertain which way the flood of anger will turn. The petty violence of those who would 'hurl the little streets upon the great' is scornfully judged and found wanting; but it is only at the climax that the failure snaps into place. Similarly Maud Gonne is seen in terms of destruction. Her beauty is like a tightened bow, her mind made simple as a fire by nobleness. Simplicity is not a quality one associates with fire, though for Yeats the association was important enough for him to remember it much later in *Vacillation*. Here the word is potent in suggesting how uncompromising intensity and dedicated single-mindedness are capable of being both noble and, in terms of a practical world, naive. The tightened bow further suggests an inherent tension in heroic beauty that necessarily issues in destructiveness. But the implication can still be that heroic beauty cannot avoid its consequences, that it must not be blamed because it cannot help itself. Once again it is not until the twist of the last line that the images lock securely into their pattern. The organising thrust is cleverly withheld and the marching suspense of the monosyllables in the eleventh line, with 'why', 'what' and 'what' reiterating the accumulated questions, is a brilliant piece of dramatic manœuvring. Then the Helen image strikes into the poem, asking the last question which the whole structure has answered, putting everything in its predestined order. It is the first demonstration, and an impressive one, of a technique which Yeats was to bring to its perfection in *The Second Coming* and *Leda and the Swan*.

Admiration for *No Second Troy* need not blind us to its shortcomings. The purpose of civilisations is not to provide bonfires for eternal or heroic beauty and Ireland has not failed because it failed to be Ilium. Certainly the poem rests on a convention, but the best poems scrutinise as well as assert their conventions. It is not unfair to describe the poem as rhetoric and its vulnerability is evident from such lines as the tenth, where the rhetoric falters in propulsive power. At the same time the momentum and driving force of the poem are reminders that rhetoric has its place though not the highest of places.

Responsibilities is usually treated as a watershed in Yeats' career with the two epigraphs to the volume carefully so distinguishing it. In fact it only confirms a movement that had long been in the making. The retreat from the dream had begun more than a decade earlier; the new style had been hammered out, both in the threatre and in two collections of verse; and even the element of social indignation (responsibility in its public aspect) had made its appearance already in *The Green Helmet*. Yet the book is a watershed if only because it decisively leaves certain fascinations behind. 'In dreams begin responsibility' marches away from the past, while at the same time suggesting that the past has not been wasted and the second epigraph suggests what the volume confirms, namely that the new poetry is Yeats' recovery of himself.

The 'violent and terrible *epistle dedicatory*', as Eliot calls it, summons up Yeats' ancestors: Jervis Yeats the 'old Dublin merchant "free of the ten and four"' (amended in a note to eight and six and in reality six and ten), John Yeats, 'old country scholar, Robert Emmet's friend', the Butlers and the Armstrongs, and Yeats' 'silent and fierce' grandfather George Pollexfen 'who thought so little of danger that he had jumped overboard in the Bay of Biscay after an old hat'. It was Pollexfen who taught Yeats the value of 'wasteful virtues' but the creative wastefulness of the writer has ebbed away in commitment to a barren passion. The poet has no child—actually or figuratively. The book is all he can offer in the name of his blood. It is both his apology and his redemption.

The last poem in the volume is a single sentence in sonnet form (barely recognisable as such), written in an angrily contorted syntax and ending with a violently realistic image which convinced Pound that Yeats had become a poet but which, ironically, is taken from Erasmus. The pun on 'passing', Unterecker notes, is something which Erasmus never thought of. Both poems owe their origin to certain statements made by George Moore in *The English Review*, but both poems are, as often happens, larger than their occasions. Here the inward presence of 'the reed-throated whisperer', the spiritual friendship of Yeats' companions of the Cheshire Cheese and the aristocratic consolations of Lady Gregory's home (Kyle-nano is one of the Seven Woods), make it possible to endure the defilement of 'priceless things'. It is through the acceptance of the fundamental literary and social values that one honours the past and survives the humiliations of the present.

Between these first and last poems the series, as Untereker points out, consists of supernatural responsibilities (*The Grey Rock*), social responsibilities (The 'Lane-pictures' and 'Playboy-riots' poems), personal responsibilities (*Friends*, and the poems to Iseult and Maud Gonne), aesthetic responsibilities and the poems on beggars and hermits which define the responsibility to irresponsibility.

The 'Lane' poems grow out of one of the three public controversies that stirred Yeats' imagination. The other two were over Parnell and over Synge's 'Playboy'. To Yeats, their moral was 'that neither religion nor politics can of itself create minds with receptivity to become wise, or just or generous enough to make a nation'. Art is presumably the indispensable third element.

The controversy began when Hugh Lane, Lady Gregory's nephew, offered his valuable collection of French paintings to Dublin if a suitable permanent gallery to house them were built. Lane's preference was for a bridge gallery by Lutyens spanning the Liffey, but Lutyens had been born English and the Dublin nationalists had the basis for an attack that began with the bridge but ended by including Lane and his paintings. An attempt to raise the money by subscription produced a discouraging response and the city's final offer was a tenth of what was required. Lane, in what Yeats described as 'a moment of pique', loaned the pictures to the London National Gallery and bequeathed them to that gallery in 1913. Later he added a codicil under which the pictures would have returned to Dublin if a building were provided for them within five years of Lane's death. Unfortunately the codicil was unwitnessed and Lane went down with the *Lusitania* before it could be witnessed.

The first poem in the series was directed against Lord Ardilaun who argued (in the best traditions of international aid after the Second World War) that money should not be given until the amount collected proved a demand for the project. Yeats, who had read Castiglione's *The Courtier* and who had also visited Italy in 1907, points out that Duke Ercole had not sought the approval of 'onion sellers' before producing Plautus, that Guidobaldo took no plebiscite among the shepherds when he built his palace (the 'grammar-school of courtesies') on 'Urbino's windy hill', and that Cosimo de Medici was indifferent to public opinion when he commissioned Michelozzo to design the library of St Mark in Florence. The poems appeals to the prospective donor to abandon the way of the Paudeens (Yeats' generic name for penny-pinchers) and to:

> Look up in the sun's eye and give
> What the exultant heart calls good (*CP*, p. 120)

The lines recall Yeats' conviction that 'only the wasteful virtues win the sun' and the fusion in *The Green Helmet* of aristocratic and heroic ideals.

> How should the world be luckier if this house,
> Where passion and precision have been one
> Time out of mind, became too ruinous
> To breed the lidless eye that loves the sun? (*CP*, p. 106)

Although Yeats' poem had been meant for another person, William Murphy, the owner of the *Evening Herald* and the *Irish Independent*, saw his reflection in it. He replied 'from what he described as "Paudeen's point of view" and "Paudeen's point of view" it was'. Yeats retaliated with *September 1913* in which the relatively bland tone of the first poem is abandoned and the jibing refrain celebrates the triumph of the Philistine and the death of ideals:

> Romantic Ireland's dead and gone,
> It's with O'Leary in the grave. (*CP*, p. 121)

Against the shopkeeping morality of those who 'fumble in a greasy till' adding 'the halfpence to the pence' the wasteful virtues are once again emphasised:

> They weighed so lightly what they gave (*CP*, p. 121)

> Was it for this the wild geese spread
> The grey wing upon every tide;
> For this that all that blood was shed,
> For this Edward Fitzgerald died,
> And Robert Emmet and Wolfe Tone,
> All that delirium of the brave? (*CP*, p. 121)

The clinical word 'delirium', placed arrestingly in the torrent of rhetoric, suggests not only how heroic action appears to the

Paudeens, but also its real nature, 'fantastic, extravagant . . . and altogether reckless', as it is in Yeats' ideal of the tragic theatre. The wild geese remind one of Cuchulain's identification of himself in *The Green Helmet* with 'the great barnacle-goose' and of Malachi Stilt-Jack in the last poems, 'a barnacle goose/Far up in the stretches of night'. These are the ideals buried with O'Leary; action capable of reaching into reality has been replaced by a 'shivering' prudence.

The next two poems assert the artist's pride and solitariness against the Paudeens. When his work comes to nothing he should 'Be secret and exult' like a 'laughing string' played 'amid a place of stone'. On a lonely height, amid stones and thorn trees, where everything stands in the eye of God, he hears the cry of the curlew and realises that no soul lacks 'a sweet crystalline cry'. 'Crystalline', with its evocations of lucidity and intricate order, suggests the coherence which the individual can achieve, even in a hostile world.

To a Shade brings us back to a world more thorny than the windswept landscape of thorn-trees. Ironically, if the ghost of Parnell were to revisit the town, it would be either to contemplate his monument (the entombment of all that he stood for), or in circumstances in which the town is given dignity by the elimination of the human element:

> When grey gulls flit about instead of men,
> And the gaunt houses put on majesty: (*CP*, p. 123)

In any case, history repeats itself in viciousness, and Lane, a man of Parnell's own 'passionate serving kind', has been insulted for his pains and disgraced for his open-handedness:

> Your enemy, an old foul mouth, had set
> The pack upon him. (*CP*, p. 123)

There is no place for the shade here, for even a marginal concession to Parnell's spirit, for the minor remnants of the noble which would permit the ghost to listen at the corners. What Parnell represents is more likely to survive in the tomb than in the reality of contemporary Ireland.

In the opening poem of the *Beggar* series, King Guare meets three beggars and offers a thousand pounds to the first of them who can fall asleep within a period of three days. They indulge in cutthroat competition to prevent each other from obtaining the prize with the result that no one is able to obtain it. At the end of the poem the old crane of Gort informs us that the best way to catch trout is to seem indifferent to catching them.

In the next poem, two hermits, one prayerful and the other flea-bitten, discuss the after-life, while the third, who has caught something of the essence of saintliness:

> Giddy with his hundredth year,
> Sang unnoticed like a bird. (*CP*, p. 128)

Beggar to Beggar Cried is said to reflect Yeats' reaction to Lady Gregory's wish that he should marry. A lass who is not too comely and not too rich, a comfortable house and the 'nightly peace' of his garden, will not drown the call into reality, 'the wind-blown clamour of the barnacle-geese'.

The poems to Iseult Gonne look back, through her, to the innocence that precedes responsibility:

> What need have you to dread
> The monstrous crying of wind? (*CP*, p. 137)

and recognise that until innocence becomes experience it must fail to understand experience.

> But I am old and you are young,
> And I speak a barbarous tongue. (*CP*, p. 137)

Fallen Majesty takes the established associations with which Yeats surrounds the figure of Maud Gonne and makes the 'burning cloud' of her presence evocative, not only of the glory of beauty, but also of an intensity that destroys itself.

Friends praises three women, Lady Gregory, Mrs Shakespeare and Maud Gonne. The poem is one of the many in this collection which show Yeats' supreme skill in weaving a complex sentence across the short span of a three or four stress line to achieve both fluency and crispness. MacNeice comments acutely that anyone 'who has tried to write such a poem, when it is not broken into short stanzas, knows how hard it is so to arrange the sentences as to avoid breaking the run of the whole, and so to control the rhythms that the poem does not get into a skid'.

The last lines of *Friends* remember Maud Gonne again in an extraordinary blend of bitterness and forgiveness:

And what of her that took
All till my youth was gone
With scarce a pitying look?
How could I praise that one?
When day begins to break
I count my good and bad,
Being wakeful for her sake,
Remembering what she had,
What eagle look still shows,
While up from my heart's root
So great a sweetness flows
I shake from head to foot. (*CP*, p. 139)

The same experience forms the climax of the *Dialogue of Self and Soul*:

When such as I cast out remorse
So great a sweetness flows into the breast
We must laugh and we must sing,
We are blest by everything,
Everything we look upon is blest. (*CP*, p. 267)

In *Vacillation* Yeats speaks of it again:

My body of a sudden blazed;
And twenty minutes more or less
It seemed, so great my happiness,
That I was blessèd and could bless. (*CP*, p. 284)

The theoretical basis of the experience is found in Yeats' 1910 essay on *J. M. Synge and the Ireland of his Time*:

There is in the creative joy an acceptance of what life brings, because we have understood the beauty of what it brings, or a hatred of death for what it takes away, which arouses within us, through some sympathy perhaps with all other men, an energy so noble, so powerful, that we laugh aloud and mock in the terror and the sweetness of our exaltation, at death and oblivion.

Some of the surplus energy without which scholarship is impossible has been spent on debating whether or not Yeats is a mystic. In this particular experience, both blazingly intense and fraught with a sense of revelation (the sweetness flowing up from the depths of his being), the apprehension is almost physical, but what is apprehended is not the world beyond, or the world transformed, but the world as it is, passionately and unflinchingly accepted.

That the Night Come sees the eternal subject in tragic perspectives, achieving its effect by a daring conflation of two images of the soul seeking the night of death and of the King pressing on to the night of marriage, with the falling rhythm of the last line perfectly expressing the stroke of oblivion. The impetuosity of the last but one line ('to bundle time away') stands in interestingly violent contrast to the repudiation of time in *The Wind Among the Reeds*.

The Cold Heaven is the most compelling and elusive poem in the volume. In the very first line 'rook-delighting', with its ominous implications, establishes the characteristic blend of terror and excitement that links this heaven to the 'thrilling region of thick-ribbed ice', the after-life that Claudio sees in *Measure for Measure*. The burning ice symbolises the dramatic situation—age thinking itself back into the hot blood of youth. Paradoxically, the wildness of the imagination and heart (wild in their intensity and in the havoc they create) are tormenting precisely because their wildness insists upon reality. The casual thoughts 'of that and this' are stripped away and the mind is driven back into its past but also into its nakedness. 'I took all the blame out of all sense and reason' affirms a sense of guilt which is all the more real for not being precisely attached, and the next line gives that guilt a physical and anguished intensity. The image of the man 'riddled with light', shot through and confounded by the devastation of understanding, passes into that of the 'confusion' of the death bed, the physical turmoil of the struggle and the mind's bewilderment as it stares into the unknown. Then, as the ghost quickens, clarity brings nakedness. Individual guilt leads into cosmic punishment. The man excessive in blaming himself is stricken by the injustice of the skies. At one level therefore a balance, or more precisely a correspondence, is preserved; but at another level the injustice done to the individual who accepts a responsibility which sense and reason forbid is frighteningly compounded by the injustice poured on him by a malignant universe.

Henn rightly considers *The Cold Heaven* the finest poem in *Responsibilities* and Hone regards its 'controlled fury' as characteristic of Yeats' work at its best. Its profound power flows from its immediacy. It is not argued but presented. Note how the qualification in the last line but one ('as the books say') is thrown into the path of the poem to be swept aside by its impetus. The suggestion that the question may be academic only proves that it is not. And the answer, apparently open, is almost closed by the pattern of the poem. It is for the engaged mind of the reader to live the conclusion.

III

When the Easter Rising of 1916 broke out Yeats was staying with the Rothensteins in Gloucestershire. He was personally acquainted with the leaders in the tragedy: he had visited Pearse's school, read and admired MacDonagh's book on Gaelic influences on English poetry, worked with James Connolly on the Wolfe Tone Memorial Committee and had lost Maud Gonne to John MacBride. His reactions to the disaster seem to have been mixed. Hone quotes him as speaking to Rothenstein of innocent and patriotic theorists carried away by the belief that they must sacrifice themselves to an abstraction. On the other hand he wrote to Lady Gregory in May that he had no idea that any public event could move him so deeply. Echoing Maud Gonne's thought that 'tragic dignity has returned to Ireland', he said: 'I am trying to write a poem on the men executed: "terrible beauty has been born again".' In July 1916 he was still divided between admiration for the bravery of the uprising and doubts about its wisdom. ' "Romantic Ireland's dead and gone" sounds old-fashioned now. It seemed true in 1913 but I did not foresee 1916. The late Dublin rebellion, whatever one can say of its wisdom, will long be remembered for its heroism. "They weighed so lightly what they gave" and gave too in some cases without hope of success.'

Easter 1916 was published by Clement Shorter in an edition of twenty-five copies. Ellmann lists two other poems on the uprising, The Rose Tree and Sixteen Dead Men, as written on 7 April and 17 December respectively. All three poems were withheld from the general public until 1920 when they appeared in the November issue of The Dial along with six other poems, including The Second Coming. Easter 1916 had been first printed slightly earlier in the New Statesman of 23 October.

Sixteen Dead Men recognises that heroism erects its own reality:

> . . . is their logic to outweigh
> MacDonagh's bony thumb? (*CP*, p. 205)

Conversely, *The Rose Tree* recognises that a certain kind of reality can only be erected by heroism:

> There's nothing but our own red blood
> Can make a right Rose Tree. (*CP*, p. 206)

Easter 1916, the most distinguished poem of the trio, is formally associated with *September 1913*, not only by its similarity of title but by its dating of 25 September (of the twenty-eight poems dated in *Collected Poems* eighteen are dated to the month). In its content the later poem takes back the earlier. Yeats had for too long lived within a political cartoon in which passion and precision were one in the big houses, in which the peasantry was full of instinctive poets and in which the commercial and contemptible middle classes added Biddy's halfpennies to Paudeen's pence. MacNeice's conclusion that big house culture consisted of nothing more than 'an obsolete bravado, an insidious bonhomie and a way with horses' can be and has been disputed, but to point out that Yeats' diagram is not wholly without a basis is not really to justify it. Fortunately *Easter 1916* is not a poem of sackcloth and ashes; it is a poem deeply troubled by the knowledge that heroic action can have more than one implication. The middle-class men coming from 'counter or desk' known only in the exchange of 'polite meaningless words', the schoolmaster who once belonged to 'the noisy set/That martyrs call the world', the 'drunken vainglorious lout' who had bitterly wronged those close to Yeats' heart, are all capable of a deeper life below the 'motley' and the 'casual comedy', a radical transformation of their appearance. But the deeper life is a divided life. Hearts dominated by a single purpose are 'enchanted to a stone' troubling the living stream. The word 'enchanted' minimises the apparent disapproval and in the vital central image, where the minute-by-minute life of the stream is perfectly seized in the description and movement, the sudden recognition comes that heroic action, however obsessed, is inalienably part of the life that it troubles:

> Minute by minute they live;
> The stone's in the midst of all. (*CP*, p. 204)

At this point, indeed, the manipulation of the imagery gives the stone permanency in the midst of transience, and, with the very next lines ('Too long a sacrifice/Can make a stone of the heart') underlining the other evocations of 'stone', the balance is complete and fully achieved poetically. It is characteristic of the subtlety of the imaginative reasoning that the heart's stoniness is born of the emotional fervour of sacrifice, but, characteristically also, this implication is cut back before it can develop to the detriment of the balance.

> And what if excess of love
> Bewildered them till they died? (*CP*, pp. 204–5)

The poem is, in fact, typical of Yeats' achievement, in which the images in the poetic organisation both challenge and amend each other, creating a total life that exists only and fully in the terms that are chosen. In these circumstances the refrain

> A terrible beauty is born,

is not, as Knights concludes, an escape from full realisation or 'a lapse into something like Yeats' earlier manner', but a consummation of the forces at work in the poem. With *Easter 1916* and with *Responsibilities* behind him, Yeats has completed his emancipation from the twilight, has securely achieved the self-conquest that is style and has fought his way into the twentieth century.

6

Metaphors for Poetry

I

IN *A Packet for Ezra Pound* Yeats informs us with disarming candour that his poetry has 'gained in self-possession and power'. 'I owe this change', he continues, 'to an incredible experience', and goes on to add that four days after his marriage his wife attempted automatic writing. What she took down was so profound and exciting that Yeats was prepared to devote the rest of his life 'to explaining and piecing together those scattered sentences'. But the spirits, with a wisdom denied to some literary critics, informed him that this was unnecessary. 'We have come to give you metaphors for poetry.' Those who are not prepared to take poetry as seriously as Yeats have seized on this remark as evidence of the essential triviality of the 'System',[1] but to Yeats himself, who had cast his life into his rhymes, the strange designs which the communicators dictated and the frustrators confused were the climax of a thirty-year search for synthesis.

Yeats' *Autobiographies* have some of the imaginative order that a literary mind cannot help seeing even when it looks back on its own life; but there is no reason to doubt his statement that the need for a centre of creative meaning, a 'religion' capable of giving birth to poetry, was present in his mind from his early twenties.

---

1. By the System is meant the blend of philosophy, mythology and expository symbolism which constitutes the substance of A Vision.

I am very religious, and deprived by Huxley and Tyndall, whom I detested, of the simple-minded religion of my childhood, I had made a new religion, almost an infallible church of poetic tradition, of a fardel of stories, and of personages, and of emotions, inseparable from their first expression, passed on from generation to generation by poets and painters with some help from philosophers and theologians. I wished for a world, where I could discover this tradition perpetually, and not in pictures and in poems only, but in tiles round the chimney piece and in the hangings that kept out the draught.

In these years when a sentence formed in Yeats' mind without his willing it, exhorting him to hammer his thoughts into unity, the synthesis he sought was a public one, expressed not only in literature, but in every aspect of the life which literature reflected. Unity of Being, 'using that term as Dante used it when he compared beauty in the *Convito* to a perfectly proportioned human body', was something that existed 'in man and race alike'. Yeats' father 'preferred a comparison to a musical instrument so strung that if we touch a string all the strings murmur faintly'; here also the comparison can be taken both as referring to the individual sensibility (the anticipation of Eliot's unified sensibility is striking), or as representing the entire creative tradition which murmurs in response to the touch of the individual talent. Later, Yeats was to see Unity of Being as more specifically correlated to a Unity of Culture, with the Renaissance marking the point of dissociation when things fell apart, both in the exterior and the inner theatre. Once again, the formulation anticipates certain theories which were later to cause excitement in the literary world.

Yeats' early attempts at synthesis, therefore, were not a bleak recognition of the need to hew his own path. Instead, he sought to discover himself in a movement and through that movement to achieve a valid and creative relationship with reality. His aim was the public and not the personal myth. Irish legend was to provide him with a mythology rooted in tradition and married 'to rock and hill'. Magic was to lead him to the great mind and the memory, the unconscious knowledge that was shared by all men. Symbolism was designed to call down the footsteps of the *anima mundi* over the heart. The 'age of criticism' was about to be succeeded by 'an age of imagination, of moods, of revelation'. This sense of an impending dispensation seems to have reached its greatest intensity in 1896 when Yeats was negotiating the purchase of Castle Rock near Lough Key as a place of retreat for the Order of Celtic Mysteries:

I had an unshakable conviction, arising how or whence I cannot tell, that invisible gates would open, as they opened for Blake, as they opened for Swedenborg, as they opened for Boehme, and that this philosophy would find its manuals for devotion in all imaginative literature, and set before Irishmen for special manual an Irish literature which, though made by many minds, would seem the work of a single mind, and turn our places of beauty or legendary association into holy symbols. (*Hados Chameliantos*)

Yeats was stubborn in admitting defeat and three years later in his controversy with Eglinton he was still referring to the 'renewal of belief' as 'the great movement of our time'. It is not until 1906 that we find him acknowledging that 'all symbolic art should arise out of a real belief, and that it cannot do so in this age proves that this age is a road and not a resting place for the imaginative arts'. After this the end is unavoidable. 'The dream of my early manhood,' Yeats wrote in sombre retrospect, 'that a modern nation can return to Unity of Culture is false; though it may be we can achieve it for some small circle of men and women and there leave it till the moon bring round its century.' The long effort at a public synthesis had collapsed and though the invisible gates were to open shortly, they were to do so for Yeats alone.

II

Although elaborate explanations of the System have been offered it still remains intimidating and exasperating to the common reader. The exposition which follows can perhaps be omitted without seriously imperilling an understanding of the poetry; it is put forward because it is necessary to know what the System says before deciding the extent to which the poetry depends on, or is enriched by, knowledge of it.

Yeats' vision is best approached as a group of interrelated symbols, which attempt to illuminate the basic pattern and rhythms of both natural and supernatural existence. He claimed, for example, that his gyres provided 'a classification . . . of every possible movement of thought and life' and in the same way he regarded his wheel as representative of 'every completed movement of thought or life, twenty-eight incarnations, a single incarnation, a single judgement or act of thought'.

The first and most inclusive of Yeats' symbols is the sphere, which represents eternal and total reality, beyond time, beyond space and, even more important, beyond conflict. Characteristically, even concord is experienced in time, not as a quality of the eternal, but in opposition to discord as one of the antinomies which shape existence. Because the ultimate reality 'falls in human consciousness into a series of antinomies' the sphere becomes manifested 'the moment it is thought of . . . as the thirteenth cone'. The thirteenth cone is the element of freedom in Yeats' otherwise determinist system. It is 'that cycle which may deliver us from the twelve cycles of space and time'. In the cyclical process of history also 'at the critical moment, the *Thirteenth Cone*, the sphere, the unique intervenes'. Although the sphere and the thirteenth cone loom large in the second edition of *A Vision* it seems that they are brought in largely to achieve what Yeats called 'the completed symbol'. They do not possess his mind imaginatively and though Ribh's fourth song is not without its subtleties, a comparison with the third section of *Burnt Norton* shows that Yeats' strength is not the poetry of the still point.

Conflict is Yeats' natural element and his important symbols, the wheel and the gyre, are fundamentally diagrams of conflict. The wheel is divided into twenty-eight phases which represent the cycle of incarnations of an individual, but which can equally represent the cyclical movement of history, or the cycle of an individual life. In the movement of the wheel as described by Yeats 'Man seeks the opposite or the opposite of his condition, attains his object so far as it is attainable, at phase fifteen and returns to phase one again'. The movement can also be described as an evolution towards increasing subjectivity and self-realisation (maximised at phase fifteen), followed by a contra-evolution towards objectivity and self-extinction (maximised at phase one). The half of the wheel in which subjectivity predominates is also described as antithetical and lunar; that in which objectivity is dominant is primary and solar.

The soul moving round the wheel is the product of four faculties

—Will and Mask, Creative Mind and Body of Fate. The Will is the normal ego, the first matter of personality. The Mask is the anti-self but paradoxically the means for the realisation of oneself. When in *The Death of Synge* Yeats suggests that 'all happiness depends on the energy to assume the mask of some other self' and that 'all joyous or creative life is a rebirth as something not oneself' he is proposing, not impersonality, but the completion of personality by projection into something beyond it. Similarly, in *Estrangement* he affirms his convictions that to live an 'arduous full life' and to impose a discipline on ourselves instead of accepting one from others we must 'imagine ourselves as different from what we are and assume that second self'. Man desires his opposite and fulfils himself in embodying his opposite and the conflict thus sought is the basis of creative development. *Ego Dominus Tuus* gives the doctrine its poetic expression:

> I call to the mysterious one who yet
> Shall walk the wet sands by the edge of the stream
> And look most like me, being indeed my double,
> And prove of all imaginable things
> The most unlike, being my anti-self. . . . (*CP*, p. 182)

The other pair in the four faculties, Creative Mind and Body of Fate, involve oppositions which are less complex or, possibly, less explored. The Creative Mind is defined by Yeats in the first edition of *A Vision* as that part of the mind which is consciously constructive and which seeks to act upon external events. The Body of Fate is the stream of phenomena or series of events that appears to the individual to be forced on him from without. At phase one (the position of the Will determines the phases) Will and Creative Mind coincide, contemplating Mask and Body of Fate, which similarly coincide at phase fifteen. At phase fifteen the positions of the pairs are reversed. These are the only two phases on the wheel where equilibrium is possible and are consequently outside the human condition. At every other phase there is a disequilibrium specific to that phase, brought about by the anti-clockwise movement of Will and Mask and the clockwise movement of Creative Mind and Body of Fate. In phases twenty-six to four, however, objectivity (except in phase twenty-seven, that of the Saint) is so predominant that the phases do not produce 'character of sufficient distinctiveness to become historical'. There are thus twenty-one basic types of human character each made up of a specific conflict between the faculties and capable of interpretation according to that conflict. The possibilities of conflict are further widened because in twenty cases out of twenty-one an individual's phase will not coincide with the historical phase into which he is born. Further combinations of disequilibrium arise because both Mask and Creative Mind can be either truly or falsely chosen. A false choice however means that the incarnation has to be repeated and the freedom that seems allowed is therefore deceptive. True freedom is the recognition of the wheel's necessity.

The gyres execute in three dimensions the process that the wheel depicts in two. These whirling, interpenetrating cones, 'living the other's death, dying the other's life', each expanding as the other contracts in time, reversing spectacularly at the flash-points of crisis, are a nearly ideal schematisation of conflict. Yeats' language as he describes them is full of the metaphors of combat. Subjectivity and objectivity are 'intersecting states struggling against one another'. The subjective cone is 'achieved and defended by continual conflict with its opposite'. Every faculty 'is alternately sword and shield' and, finally, to use an eloquent image from *Per Amica Silentia Lunae*, 'Every movement, in feeling or in thought, prepares in the dark, by its own increasing clarity and confidence, its own executioner'. The gyres stand basically for the conflict between objective and subjective, between the 'emotional and aesthetic' and the 'reasonable and moral', but they can also stand for any of the great oppositions—love and hate, demon and beast, the religious and the secular, permanence and change, the natural and the supernatural—which shape human and historical existence through their recurrent and inconclusive battles. Once again, the possibilities of conflict multiply since 'gyres may be interrupted or twisted by greater gyres, divide into two lesser gyres or multiply into four and so on'. Even individuals can be primary and antithetical to one another to such an extent 'that they form a common gyre or series of gyres'.

History, as might be expected, consists of wheels within wheels or gyres twisting gyres. The wheel of a civilisation lasts for a millennium, the wheel of an era for two, and there are larger revolutions behind these which it is perhaps confusing to consider. The wheel of the Pre-Christian era begins with the rape of Leda ('the annunciation that founded Greece') and ends with the birth of Christ. Phidias represents the climax of the second Greek civilisation; the first is too remote for its cyclical course to be charted. In the Christian era Byzantium (dated, as Yeats admits, with some flexibility) represents the full moon of the civilisation that ended at A.D. 1000, and the Renaissance the climax of self-realisation of the civilisation now sweeping to its reversal. Nineteen-twenty-five, when Yeats was writing this particular chapter of *A Vision*, is reckoned at phase twenty-three on the gyre of the civilisation and between phase twenty-five and twenty-six on the gyre of the era. The main combatant gyres in the historical process are the religious and the secular but almost equally important is the contest between Symbolic Europe and Symbolic Asia. The former is regarded as antithetical and lunar, the latter as primary and solar. Christ was begotten by the West upon the East; the coming dispensation will be begotten by the East upon the West. Religious life became primary, and secular life antithetical, with the coming of Christ; with the Second Coming these attributions will be reversed. These are the crisis points in the larger gyre of the era; in the smaller gyres of civilisations Persia fell to Phidias' westward-moving art, Rome to the eastward-moving art of Byzantium and Byzantium in its turn to the westward movement of the Renaissance. 'Each age unwinds the thread another age had wound.'

The natural and supernatural worlds are linked in a series of correspondences of the sort that would delight the Elizabethan mind. The Daimon corresponds to the earthly personality, but 'Nations, culture, schools of thought' may also have their Daimons. The Four Principles of Spirit and Celestial Body (mind and its object) and Husk and Passionate Body (sense and its object) corres- pond to the four faculties. The Principles are described as the 'innate ground of the *Faculties*', and as 'the *Faculties* transferred, as it weer, from a concave to a convex mirror or vice versa'. They inform the Faculties, but 'it is the *Faculties* alone that are apparent and conscious in human history'. Like the Faculties, the Principles have their gyres and wheels, but these include not only the time between birth and death but also the time between death and rebirth. The wheel of the Principles completes its movement in four thousand years and instead of being divided according to the phases of the moon is divided according to the signs of the zodiac. Problems consequently arise in synchronising the movement of the lower wheel with the higher, which are perhaps incapable of solution. In general, the period between death and birth corresponds to day in the cycle of night and day and to summer (the period between Aries and Scorpio) in the Daimonic year. There are therefore six stages in the passage from death to rebirth. The first stage, called *The Vision of the Blood Kindred*, is a synthesis of the past, a vision 'of all those bound to us through *Husk* and *Passionate Body*'. The second stage, that of the *Dreaming Back* and the *Return*, is a meditation over the past and a reliving of it, after which *Husk* and *Passionate Body* fade away. Then follows the stage of the *Shiftings* in which 'the *Spirit* is purified of good and evil'. The fourth stage is that of the *Marriage* or the *Beatitude* in which 'good and evil vanish into the whole', the *Celestial Body* falls away and 'Christ is revealed'. In the fifth stage of *Purification* a new *Husk* and *Passionate Body* are acquired. The last stage is that of *Foreknowledge* in which the life to come is both foreseen and accepted.

Ellmann rightly stresses the continuity between Yeats' earlier and later symbolism. The sun and the moon become the primary and antithetical, the four elements become the four faculties, the rose becomes the sphere and the fixed cross of the antinomies the whirling gyres. Except for the sphere, the dynamic has everywhere superseded the static. Struggle and combat replace consummation and repose. Even the sphere itself is most vividly described in an image, not of rest, but of contrary efforts, that cancel each other perfectly: 'a being racing into the future passes a being racing into the past, two footprints perpetually obliterating each other, toe to heel, heel to toe'.

'My instructors,' says Yeats, 'identify consciousness with conflict, not with knowledge, substitute for subject and object and their attendant knowledge a struggle towards harmony, towards Unity of Being. Logical and emotional conflict alike lead towards a reality which is concrete, sensuous, bodily.' This is a statement which annotates one of Yeats' last and most eloquent convictions: 'Man can embody truth but he cannot know it.' Reality cannot be analysed. It can only be experienced, and the wisest man is he who has lived most totally and profoundly. 'All knowledge is bio-graphy', to quote one of Yeats' instructive over-statements. In such a philosophy good and evil take secondary places and the decisive terms are completeness and incompleteness. The Mask extends the personality and for that extension to be maximised it must be all that is 'handled least, least looked upon'. The gyres enlarge consciousness through conflict. The twelve cycles of twenty-eight incarnations compel one to live completely and understandingly through every possible permutation of human nature. Escape is achieved only by those who accept necessity, by individuals who know 'how to exhaust their possible lives, to set, as it were, the hands of the clock racing'. Even Unity of Being is achieved in earthly existence by 'some man, who, while struggling with his fate and his destiny until every energy of his being has been roused, is content that he should struggle with no final conquest'. Thus, in the end, it is the struggle not the objective which matters. Harmony demands completeness. Unless it includes all, that which it fails to include becomes its antagonist. Complete harmony is the sphere, lying beyond human consciousness; but within that consciousness even harmony is achieved in terms of conflict. 'I find my peace', Yeats wrote to Ethel Mannin, 'by pitting my sole nature against something and the greater the tension the greater my self-knowledge.' The only reality we can know is 'concrete, sensuous bodily', and therefore inevitably partial and incomplete. It is the failure and the struggle, undyingly renewed.

Any account of *A Vision* is necessarily a diagram of a diagram but the exercise is a necessary prelude to the examination of its meaning. Some of the claims made for it are evidently incapable of being substantiated. It is argued for example that the wheel represents the cycle of an individual life, but it can hardly be maintained that Yeats reached the full moon of self-realisation in 1902 (the period of the self-effacing rhythm) and that his later work represents a progressive extinction of personality. It is also argued that the gyres and the wheel represent 'every completed movement of thought', but a poem like *Leda and the Swan*, though cyclic in the view of life it urges, seems to be far from cyclic in its structure. Yeats' typical movement is the progress (sometimes relentless and at others deceptively casual) towards a climax that is prepared for and yet withheld until it sets the whole poem in order by its impact. Again it is argued that the System provides a complete classification of human nature ('a form of science for the study of human nature' is how Yeats describes it in a letter to L. A. G. Strong), but some of the couplings—Lady Gregory with Queen Victoria, Calvin with George Herbert and even the well-known one of Shakespeare with Napoleon—seem deliberately provocative rather than profound. Yeats is said to have altered Pound's phase after watching him feed the Rapallo cats and this is not the only occasion on which he proved to be more pragmatic than his critics.

The inference is that *A Vision* needs to be imaginatively rather than literally received. It would not be necessary to establish this conclusion so laboriously if the details of Yeats' geometry did not seem to invite a literal and quasi-scientific attention. Indeed the abracadabra which surrounds the System has led to much confusion (some of it intended) and has mesmerised readers into believing that what it presents is bizarre, esoteric or, at the least, extremely individual. Actually, several of the ingredients of the System are wholly conventional and the massive attempts made to rehabilitate it only break down what should be an open door. Among those who adhere to the world's religions there are more people who believe in reincarnation than people who do not. The cyclical view of history is not unusual. As Northrop Frye remarks, most poets and critics are Spenglerians, several of them considerably before Spengler. The gyres have sporadic precedents (which Yeats is careful to point out) and in any case the interpretation of change in terms of conflict is almost venerable in its origins. Even today one need only open a typical history of English Literature to find the classical and romantic gyres locked in tedious and interminable combat. Finally, the System has unexpected links with contemporary thought. Though Yeats is careful to distinguish a 'contrary' from a 'negation' his view of the character (not the teleology) of the socio-historic process is intriguingly reminiscent of the Marxian view. The interpenetration of opposites (as in the gyres), the growth of quantitative into qualitative changes, the transformation of history at the flash-points of revolutionary crisis and the idea of freedom as the recognition of necessity are all part of the vocabulary of Communist thought. Yeats' use of these characteristics is of course very much his own;

the point is simply that the System, both in its content and in some of its dispositions, originates in a *milieu* which is considerably wider than the mind of the man.

The elements of the System are drawn from many sources; but the synthesis Yeats makes of it is unmistakably Yeatsian, a diagram not merely of reality but of the immediate reality of his life. As early as 1901 Yeats had suggested that 'there is some one myth for every man which, if we but knew it, would make us understand all he did and thought', and it is not uninstructive to look at *A Vision* in this light. Yeats, to use his own description of Blake, was 'a man crying out for a mythology and trying to make one because he could not find one to his hand'. The mind of the poet demands myth and not philosophy, 'not abstract truth, but a kind of vision of reality which satisfies the whole being'. 'I have constructed a myth,' Yeats wrote to Olivia Shakespeare, 'but then one can believe in a myth—one only assents to philosophy.' In the introduction to *The Resurrection* he is even more emphatic: 'For years I have been preoccupied with a myth that was itself a reply to a myth. I do not mean a fiction, but one of those statements our nature is compelled to make and employ as a truth though there cannot be sufficient evidence.'

Yeats describes *A Vision* in many ways but most frequently as a myth. Unfortunately, its presentation makes it difficult to receive it as such. It is too abstract and too schematic to possess the imagination. Yeats himself was sufficiently aware of this aspect of his system to describe his 'circuits of sun and moon' as 'stylistic arrangements of experience comparable to the cubes in the drawings of Wyndham Lewis and to the ovoids in the sculpture of Brancusi'. Here the diagrams of *A Vision* are seen as symbolic forms, rather than full-blooded mythologies. Yeats then adds significantly (and a little obscurely) that these stylistic arrangements have helped him 'to hold in a single thought reality and justice'. 'Justice' can perhaps be interpreted as justice to the creative needs of the artist, to his hunger for significance and order. 'I wished for a system of thought', Yeats wrote, 'that would leave the imagination free to create and yet make all that it created, or could create, part of the one history and that the soul's. The Greeks certainly had such a system and so had Dante . . . and I think no man since.'

A Vision provided Yeats with a framework that made all that

he imagined 'part of the one history'. Every event found its reverberation elsewhere. If the string of a single experience was touched,
all the strings of reality murmured in response. Each thought and
emotion that the man had lived through could be drawn into the
unity of what the poet created. A setting was provided for Yeats'
poetic history and for the commitments that history had developed
—the theory of the Mask, the belief in magic, the failure of the invisible gates to open, the passionate pursuit of Unity of Being, the
conviction that, since the Middle Ages, minds as well as things had
progressively fallen apart. In this way a peculiarly authoritative
connection was created between Yeats' life and his 'philosophy'.
The System became the interpretation of his life and his life, conversely, the experience of the System. This feeling that his experience was naturally meaningful, that it could be made responsible to a
single synthesis, gave Yeats' poetry authority and a sense of direction, his imagination was set free to create by the conviction that
its products would vivify the largest possible contexts.

The stubborn question remains of how important *A Vision* is in
the interpretation of Yeats' poetry. There are many who argue that
it is all-important and that Yeats' later work can only be fully known
or even essentially known when it is approached through a full
knowledge of the System. There are others who suggest that to
admire the poetry is to endorse the philosophy, not necessarily by
accepting it, but at least by recognising that the thought contained
in it is significant, intelligent and even profound. It is possible to
accept Stock's view that great poetry does not grow out of flabby
thought and yet to feel that the core of Yeats' thought is in his
poetry and that only in the poetry does it live with sufficient passion
and authority for disbelief to be suspended in its presence. Perhaps
one should go further and suggest that what is in the poetry is not
'thought' but embodiment. Yeats may take the System as his point
of departure but a time must come when the poem begins to live in
its own logic and one is conscious only of 'bird and woman blotting
out the Babylonian mathematical starlight'. The best poems leave
the System behind them and give poetic flesh and blood to certain
deep insights about the quality of existence which the System cer-
tianly implies but which are equally certainly implied by other
systems. It is the possession of this common ground of experience

which makes the poetry first viable and then vital. The act of writing in poetic language is a recognition that others have visions besides yourself and that what you see must be made valid in their sight. Yeats himself recognised this responsibility, the responsibility of all poets to achieve a public language: 'that word which I had not thought of myself is a word I want'. One could add his favourite quotation from Goethe: 'A poet needs all philosophy but should keep it out of his work.' The *Geeta* that he proposes to leave to posterity is significantly 'not doctrine, but song'. Reality is 'concrete, sensuous, bodily' and if one believes in myth and only assents to philosophy it is because 'belief is love and the concrete alone is loved'. Poetry represents the incarnate insight, the living, demanding and accepting body, and among scholars there must be some to doubt that the body is best known by scrutinising the skeleton.

The danger of reading Yeats' poetry as *A Vision* versified is that the excellence of the poetry tends to depend on the efficiency with which *A Vision* is rendered. Once this criterion is abandoned, as it should be, then the alternative must be that the poem establishes and justifies itself. Through the thrust of its images and the organising force of its structure it must develop its own penetration into the meaning of experience. If what it says, or rather what it is, is valid it is not because the System so decrees but because the poem itself prevents it from being otherwise. Yeats' poems survive these formidable demands and to demand less from them is to decline to do them justice. Allen Tate points to a real danger when he suggests that one consequence of Yeatsian scholarship may be 'the occultation of a poetry which I believe is nearer the centre of our main traditions of sensibility and thought than the poetry of Eliot or of Pound'. One must also beware of concluding that the occult reading is necessarily the central one. When Adams tells us that the airman in *An Irish Airman foresees his Death* 'achieves a vortex of timeless vision between past and future where present is really eternity' one has to remember that the public meaning of the poem is different and possibly richer. When the rough beast slouches towards Bethlehem in *The Second Coming* the poetry invests the monster with certain qualities which are not necessarily typical of an 'antithetical influx'. At the climax of *Among School Children* it is perhaps unnecessary to recall that Yeats describes the Thirteenth Cone in terms of blossoming and dancing. It is to the poetry that we should direct ourselves, and though esoteric interpretation is sometimes helpful and at other times necessary, it has to be controlled by a firm sense of the poem. The poems at their best achieve a public language and a created and potent public meaning. Yeats' spiritual advisers were also telling his readers of the importance of putting first things first.

7

Four Plays for Dancers

IN THE evolution of any poetic dramatist a time ought to come when life to Shakespeare appears to be death to him. What has been done supremely well cannot be done again; and the problem then becomes the nearly insoluble one of doing something which is radically different and essentially dramatic, which is creative in its own right and not a reflection of the past, either in mimicry or in rebellion. With Yeats there were other complications in the movement of dissent. Character and plot were resources that had become vulgarised in the naturalistic theatre and the poetic drama had to be held away from them—distanced by legend or by specific conventions—if it was to engender a poetic response. The 'Playboy riots' had discredited the popular theatre and artistic salvation now had to be aristocratic. 'I have invented a form of drama', Yeats wrote, 'distinguished, indirect and symbolic, and having no need of mob or Press to pay its way.' He invented it partially because modern poetic drama 'always dominated by the example of Shakespeare' sought to 'restore an irrevocable past'. In rejecting one tradition he was guided to another, that of the *Noh* drama of Japan, with its five-hundred-year continuity of writing and performance, played before a military aristocracy, which Yeats wishfully visualised as combining the best qualities of Achilles and Walter Pater.

The *Noh* plays would not have seized Yeats' imagination so firmly if his own mind had not been moving towards similar conventions. As early as 1903 he argued that gesture should be simplified so that it could 'accompany speech without being its rival', that scenery should be 'little more than an unobtrusive pattern', that everything 'that draws the attention away from the sound of the voice or from the few moments of intense expression' should be rejected, and that one should 'from time to time substitute for the movement that the eye sees the nobler movement that the heart sees, the rhythmical movements that seem to flow up into the imagination from some deeper life than that of the individual soul'. These are notable premonitions of a theatre which Fenollosa characterises by its 'concentration', by its union of costume, motion, verse and drama to produce 'a single clarified impression', and by its heightening of 'some primary human relation or emotion' through the careful exclusion of 'all such obtrusive elements as a mimetic realism or vulgar sensation might demand'. Yeats' movement towards this form is further strengthened by the theorising surrounding *Deirdre* in which 'rhythm, balance, pattern' are summoned to fill the vacuum left by lessening of character and by the practice of the play itself, in which the two musicians establish a convention that continues into the *Noh* plays. In addition, the intellectual excitement which Yeats' theories of the Mask generated found its dramatic correlative in a tradition where three hundred masks, many of them works of art, were needed to perform the repertory. *A Vision* helped by philosophising the evidence of the 'Playboyriots' and urging Yeats in the direction of the Salon. Popular art had to be realistic in an objective—solar age. The lunar man (Yeats was a phase seventeen product) could find himself only in a minority accomplishment.

'I want to create for myself an unpopular theatre', Yeats wrote 'and an audience like a secret society where admission is by favour and never to many.' Those who were favoured had to be chosen with care: 'Instead of advertisements in the Press I need a hostess.' An audience of fifty was the objective and when three hundred people attended the second performance of *At the Hawk's Well* 'once more my muses were but half-welcome'. To this *élite* Yeats promised 'a mysterious art . . . doing its work by suggestion, not by direct statement, a complexity of rhythm, colour, gesture, not space-pervading like the intellect but a memory and a prophecy; a mode of drama Shelley and Keats could have used without ceasing to be themselves, and for which even Blake in the *Book of Thel* might not have been too obscure'. These remarks are so strong an invitation to esoteric reading that one has to balance them by Yeats' much later description of his *Noh* plays as an attempt to think like a wise man but to express himself like the common people, and to write in a blank verse 'as close to common speech as the subject permitted'. The critic will find his position between these extremities, perhaps guided by the truism that dramatic effect is what matters in a drama, and that the poet in the theatre is committed in the first place to a theatrical strategy.

'All imaginative art', Yeats said, in a conclusion already touched on, 'remains at a distance and this distance, once chosen, must be firmly held against a pushing world.' The distance chosen in the *Noh* plays is one which seems to separate from the world and us 'a group of figures, images, symbols' and which, by so doing, enables us to pass 'for a few moments into a deep of the mind that had hitherto been too subtle for our habitation'. All elements in the artistic fusion contribute to this distancing. The dancer throws out an arm 'to recede from us into some more powerful life'. The masks that the actors wear are 'images of those profound emotions that exist only in solitude and silence'. But aesthetic distance combines with aesthetic intimacy. The players enter through the audience, drawing the small gathering into the deep of the mind. It is the entire room, including both actors and listeners, which is enclosed against the pushing world. The fusion of resources draws the whole mind into the act of participation, the moment of clarified insight. 'I believe myself to be a dramatist,' Yeats protested, presumably to those who regarded the *Noh* as the anti-self of the drama. His description of how the dramatist recognises himself is significant: 'I desire to show events and not merely tell of them . . . and I seem to myself most alive at the moment when a room full of people share the one lofty emotion.'

At the Hawk's Well, Yeats' first experiment in the new form, is a taut, brief study of the anatomy of failure written in a verse as bleakly evocative as the landscape it brings to the mind's eye. The world in which it moves is akin to that of the waste land. The well, into which three withered hazels drop their nuts, choked with leaves which the wind swirls and diminishes, has three times in fifty years filled with a mere cupful of water that disappeared almost as soon as it splashed. An old man, bent double like the thorn trees, has sat by the well's edge, waiting for the 'miraculous flood', snaring the birds and eating grass for food. He has never moved too far away to hear the faint and fleeting sound of the water, but, three times, awakening from a sudden sleep, he has found the stones wet and the water gone. Cuchulain who, unlike the old man, is 'not of those who hate the living world', arrives confident in his good fortune ('For never/ Have I had long to wait for anything'). The guardian of the well, a girl, enters into the state of possession, 'a horrible deathless body sliding through the veins of a sudden', that accompanies the brief filling of the well. She assumes the form of a hawk and dances. The old man, unable to look at her 'unfaltering, unmoistened eyes', falls into his sleep. Cuchulain, who does look into the dancer's gaze, is led by her away from the well, as the water fills and empties. He returns to find himself cheated of his objective and to find the women of the hills arming against him. Henceforward he can never know tranquillity. Shouldering his spear and 'no longer as if in a dream', he goes back into the battle of life.

Interpretations of the symbolism are not lacking but it is best to keep the pattern generalised so that the quest can be anybody's quest, the water, fulfilment as each man wishes to find it, and the failure, defeat, tasted by each in his own way. The point of the pattern is that failure is inevitable. The old man is defeated through his prudence, Cuchulain through his courage. Whether one looks into the hawk's eyes or not, those who seek wisdom must learn to live with frustration. The closing song ends by recommending a married life by the fireside, with children and dogs on the floor, where a hand on the bell can call the milch cows to the entrance. Wilson takes the lyric at its face value, seeing in it a resignation akin to the 'Teach us to care and not to care' of *Ash Wednesday*. But it is at least possible that Yeats' irony is sufficiently alert to leave the conclusion open. The hero finds his mask in defeat but that does not mean that he should insulate himself from the actions that lead to defeat. Only an idiot would praise 'a withered tree' and 'dry stones in a well', but perhaps this conclusion really means that those who seek fulfilment will always seem fools by certain standards. Much of the effect of the play certainly resides in the bleak, clean, almost dispassionate honesty with which the rewards that await

D

the quester are stated; the poem is weighted towards security so that those who choose something else do so in a place that the salt sea-wind has stripped bare of illusions.

II

The Only Jealousy of Emer is the most intricately and satisfyingly designed of the *Noh* plays; Yeats tells us that he wrote it for 'some country where all classes share in a half-mythological, half-philosophical folk-belief which the writer and his small audience lift into a new subtlety'. In what is presumably a reference to *A Vision* he adds: 'I have now found all the mythology and philosophy I need.' Some writers have concluded that he found even more than he needed since *Fighting the Waves*, the prose version of *The Only Jealousy of Emer*, omits nearly all the discussion on the problems of living in the fifteenth phase.

The dramatic kernel of the play can be briefly stated. The body of Cuchulain, washed ashore after his combat with the waves, is tended in a fisherman's house by Emer, his wife, and Eithne Inguba, his mistress. Bricriu, maker of discord, possesses Cuchulain's body. He demands as the price of Cuchulain's ransom from the Sidhe the renunciation of the most precious thing that Emer possesses, namely her love for Cuchulain. Emer protests and hesitates; then as Fand, the Woman of the Sidhe, seems on the verge of claiming Cuchulain's soul she makes her renunciation and Cuchulain returns to the world in words that are pregnant both with terror and irony:

> Your arms, your arms! O Eithne Inguba,
> I have been in some strange place and am afraid. (*CPl*, p. 294)

The direct impact of the play is partly that of folk-legend and partly through the dilemma of Emer, who must renounce everything to witness the victory of another and who can bring Cuchulain back from death only at the price of all that is vital in her own life. Once again we face the pattern of failure, but this time the protagonist knows the pattern. Man cannot choose happiness but he can choose his particular unhappiness. In performance the play must derive additional tension from the simultaneous presence on stage of the figure of Cuchulain with Emer beside it and the Ghost of Cuchulain confronting the dance of Fand and the allurement of eternity. As Fand makes her bid for Cuchulain and Cuchulain feels the pull of loyalty to Emer, the effect is surely reinforced because Emer is not only in the hero's mind but on stage before the audience and on the verge of her ultimate act of loyalty.

The lyrics which enclose the dramatic core, the first opulent in its beauty, the final one cryptic in its resignation, deal with the soul's effort to realise itself, with physical beauty as the sign of its achievement. The first stanza of the opening song celebrates the attainment of beauty by the mind, the second the attainment of beauty in the blood, and the run of the verse, exactly repeated in each stanza, reminds us that all perfect things are rooted indistinguishably both in reason and violence. Bird and shell suggest the fragility of earthly beauty, the migration of the soul and its recurring rebirth. The musicians describe white shell and white wing alike as frail and unserviceable, knowing only change and its endlessness. The stage is thus set for Fand, a being of the fifteenth crescent, who offers Cuchulain not only beauty which is absolute (and therefore statue-like, beyond the human) but liberation from the wheel of rebirth, from memory and 'intricacies of blind remorse'. It seems necessary to interpret Fand's role in this way and Wilson's sensitive and erudite reading should be accepted, not because of its subtlety, but because it makes deeper dramatic sense than any alternative. The main apparent argument against it is the difficulty of accepting the Woman of the Sidhe, who, in *At the Hawk's Well*, was the means of Cuchulain's defeat, as transformed into the means of his potential salvation. The play touches briefly on this paradox:

> Hold out your arms and hands again;
> You were not so dumbfounded when
> I was that bird of prey, and yet
> I am all woman now. (*CPl*, p. 292)

The change can of course be rationalised; yesterday's scourge can become today's deliverance. But the irony is intended to cut deeper. The man who looked into the hawk's eyes cannot look into the eyes of the woman. It is possible to face the battle of life but not the peace of eternity. It was never really possible to have drunk the water of the hawk's well.

The fifteenth crescent is beyond the human and so the perfection which Fand stands for is seen in terms of a brilliance surpassing all memories, the attachments of time which are beauty's 'bitterest enemy'. But the light of the full moon is also bewildering. It is the vesture of the totally realised self and dazzles man by a reality which he cannot continuously bear. Apart from this, Fand is studiously described in terms which are non-human. She is a statue in the last song and an idol in the stage directions. Even the fact that her heart can beat at all, that she is capable of feeling desire, means that she lacks perfection 'by an hour or so'. Her interchange with Cuchulain is set in a rhymed tetrameter carefully segregated from the rest of the play, not only by its metrics but by its remote, stylised, deliberately abstract quality. Only at one point does the mask drop to remind one (perhaps a little too sharply) that women will be women even in the fifteenth crescent.

> Being among the dead you love her
> That valued every slut above her
> While you still lived. (*CPl*, p. 293)

Cuchulain, himself of the twelfth and the heroes' crescent, is unable to ascend to the fifteenth. He is dragged down by memories, by the chain of time, the cycle of action and expiation, but ironically those memories are of Emer and flood into his mind as Emer meditates her ultimate act of loyalty. The spectacle of the man brought back into time by his own remembrances and by the will of his wife to 'save' him is potent in laying bare the blindness within which even renunciation has to work. At the dramatic level Emer saves Cuchulain only to lose him to Eithne Inguba. At the symbolic level she saves him only in order to doom him to the wheel. The supreme sacrifice achieves no objective except the frustration of a higher design, and the only real victor is Bricriu, maker of discord, the agent of those laws of conflict which preside inexorably over the human condition. The 'bitter reward of many a tragic tomb' is that of man struggling to perfect himself through thought, pain and even violence, reaching to and falling short of eternity, and spinning away out of sight of the stars into the objective darkness, committed

once again to the entire cycle of rebirth. This almost desperate conclusion is rendered through poetry which, both by lyric stasis and
by indirection, distances a truth which might otherwise be un-
bearable. But there is no mistaking the grimness of the moral. The
reality of Emer's renunciation is that man is not only doomed to
fail but defeats himself by the very nobility of his effort to save
himself.

<h1 style="text-align:center">III</h1>

The theme of *The Dreaming of the Bones*, Yeats tells us, 'is
derived from the world-wide belief that the dead dream back, for a
certain time, through the more personal thoughts and deeds of life.
The wicked, according to Cornelius Agrippa, dream themselves to
be consumed by flames and persecuted by demons. . . . The lovers
in my play have lost themselves in a different but still self-created
winding of the labyrinth of conscience.'

The dead who dream back in Yeats' play are Dervorgilla and her
king and lover', Diarmuid, who

> Was overthrown in battle by her husband,
> And for her sake and for his own, being blind
> And bitter and bitterly in love, he brought
> A foreign army from across the sea. (*CPl*, p. 442)

For their betrayal of a nation the two are trapped in the labyrinth of
their guilt, condemned to a self-inflicted penance in which the
recurrent crises of anguish come when their eyes meet and their
lips are unable to do so:

> . . . When he has bent his head
> Close to her head, or hand would slip in hand,
> The memory of their crime flows up between
> And drives them apart. (*CPl*, p. 441)

The ghosts of the lovers are encountered among the grey and
desolate hills on the borders of Clare and Galway, in accordance
with the traditions of the *Noh* where the central situation 'is often
the meeting with ghost, god, or goddess at some holy place or much-
legended tomb'. However, the traveller meeting the ghosts is not, as

tradition prescribes, 'a Buddhist priest', but a young man who has taken part in the Easter uprising. The play is thus given a contemporary and political orientation for which there is no warrant in the *Noh*. One result of the innovation is that it enables Yeats to suggest that the uprising is the consequence of the seven-centuries-old betrayal and gives an immediate bitterness to the young man's protestation that Diarmuid and Dervorgilla can never be forgiven. It also enables the crowing of the 'Red Bird of March' to be interpreted as a symbol of impending and revolutionary change. Yeats himself was not wholly convinced by these undertones and expressed to Lady Gregory his fear that the play was 'only too powerful politically'. There are indeed moments of didacticism in it that are strangely at variance with the mood of the rest.

> For though we have neither coal, nor iron ore,
> To make us wealthy and corrupt the air,
> Our country, if that crime were uncommitted,
> Had been most beautiful. (*CPl*, p. 443)

Apart from its contemporary twist, the play is the most successful of the *Four Plays for Dancers* in assimilating the atmosphere of the *Noh*. The sense of place and of local legend is sharply realised and the use of place-names is, as Wilson points out, unlike anything anywhere else in Yeats. The image clusters in the songs embody Yeats' understanding of the language of the *Noh* as 'a playing upon a single metaphor, as deliberate as the echoing rhythm of line in Chinese or Japanese painting'. Resemblances to a particular *Noh* play, *Nishikigi*, which Yeats discusses in *Certain Noble Plays of Japan*, are indeed so striking that Wilson considers Yeats' play to be virtually a re-creation of the Japanese original. But it is not only Japanese tradition that is absorbed. Hone notes that Diarmuid and Dervorgilla are an Irish Paolo and Francesca, and Eliot agrees that Yeats' tormented lovers have 'something of the universality' of Dante's lovers.

One possible criticism of the play is that it contains no central action to unravel its significance. Diarmuid and Dervorgilla disclose their identities gradually to the young man, but the forgiveness they seek from the living cannot be given. They enter again the dance of their anguish, reaching their hands up to the unattainable sleep that 'lingers always in the abyss of the sky'. The clouds envelop the mountain-top, shrouding once more what has been momentarily revealed. Even if, as Wilson suggests, we take the cock as an emblem of reincarnation, signifying the release of the lovers into time and their liberation from the labyrinth of their penance, the objection would still remain that the symbol is not given any dramatic substance. It may equally well be read as implying that morning breaks for everyone but the lovers. The play is essentially static, and perhaps its most serious weakness is not that Diarmuid and Dervorgilla are not forgiven but that the soldier has no basis for forgiveness. He faces no conflict and in the end makes no choice. He looks back into the past but his attitude to it is already decided. He is too much its victim to be able to redeem it.

IV

Calvary, the last of the *Four Plays for Dancers*, uses the *Noh* form for something approaching a drama of ideas. Its development however is not argumentative; the positions presented in it are related to each other rather than modified by debate and the whole has to be held in the mind and played back for its structure to be confirmed.

The play, which, as Wilson notes, owes much to Oscar Wilde's *The Doer of Good*, surrounds Christ 'with the images of those He cannot save'. These include the birds 'who have served neither God nor Caesar', Lazarus and Judas, 'types of that intellectual despair' that lies beyond Christ's sympathy, and the Roman Soldiers who represent 'a form of objectivity that lay beyond His help'. This part of Yeats' note suggests that four different images of failure are being presented but the play itself establishes links between three of them. The refrain of the opening song tells us that 'God has not died for the white heron'. When Judas plans his betrayal

> There was no living thing near me but a heron
> So full of itself that it seemed terrified. (*CPl*, p. 454)

Similarly, Lazarus in denying Christ goes to search

> Among the desert places where there is nothing
> But howling wind and solitary birds (*CPl*, p. 452)

The central lyric in the play brings together the bird images of the opening and closing songs, and clearly suggests one side of their significance:

> Take but His love away,
> Their love becomes a feather
> Of Eagle, Swan or Gull,
> Or a drowned Heron's feather
> Tossed hither and thither
> Upon the bitter spray
> And the moon at the full. (*CPl*, p. 453)

The full moon, of course, stands for maximum subjectivity and Yeats tells us in his note that 'such lonely birds as the heron, hawk, eagle, and swan, are the natural symbols of subjectivity, especially when floating or alighting upon some pool or river'. Christ's love is therefore a pull towards objectivity but it is typical of the instinctive justice of Yeats' poetry that the alternative against which it pulls is shown as drowned and drifting, tossed on the bitter spray of change and reincarnation. Nevertheless, it remains the alternative that certain men must follow and the concluding lyric restores our confidence in its images, showing us the gull protected by the 'great wave's hollowing crest', the ger-eagle 'content with his savage heart' and the swan needing nothing but the companionship of his kind. All these are images of loneliness and Yeats' note makes it clear that he distinguishes between subjective loneliness which always seeks that 'which is unique or personal' and objective loneliness which is a loneliness of person, not of thought, and which 'always seeks the welfare of some cause or institution'.

I have used my bird-symbolism in these songs to increase the objective loneliness of Christ by contrasting it with a loneliness, opposite in kind, that unlike His, can be, whether joyous or sorrowful, sufficient to itself.

Both this statement, and the imagery of the play, make it difficult to accept Ure's conclusion that Christ is like the birds although he has not appeared to them. In fact the association of Christ with Yeatsian objectivity (the opposite of what the birds represent) goes back to Yeats' reading of Neitzsche from whom he seems to have acquired both the subjective-objective antithesis and his initial ideas about the Mask. Lazarus and Judas also are less types of 'intellectual despair' than seekers after identity, the one asserting the right to his own death, the other seeking by betrayal to defend his personality against a faith that would otherwise overwhelm him. In this sense they are allied to the subjectives. The subjective man seeks self-realisation and self-sufficiency, and isolation and solitude are his strength. The objective man seeks conversion, and loneliness is his weakness, born whenever the Messiah discovers someone for whom he is unable to die. The play is not necessarily an exposure of the failure of Christianity; but it is certainly a reminder that there will be many who require a different faith.

V

Yeats' four ventures in the *Noh* form include a play of ideas, a ghost play in a modern political context and two studies in the irony of action, set in the framework of the Cuchulain myth. This is a surprisingly varied accomplishment and it is also solid enough to substantiate the obvious claim that a form developed through five hundred years of dramatic usage is unlikely to be inherently un-dramatic. Yeats' achievement is also more accessible than some of his own remarks suggest; though a full education in the system cannot be without its rewards, it is reassuring to get close to what Wilson calls the maximum reading, on the basis of the play itself, the notes which Yeats has provided, and an elementary knowledge of the wheel. The truth is that the special preparation required to read Yeats, even at his most esoteric, is far less than that required for Pound and for the Eliot of *The Waste Land.* This is as it should be, particularly in the plays. A living theatre can and possibly has to be the concern of a minority; but it cannot be a theatre only for initiates.

If, in the end, the *Noh* plays leave a certain sense of inadequacy it is largely because Yeats' best work provides us with a standard to apply to his lesser achievements. The conclusion is that Yeats is not fundamentally a dramatist, not because he lacks the dramatic imagination but because that imagination is most powerfully and most characteristically at work in his poetry rather than in his drama. It is no accident that the highest accomplishment of these plays (and of the later plays which bear the impress of the *Noh* form) is, almost without exception, in the songs. Yeats' characteristic approach to experience is through the fundamental forces that give experience its quality, rather than through the dispositions of plot and the nuclei of character. His is a symbolic art with the dance on the surface, reflecting the rhythm below, the immediate pattern suggesting the fundamental geometry. His deepest concern is with man rather than men, whereas Shakespeare was concerned equally deeply in both. The result is not necessarily a gain in subtlety—the deeps of the mind are no deeper than those which Jacobean tragedy explores—but it does involve some sacrifice of solidity, of the powerfully maintained connection between the natural and the symbolic, between the exterior movement and the inner life, which, in Yeats' phrase, presses for expression through the characters. Even in the more comparable area of Greek drama, Aeschylus, who deliberately restrains his interest in character so that attention is focussed less on his protagonists than on the forces of which they are the agents, is nevertheless able to reach through the central action to a web of cause and consequence which the economy of the *Noh* excludes. Perhaps we may regret that the possibilities opened by *On Baile's Strand* were not explored and that Yeats' preferences lay in a different direction. But it is foolish to prescribe lines of development, and in any case the solution to a contemporary aesthetic problem is never clear until it is created. Yeats' attempt on the drama was intelligent and courageous and neither its tenacity nor the extent of its success should be minimised. Nevertheless, it remains, among other things, a formidable testimony to the difficulties of writing poetic drama in our time.

8

Dancer and Swan

I

The Wild Swans at Coole begins with the muted melancholy of the title poem and ends with the bleak ambivalences of *The Double Vision of Michael Robartes*. Between the sense of withering away and its growing knowledge of the truth, the collection stands judiciously balanced. It moves through the death of friends and the persistence of love to a harsher world which the light of the Vision dominates.

The opening poem begins in the tones of ordinary speech, with the 'nine and fifty swans' adding an accurately judged touch of photographic precision to a landscape which is otherwise carefully symbolic. It is a measure of Yeats' achievement that the language is held so effortlessly at this level, where the interior meaning is achieved without remoteness and the poem moves in the foreground of particularity without obscuring its hinterlands. The details accumulate and with them consciousness of the autumnal mood, the 'October twilight' setting and the dry, woodland paths on which the poet walks, contrasted with the 'brimming water' on which the swans float and from which they rise in clamorous brilliance. The 'nine and fifty' now takes it place in the symbolic picture, ranging itself against the nineteen autumns, setting the details of constancy and of undying recurrence against the inexorable arithmetic of decay. The bell beat of the swans' wings, that once brought exultation, now rings in the knowledge that a phase of life is ending; the two lines with their finely realised fusion of heaviness and elatedness give the recognition an almost physical impact.

It is tempting to marry these swans to other swans in other poems by Yeats, but they are meant to remain slightly mysterious and to create broken rings of meaning in the sky. In one sense they stand for the life-force; their hearts do not grow old, they find the streams companionable despite their coldness, passion and conquest attend them unsought, and their vigour is such that they climb the air instead of flying through it. In another sense the swans stand for the union of time and the timeless, as the dancer symbol does in the last poem of the collection. In a third sense they stand for inspiration, building by the lake's edge where the wind blows among the reeds. The poet awakes into reality to find them gone, but perhaps the dream which they inhabit remains at his calling and perhaps the sources of life lie in the dreams of poetry. The suggestion that the power of poetry has deserted the poet is probably offered in order to be rejected by the poem. The imagination does not age any more than the swans do. The poem is deceptively matter-of-fact, firmly rooted in the landscape of the everyday, yet, in its very unfolding, it charges itself with meaning. Symbolic speech is not simply professed but possessed.

Yeats, who almost always thought that his last play was his best, was more cautious in judging his poetry; *The Two Trees, Lapis Lazuli* and *In Memory of Major Robert Gregory* are among the few poems that he commends. The Gregory Elegy is the first of the poems to be set in Thoor Ballylee—the ruined tower with the cottage below it, which Yeats purchased from the Congested Districts Board for thirty-five pounds, and which was destined to become the twentieth century's most important piece of symbolic property. Yeats was to spend several times the purchase price on renovations which, like the revisions to his poetry, were never quite completed. At the time he wrote the poem, however, (May–June 1918) he could describe himself as 'almost settled in our house' and the detail invites the reader into the poem, making him a privileged guest beside the 'fire of turf'. The fire in due course becomes the poem's central symbol. The 'entire combustible world' burning like dried straw in it goes 'black-out' in the blaze of total accomplishment. The poem obliterates the border between fireside speech and poetry as it moves to and fro across it; the seamlessness of the language forces recognition of the continuity between the immediate and the ultimate, the transformation of actual men into myth. Johnson, Pollexfen and Synge, brought before us in the apparently casual flow of reminiscence, are all carefully chosen from the dead. Johnson is the scholar, Pollexfen the horseman, and Synge the artist, whose country of the heart is a 'desolate stony place', akin to Gregory's landscape of 'cold Clare rock and Galway rock and thorn'. Gregory is the fusion of all these partial men—'Soldier, scholar, horseman, he'—a 'perfect man' who, like Sidney, fell in battle. Death does not destroy him but does him a discourtesy; the conceit is one of Yeats' masterly touches, a sudden tensing in the run of conversation, bringing us back to the fireside and the host, and subtly reminding us of the limits of death's victories.

Yeats had consulted Gregory about the renovation of the tower ('What other could so well have counselled us/In all lovely intricacies of a house'), and Gregory's painting of the Tower is reproduced in Hone's biography. These facts bring him into the fireside circle and indeed suggest that he ought to have been one of the hosts: 'He might have been your heartiest welcomer.' Here, as elsewhere, the poem stays close to its roots, to the ordinary solid world which it dignifies. But in the thrice-repeated 'Soldier, scholar, horseman, he', it also moves forward unhesitatingly to its climax. The line is first linked with intensity, then with perfection, then with 'all life's epitome', and then, seizing on the implication that the epitome must be brief and combining it with the image of the bare, blacked-out chimney, the monosyllables toll in their tragic recognition.

What made us dream that he could comb grey hair? (*CP*, p. 151)

Kermode, who notes that the stanza Yeats uses here and in *A Prayer for my Daughter* is taken from Cowley, comments on the manner in which Yeats is able to vary the pace and weight of the last line. Another dramatic example is at the close of the poem:

.... but a thought
Of that late death took all my heart for speech. (*CP*, p. 152)

Here the 'grievous congestion' of the monosyllables expresses, as no other device can do, an emotion before which even the achieved eloquence of the poem must be silent.

It is possible to read the Gregory Elegy as a statement of the difficulties encountered by subjective men in an objective age, and of the impossibility of achieving unity of being in contemporary life. But the idea that those whom the Gods love die young is older than the system and does not divert one from the poem's central meaning.

An *Irish Airman foresees his Death* achieves its effect through a nearly perfect neutralisation of forces. The 'lonely impulse' that drives the airman to his destiny is like Sartre's *acte gratuit*, freed from all motivation and therefore totally self-expressive.

> Those that I fight I do not hate,
> Those that I guard I do not love;
>
> .   .   .   .
>
> Nor law, nor duty bade me fight,
> Nor public men, nor cheering crowds (*CP*, p. 152)

The language itself, bleakly indifferent, inexorably denying all public or private causes, encloses, as it were by exclusion, a cold, hard centre of the will. The verbal balance is planned precisely to complement the actual and in the complete equilibrium that is achieved nothing matters but the solitary, alienated urge to self-realisation. The poem can hardly be taken as a recommendation for living or for dying; but few poems are more impressive in conveying the cold, detached and total recognition which, it is sometimes said, precedes the moment of death.

Men Improve with the Years is described by Kenner as counter-rhetoric to the *Irish Airman*. The poem has sufficient irony to suggest that the Triton worn out with dreams may have wisdom on his side and that withering away may have as much to commend it as dying self-expressively.

Growing old is the theme of the first group of 'love' poems in which 'The living beauty is for younger men', and dumb-bells which prolong the day of youth cannot arrest the ageing of the heart. But men continue to improve with the years and those that have paid the price of service to beauty (the word enlarges subtly to suggest both the artistic and the physical ideal) will dine at journey's end with Landor and with Donne. The pairing is an unusual one reflectin, perhaps, Landor's membership of the seventeenth crescent and Yeats' enthusiastic reading of Grierson's edition of Donne.

Improving with the years is given another twist in *Lines Written in Dejection*, in which the poet sees himself, after fifty, moving into the solar phase of his life. The 'heroic moon' of self-realisation has vanished and the 'timid sun' of objectivity has to be endured. But the progress is also from dream to reality; the wild witches who are also noble ladies have ceased to exercise their fascination over the poet and he can now move into the bleak landscape of the 'embittered' but de-romanticised sun. Timidity is in any case hardly the sun's primary characteristic; the inconsistency invites us to read the poem ironically and perhaps suggests that the poet is capable of defeating even his own system.

In the next poem, the solar phase is given its mask and the mask, characteristically, is not that of senility or weather-beaten wisdom, but of the dawn, 'ignorant and wanton' in its vitality, and carrying its traditional associations of rebirth. We are presented with a kind of experienced innocence, a mind that has looked upon everything but which refuses to be tied to knowledge when 'no knowledge is worth a straw'. Apart from its theme, *The Dawn*, as B. L. Reid notes, is striking in its brilliance of epithet, 'that inspired power of vision packed and crowded into compressed speech which may be Yeats' greatest legacy to modern poetry'.

On Woman, the next poem in the sequence, takes up the idea of rebirth and fits it into the wheel. Woman is now the symbol of the ignorant, wanton dawn, the sheath that covers man's thought, the completion of the body. The shudder that makes man and woman one tempers and strengthens the iron; both the imagery and the clipped line with its stabbing assonances are carefully controlled to suggest the harshness rather than the sweetness of fulfilment. It may be too late to seek fulfilment in this life but when man is reshaped for his next birth in the pestle of the moon (an image which, Miner tells us, has its origin in Japanese legend) the dance of torment can be entered again and re-enacted in all its implications. The only difference will be that this time the dance may bring Solomon's wisdom.

The Fisherman, the most eloquent of *The Dawn* poems, imagines a man in grey Connemara cloth, in the bleak clean landscape of Galway rock and thorn, one of those 'upstanding men' who in *The Tower* are to receive the inheritance of Yeats' pride. He represents isolation, self-containment, natural life, as opposed to social squabbling and, even though he does not exist, he remains the symbol into which the mind's eye looks. He is the image of the race the poet would write for, the ideal imagined in disdain of the actual, and the shrill sterility of the world against which he stands is power-fully and precisely realised. The short, end-stopped lines with their sledge-hammer repetitions, their impact increased by the complete absence of internal pauses, fall in a mounting fusillade of indictment. Once again, as in the *Irish Airman*, the metrics and the verbal pattern make the emotion both exact and alive. The whole central section presents itself as a systematic 'beating down' rising inexorably to its embittered climax.

> The beating down of the wise,
> And great Art beaten down. (*CP*, p. 67)

Against this 'reality' the Fisherman is set, the image of instinctive dignity and homespun virtues, climbing away from mob hysteria to a different world 'where stone is black under froth'. The poem that ought to be written to him is, of course, the poem which has just concluded, a poem 'Cold/And passionate as the dawn'.

The heart has certainly not grown old in the group of poems to Maud Gonne, and the poet, the channels of whose blood were frozen less than a score of poems earlier, now sings 'stubborn with his passion' and 'when age might well have chilled his blood'. *A Thought from Propertius* and *A Deep-Sworn Vow* are the most strik-ing poems in this group: brief, intense and controlled explosions of passion, both of them remarkable for the complete assurance with which they negotiate their imaginative rights. The first poem builds up a sense of spirituality into which the sensual detail of the second line is swept. Then, the counter-movement crashes deliberately against the image of holiness that has been erected. Yet the effect is not one of desecration but of balance; the poem is made more valid and secure by the violent challenge to the spiritual which it accommodates. *A Deep-Sworn Vow* is another poem written in this central area where opposites meet and mingle, with the poem the ground of their creative intertwining. In it perilous adventure, dreaming and mere drunkenness are daringly juxtaposed and made

not only to co-exist but to give their characteristic qualities to each
other, so that each meets the same face as its consummation. In one
sense the juxtapositions measure the depth of the 'deep-sworn vow'
—a commitment so basic that it confronts the personality wherever
and however it is exercised. More fundamentally, however, the
juxtapositions suggest the indivisibility of experience; the dreaming
of desire and the dangerous clambering to imaginative summits,
death in love and death in high adventure, the excitement of wine
and of a deeper fulfilment, are driven together in an organic reci-
procity where all elements share the same dignity and commonness.
It is the everyday roughage of experience which enables it to be
shaped towards nobility.

Ego Dominus Tuus, a dialogue on the Mask, steers the collection
away from the personal and into the abstract world, the revealed
truth that is affirmed in *A Vision*. The participants, who have been
irreverently rechristened as Hic and Willie, explore the paradox that
self-realisation is best achieved by imaginative entry into the anti-
self. Dante, who is put forward as a stumbling block to this theory,
is seized on as the classic example of a man finding himself by
absorption in the mask. The quest for happiness and the lyric cele-
bration of happiness when found, are artistic illusions. Poetry,
whatever its achieved qualities and balance, can arise only out of
'tragic war', the deliberate courting of a conflict in which man and
mask are inexorably engaged. The poem then twists into typical
Yeatsian irony as Hic reproaches Ille with leaving his lamp burning
'beside an open book' and tracing 'characters upon the sands'. We
have to remember that Yeats' mythical tribe, the Judwalis or Dia-
grammatists, taught their children dances 'which leave upon the sand
traces full of symbolic meaning' and that, in the first edition of *A
Vision*, Kusta ben Luka's children were to dance the Great Wheel on
the sand before a Caliph. In this context Ille's retort that he seeks an
image not a book, a truth in the present rather than an example
from the past, acquires additional significance and it is no accident
that the 'mysterious one', who is to become his mask and who is
vaguely reminiscent of the Fisherman, walks 'the wet sands by the
edge of the stream'. To compound the irony, Yeats eventually finds
a book in seeking an image—the mythical *Speculum Angelorum et
Hominum* of Giraldus. The climactic paradox is that the road away

from the self, whether it leads one towards the image or towards the book of revelation, also winds back decisively into the self:

> Those men that in their writings are most wise
> Own nothing but their blind, stupefied hearts. (*CP*, p. 182)

The Phases of the Moon is described by Yeats as to some extent 'a text for exposition'. The setting is Thoor Ballylee, with the poet in his tower, as in *Ego Dominus Tuus*, poring by lamplight over his books and manuscripts. Robartes and Aherne, who, Yeats tells us, 'have once again become part of the phantasmagoria through which I can alone express my convictions about the world', enter clad in symbolic Connemara cloth. Standing on the bridge which leads to the tower, Robartes affirms that the poet's quest is fated to end in failure. Ille, who sought an image not a book, can now only find images and ponders over books in vain. Aherne suggests that they enlighten Yeats with a fragment of the truth just sufficient to make clear the dimensions of his failure, but Robartes, whose complaint against Yeats is not only that Yeats declared him dead but did so in a style borrowed from Pater, refuses to knock at the poet's door. Instead, the two go over the twenty-eight phases of the moon in language that is striking but also suggests the distance between poetry that is lived and philosophy that is versified. In the rigid determinism of the wheel they find one possibility of escape. Between the bodily deformity of the Hunchback (phase twenty-six) and the mental deformity of the Fool (phase twenty-eight) comes the phase of the Saint when the burning bow can shoot an arrow

> Out of the up and down, the wagon wheel
> Of beauty's cruelty and wisdom's chatter
> Out of that raving tide. (*CP*, p. 188)

Aherne amuses himself with the thought of tantalising Yeats into madness, by ringing the bell, pretending to be a drunken lout and enigmatically muttering: 'Hunchback and Saint and Fool'. A bat, symbolic of the utter darkness that precedes a new cycle of incarnations, rises from the hazels that once grew beside the Hawk's Well. The light in the Tower is put out and both the poem and the quest are over. The obvious irony is the one that enables Yeats to stand outside and contrive the phantasmagoria in which he himself,

Robartes and Aherne are involved. But the apparatus also enables the poet to make his philosophy part of the phantasmagoria and so to urge it upon the reader without straining his capacity for the suspension of disbelief.

The Double Vision of Michael Robartes brings the collection to a close. Between Coole Part and Cashel Rock there is a progression in bleakness and the swans which threatened to fly away are replaced by the starker symbols of a new knowledge. The vision is double because only the sphere can be single; the antinomies that control consciousness cannot be transcended and one needs the guidance of vision even to be aware that they are antinomies. The first revelation is of the darkness of phase one (which the bat in *The Phases of the Moon* prefigures). The old moon has 'vanished from the sky' and the new 'still hides her horn'. Behind existence, the forces that pound the particular into men are mechanical and puppet-like demiurges that transmit their mindless obedience to their creations. The second revelation is born from the fifteenth crescent. Between the sphinx whose moonlit eyes gaze upon all things known and unknown and the Buddha whose moonlit eyeballs are fixed on all things loved and unloved is the dancer who overcomes the antithesis and who by her reconciliation of stillness and motion also incarnates the fifteenth phase in time.

> Mind moved yet seemed to stop
> As 'twere a spinning top. (*CP*, p. 193)

The symbol looks forward to the climax of *Among School Children* and to the grimmer dance of *A Full Moon in March*, where the severed head symbolises an opposition of principle which must be destroyed before it can be embraced. This particular dancer, who dances out of thought and into bodily perfection, also takes us into the first poem of the next volume, where Michael Robartes teaches the thinking of the body to a dancer who has evidently gone to the wrong school. The important point to note is that the dancer reconciles only the antitheses within the fifteenth phase itself. She cannot reconcile the first phase to the fifteenth and the visions appropriate to each remain symbolically segregated in different sections of the poem. Man remains 'caught between the pull/Of the dark moon and the full', though artistic vision is dominated by elemental order (the dancer) rather than by her opposite, elemental chaos. It is the presence of the dancer that makes one feel undone 'by Homer's Paragon' and if Helen 'never gave the burning town a thought', that merely reminds us that all vision exacts its price from the artist, even though no single vision can encompass the whole truth.

The Wild Swans at Coole marks the kind of decisive movement forward in Yeats' development that can only be predicted after it has been achieved. In *Responsibilities* it seems that Yeats' spectacular technical powers are applied to the poetic experience rather than made to grow out of it. Indignation with the Paudeens never attains the status it achieves in *The Fisherman* where metrics and emotion are startlingly and indissolubly welded. The self-contempt of the earlier collection, except when it is disciplined by irony, is capable of approaching self-indulgence. The attitudes are designed to shock the reader into attention and do so with almost uniform success; but the tactics, however confidently carried out, are impressive primarily as tactics which are not absorbed into the thinking of the body. In *The Wild Swans*, the civilised sadness of the Gregory Elegy, the taut, fully shaped beauty of the love lyrics and the title poem itself, completely possessed and formed by its central symbol, bring us into a world where ordinary speech is invested with fundamental meaning and the objects of an everyday world seem charged with forces beyond them that find their expression in them. The reader can only be amused by Middleton Murry's conclusion that '*The Wild Swans at Coole* is indeed a swan song. It is eloquent of final defeat; the following of a lonely path has ended in the poet's sinking exhausted in a wilderness of grey'. The comment should do more than remind us that critics are not always reliable judges of poetry; there are also ironical and salutary occasions when it is the poems that pass judgement on the critics.

II

Michael Robartes and the Dancer, a brief and not very memorable volume, remarkable chiefly for *Easter 1916* and *The Second Coming*, is nevertheless carefully fitted into the continuity of *Collected Poems*. The last poem of the previous collection leads into it and after Robartes has expounded and Solomon and Sheba have celebrated the thinking of the body, the gyre narrows to two poems of personal reassurance. In *Demon and Beast* the system moves again into the foreground and the poems on the Easter uprising which follow are tremors of apocalyptic violence which reach their prophetic climax in *The Second Coming*. Yeats' prayer for his daughter gains in strength against this threatening background, which makes the appeal to custom and ceremony something more than nostalgia for an aristocratic past. Once again the field of vision narrows to the personal, though with the weight of historical consciousness behind it. The last poem on Thoor Ballylee once again prepares the entry into the next volume.

The theme of the title poem has already been indicated; it is not substantially altered by Henn's disclosure that the lady is actually Iseult Gonne. Distracted by the dragon of the abstract (which also suggests dedication to impersonal causes), she is advised to concentrate on what her looking glass reveals and in a characteristic reversal of Yeats' favourite simile from the *Iliad*, to 'Go pluck Athene by the hair'. The plain man's insistence that the business of women is to be beautiful saves the thought of the poem from its own dragons and is urged with ironic offhandedness.

> And may the Devil take the rest. (*CP*, p.197)

The aim, however, is not to eliminate thought but to absorb it into something more immediate. The figures of the Sistine roof rule by supernatural right without ceasing to be sinew, and Robartes' final instructions, fortified by mythical Latin authorities, are to:

> banish every thought, unless
> The lineaments that please their view
> When the long looking-glass is full,
> Even from the foot-sole think it too. (*CP*, p. 198)

Solomon and Sheba, who practise the wisdom of the body, are presented to us in the next poem as having very nearly achieved the emancipation of the fifteenth night. A cock that 'crowed out eternity' three hundred years before the fall is deceived into imagining that the foul world is dead, that the consequences of the 'brigand apple' have died out, that chance and choice have been united (a

characteristic of the fifteenth phase) and that the time has arrived
to crow in eternity again. The witch who knows wisdom in all its
discordant cacophony

> Who understood
> Whatever has been said, sighed, sung,
> Howled, miau-d, barked, brayed, belled, yelled, cried, crowed, (*CP*, p. 199)

informs the lovers how close they have been to perfection. But the
world still 'stays' and the cockerel was deceived:

> Maybe an image is too strong
> Or maybe is not strong enough. (*CP*, p. 200)

The response to failure,

> the moon is wilder every minute.
> O! Solomon! let us try again. (*CP*, p. 200)

is Yeatsian because of the surrounding recognition that fulfilment
can only be glimpsed, that the unity in which 'oil and wick are
burned in one' entails the ending of the world, and that man's
natural condition is the cruelty of the search and the despair of the
bride-bed. The hushed last stanza in which the only sound is that of
a petal falling, and the only suggestion of the human is the sight of
the crushed grass where Solomon and Sheba have lain, conveys
vividly the sense of a reality that must always remain essentially
inviolate.

Demon and Beast recognises, in different terms, the impossibility
of fulfilment. Victory can belong to either of the contending forces
within man, but man himself can neither unite nor triumph over
these forces.

> Yet I am certain as can be
> That every natural victory
> Belongs to beast or demon,
> That never yet had freeman
> Right mastery of natural things. (*CP*, p. 210)

The 'sweetness' of insight is only an uneasy truce in this struggle,
what Cuchulain much earlier had called 'a brief forgiveness between
opposites'. Wisdom is the product of old age and 'chilled blood', of
the struggle dying down as the vigour of existence ebbs, the insight
achieved by St Anthony as he withered to 'a bag of bones' in the

monastic colony near Thebes. But wisdom is not an unequal exchange for power; the last line with its challengingly, confident
Yeatsian question—'What had the Caesars but their thrones?'—
sets the surface poverty of truth against the exterior richness of the
temporal so that the inner wealth of the former can be ironically
defined.

When Yeats first published *Michael Robartes and the Dancer* he
included a foreword to it that remains of critical significance. Having
reminded us of his favourite quotation from Goethe, he adds that
after writing the first few poems in the collection, he came into
possession of Robartes' exposition of the *Speculum Angelorum et
Hominum* of Giraldus. In the 'excitement of arranging and editing'
he could 'no more keep out of philosophy than could Goethe himself at certain periods of his life'. He has tried to 'make understanding easy' by two notes which he tells us almost apologetically, are
'much shorter than those Dante wrote on certain of his odes in the
Convito'. But he recognises that he may not have succeeded: 'It is
hard for a writer who has spent much labour on his style, to remember that thought, which seems to him natural and logical like that
style, may be unintelligible to others'. A reassurance to the common
reader follows:

The first excitement over, and the thought changed into settled conviction,
his interest in simple, that is to say in normal emotion, is always I think
increased; he is no longer looking for candlestick and matches but at the
objects in the room.

No firmer statement could be made of the poet's commitment to
achieve a public language and to create a meaning that is generally
accessible. The role of the System is also clearly defined; it is a
means of illumination but interest has to remain centred in the
objects themselves and not in the method of lighting. In subsequent
editions, Yeats left out the foreword as well as the note to *The Second
Coming*; the deletions seem to reflect his growing confidence that the
poem was capable of standing on its own text.

The Second Coming is one of the half-dozen or so poems by Yeats
which specifically mention gyres. His restraint in using this technical
term is significant and in fact no special knowledge is needed to
respond to the sense of circling, inexorable movement which the

first line conveys, both through the repetition of 'turning' and the fourfold repetition of the *in* sound. 'Widening' suggests first the increasing scope of the movement and, in conjunction with the next line, its increasing uncontrollability. The sound echo between 'falcon' and 'falconer' dramatises the growing loss of contact. The next line extends disintegration from the circumference to the core. The centre cannot hold and the forces of disorder, previously only deaf to the voice of the falconer, now become eruptively dominant. 'Mere anarchy is loosed upon the world'; the word 'loosed' finely conveys both the ebbing power of coherence at the centre, and the unleashing of destruction as an active, rending force. 'Mere anarchy', with its suggestion of worse things to come, is carried to a climax in 'blood-dimmed tide', an image potent in its fusion of blind passion with apocalyptic, world-destroying violence. Against these catastrophic forces, the ceremony of innocence is a frail dyke indeed and the very word 'ceremony' helps to suggest the almost formal character of the resistance. The stanza drives to a conclusion which might seem a piece of generalising, were it not for the rage of imagination behind it. Backed up by the poem, it is decisively, angrily concrete. The wisdom of the best, the centre of conviction, the moral basis of order has collapsed; the world lies open to the 'passionate intensity' of those who plunge forward on the blood-dimmed tide.

The tide, with its evocations of the deluge and the flood, prepares us for an impending revelation; and the expectation is strengthened by the repetition of certain key phrases—'Surely', 'is at hand', and 'the Second Coming'. Carefully controlled repetition is in fact an important feature of the poem, and is clearly intended to carry a certain sense of history into the poem's tactics. The Second Coming itself is repetition with a difference.

As the poem moves into the dimensions of prophecy, the shape of its revelation is established with ominous vagueness. The image out of *Spiritus Mundi* is vast not only in sheer size, but because it is beyond comprehension, because its consequences have still to be fully grasped. It troubles the sight—the word with its almost physical sense of an effort to focus, conveys not only the fitful, elusive character of revelation but the grim implications of the revelation itself. 'Somewhere in sands of the desert' leaves the location purposefully vague, while the wave-like motion realises with poetic accuracy the landscape of undulating desert sand. The shape with lion body and the head of a man could, in a different context, suggest the union of power and intelligence, but the first stanza has foreclosed this possibility and the next line moves the shape forward into a frame of mindless and merciless violence. Searchers after the System may find it difficult to reconcile a 'gaze blank and pitiless as the sun' with an antithetical-lunar dispensation, but the image remains threateningly appropriate to those who believe that the poem has its own rights. 'Moving its slow thighs' once again conveys with Yeats' unfailing immediacy, the clumsy, powerful, stirring of the shape into life. The shadows of the desert birds reel away from it in the giddiness of nightmare but also because, accustomed as they are to death, they find themselves in a presence from which they are obliged to recoil. As the darkness drops over the desert of prophecy, we realise that every civilisation chooses its executioner. Every order, because it is order, has its own shape of exclusion, but the things it excludes must one day rise to destroy it. Each stony sleep creates its specific nightmare and, in the rocking cradle, looks on the birth of its death. The shape moves into ferocious actuality, each monosyllable a step forward by the rough beast, with the *ou* sound four times repeated, conveying with almost tactile immediacy the shambling progress of the nightmare into life. Even the word 'Bethlehem' with its evocations of love and mercy is almost spat out in the run of the verse. The grim authenticity of the last lines is profound evidence of the poem's loyalty to its logic, of its determination not to stop short of total honesty.

The impact of *The Second Coming* derives from its archetypal power, a power that takes the poem beyond its 'thought', into a deeper world of mythical embodiment. Even the genesis of the poem reveals its thrust towards the archetypal; Stallworthy's presentation of the various manuscript drafts shows how specific references to Pitt, Burke and the German advance into Russia were discarded and how, in its evolution, the poem moved steadily to its twin objectives of universality and immediacy. Yeats himself seems to have been prepared to learn something from the poem. His original note saw in it the end of 'our scientific, democratic, fact-accumulating, heterogeneous civilisation' and there is nothing to suggest that he regretted the ending. Later, however, the poem became symbolic to him of 'the growing murderousness of the world' and in 1938 he was quoting it to Ethel Mannin as evidence of his attitude to fascism: 'Every nerve trembles with horror at what is happening in Europe.' *A Vision* which describes an antithetical dispensation as 'expressive, hierarchical, multiple, masculine, harsh, surgical' seems to inherit something from the rough beast and Yeats' comment that 'a civilisation is a struggle to keep self-control' is acted out in the first stanza of the poem with an authenticity unattainable even in poetic prose. The poem lives outside the philosophic texts and, if anything, illuminates those texts; but it is always considerably more than the texts. At the critical moment, Yeats tells us, 'the *Thirteenth Cone* the sphere, the unique intervenes'. It has to be so with the poetic imagination at its most creative.

A Prayer for my Daughter follows designedly upon *The Second Coming*. The sombre auguries of the latter poem define the 'great gloom' now in the poet's mind. The storm of change howls angrily once more and the poet's child sleeps in a cradle which the earlier poem had used for a more sinister birth. The 'haystack and roof-levelling wind/Bred on the Atlantic' is opposed only by 'Gregory's wood and one bare hill'. It screams (the word is deliberate in its suggestion of hysteria) upon the tower, below the arches of the bridge and in the elms above the flooded stream that suggests the forthcoming inundation. The sea that once gave birth to Venus now threatens with the future years, dancing frenziedly out of its murderous innocence.

Written in the same stanza as *In Memory of Major Robert Gregory*, the poem is consciously and deceptively discursive. The conversational tone and the apparent meandering are meant to give authenticity to the prayer, to the stream of hope and anxiety in the poet's mind. Nevertheless, as the poem proceeds, its chosen symbols gather weight and meaning and the last stanza knits them into a fully controlled order. Thus, the wind bred from the sea's murderous innocence, changes startlingly but convincingly into the wind of intellectual hatred. It emanates from an old bellows, exchanged for the horn of plenty, by a member of that class of opinionated idealists whose destiny is to climb upon waggonettes to scream. It batters not only Gregory's wood but the 'flourishing hidden tree' which Yeats visualises as the ideal image of his daughter's future. The tree, in turn, is a tree of self fulfilment, of inner life around which thoughts cluster like linnets. But it also comes to stand for constancy and for the life of tradition; it is 'like some green laurel/ Rooted in one dear perpetual place'. The innocence achieved when the wind had failed to tear the linnet from the leaf is 'radical' as opposed to 'murderous' innocence. It is self-contained, organic, expressive of the will of Heaven, finding its fulfilment in itself and not in working on the happiness of others. The last four lines of the poem confirm and make explicit the evolving design.

> How but in custom and in ceremony
> Are innocence and beauty born?
> Ceremony's a name for the rich horn,
> And custom for the spreading laurel tree. (*CP*, p. 214)

The last poem in the collection is an inscription to be carved on a stone at Thoor Ballylee. Yeats foresees the coming doom and asks that 'these character remain/When all is ruin once again'. The poem deals nominally with the restoration of the Tower but more fundamentally with its perfecting as a poetic symbol, a process which began in a previous volume and is to continue splendidly into the next. In the end we are reminded of the ancient poetic convention of the triumph of the imagination over time.

> Not marble nor the gilded monuments
> Of princes shall outlive this powerful rhyme.

9

Tower and Stair

I

WITH *The Tower* and *The Winding Stair* Yeats' writing comes fully into its strength and words respond completely to the poem's call to order. To say that Yeats was incapable of writing a bad poem during this phase is an exaggeration, but one within the limits of critical licence. His best poems have the quality of greatness; they reward and yet defeat analysis, remaining obstinately superior to the sum of everything that can be said about them. Nevertheless, though the content of greatness remains permanently elusive, the style of greatness invites critical definition; the suggestion made here is that Yeats' poetry achieves the self-conquest which he himself called style by a sensitive engaging of extremities, in which commitment to either extremity is avoided and the poem grows out of the creative tension between them. His poetry succeeds, in other words, because it is securely the poetry of the mainstream.

The creation of a middleground is far from easy. The distance is not very great between the pulls and counter-pulls which give a poem its shapeliness and tautness, and those which are capable of tearing the living centre of the poem apart. A deep sense of judgement is needed to evolve what Cuchulain terms 'a brief forgiveness between opposites', to ensure that the 'momentary peace' which Dylan Thomas calls a poem is achieved securely in the 'womb of war'. Yeats holds this balance firmly in his best work and even in his 'bitter' political poems (the word is one which he himself popularised) the very intensity of the bitterness asserts the presence of certain values which reality degrades. The phantoms which Yeats sees are of the heart's fullness as well as of the coming emptiness. If history sweeps to a climax of nihilism and violence it is because knowledge and power are not united, because wisdom is the property of the dead, because the best have succumbed to loss of conviction while the worst are full of passionate intensity. History fails us and failure is in the nature of history; but the poet knows the synthesis and implies it in his poetry, even though he knows also that the synthesis is unattainable. Finally, the man who sees the nature of failure is not simply its analyst but its victim. His bitterness and anger flow out of his involvement, and for that reason speak more directly to us than the detachment and remote, tragic ecstasy of the seer of Old Rocky Face or of the hermit's cave on Mount Meru.

Sailing to Byzantium which begins *The Tower* is a poem Yeats was destined to write. The distillation of his poetic life pours into it and yet, in the end, it shapes and defines itself. It is interesting to know that the 'salmon falls' are in the Sligo River, that the soul clapping its hands recalls Blake's vision of his dead brother, that Yeats before writing the poem had embarked on a systematic study of Byzantine art and history, and that he draws on visual memories of the mosaics at Ravenna, Palermo and Cefalu and possibly of the Stadhus at Stockholm. More important, perhaps, is Yeats' conviction that 'in early Byzantium, maybe never before or since in recorded history, religious, aesthetic and practical life were one', that architect and artificer 'spoke to the multitude and the few alike' and that 'building, picture, pattern, metal work of rail and lamp' were made to synthesise into a 'single image'. Yet, even these comments should be used with caution. Byzantium may represent transcendence, the world out of nature, the artifice of eternity; but the poem itself embodies Blake's proposition that eternity is in love with the productions of time.

The heart of the poem lies in its deep sense of the organic continuity between the worlds of flesh and spirit, in the union which the language itself achieves between monumental form and ardent energy. In four taut stanzas of *Ottava Rima* the great contraries of youth and age, life and death, change and the changeless and nature and art disclose themselves in a creative interdependence where each demands the other for its completion. Whatever may be the nominal thrust of the poem, the undertow of the imagery reshapes it so that the very movement of rejection re-creates the thing that is rejected. The sensual music of youth is richly recognised and is reflected in the contrapuntal music which the soul sings to redeem its tattered body. 'Monuments of unageing intellect' evolve subtly into monuments of magnificence; the inner life assumes the organic richness of the natural world from which it is disengaged. Standing in the gold mosaic of art and in the holy fires of reality, descending into the gyres of the soul's history, the sages incarnate both energy and stillness, the indestructible and its perpetual involvement in change. The interdependence extends even to minor details of language so that 'fastened' (a word suggesting an artificial linkage) is used to describe the soul's relationship to the 'dying animal', while 'gather' (a word suggesting a spontaneous natural process) describes its absorption into the '*artifice* of eternity'. Finally, there is the golden bird of Byzantium (whether derived from Gibbon or Hans Andersen), presented to us in terms which at first suggest an uncompromising cleavage between the natural and the supernatural. However, the bird sings, not of eternity, but of 'what is past or passing or to come' thereby clearly echoing, even in its cadence, the sensual music of 'whatever is begotten, born and dies'. This particular paradox was too much for Sturge Moore, and the bird of the second Byzantine poem 'more miracle than bird or handiwork', scorning aloud the mire and blood of existence, is held to reflect Yeats' reaction to Moore's objection. The suggestion is made that on this particular occasion the poem may have been wiser than either Moore or Yeats.

The Tower etches new lines into the mask of age. The 'tattered coat upon a stick' becomes 'a sort of battered kettle at the heel', and the singing soul, which once studied its own magnificence, must now bid the 'Muse go pack', deal in 'abstract things' and choose 'Plato and Plotinus for a friend'. Once again the movement is qualified by the undertow; the 'excited, passionate, fantastical' imagination is still capable of writing poetry, and exhibits that power in the off-hand diction and in the exuberant energy which overflows the quatrains.

Before the 'mocking muses' are dismissed, the ghosts of the past who peopled the Tower and its neighbourhood are summoned. There is Mrs French, whose obedient servant tried to convert fantasy into reality, Mary Hynes, whose beauty, celebrated by the blind poet Raftery, caused men to mistake the moonlight of the dream for the daylight of actuality, and Hanrahan, Yeats' creation, frenziedly pursuing the hare and hounds, which his own imagination had conjured from his cards. The poet unites the imagined and the actual, mixing daylight and moonlight in 'one inextricable beam'; though his madness cannot console the 'ancient bankrupt master' of the Tower, harassed with mundane anxieties, the Tower itself remains a poetic symbol peopled with men-at-arms and images from the great memory.

In the end, all are dismissed except Hanrahan, whose 'deep considering mind', refined by lechery, is ironically the repository of wisdom. The questioning turns towards Helen—Maud who has betrayed all living hearts; to have lost her through pride, cowardice, or over-scrupulousness is an error, the memory of which blots out the sun and which even the poet's power is incapable of redeeming.

The 'rooting of mythology in the earth' is Yeats' description of his art to Sturge Moore and his poetry exemplifies this precept, making familiar woods and rivers fade into symbol, obliterating the boundary between the legendary and the actual, mixing daylight and moonlight in one inextricable beam. The pride of the people of Burke and Grattan should be looked at in this way, but even the larger context does not fully define the legacy. It is, as the subsequent images make clear, an *élan* that is unattached, an effervescence of nature, the rejoicing of the life-force in itself. Eventually, it is the wisdom of the *anima mundi*, the instinct that enables the daws to build their nest outside the peephole of the tower, the continuity that endures through death and birth, uniting them in a single vital process. Something far deeper than snobbery is being handed on and neither snobbery, nor Yeats' swagger at its most assured, could sustain the poem in its climactic cry of defiance.

> I mock Plotinus' thought
> And cry in Plato's teeth,
> Death and life were not
> Till man made up the whole,
> Made lock, stock and barrel
> Out of his bitter soul,
> Aye, sun and moon and star, all . . . (*CP*, p. 223)

The wheel of the poem has completed its circle and insured itself against the charge of rhetoric. The seemingly arrogant claim that man makes reality is set against, and reached through, the background of his madness, the massive errors that he commits in action, his humiliation by the ageing of his body. It is the counter-truth that proclaims man's dual nature, the inextricable mingling of the absurd and the heroic. The manner in which the poetry absorbs the colloquialism of 'lock, stock and barrel' is further proof of its validity; rhetoric would be incapable of accepting such a risk. So the circuit is closed imaginatively; Plato and Plotinus are accepted in order to be set aside; the madness of the artist becomes the superhuman dream in which reality is mirrored.

Faith and pride are left to the plenitude of life. The 'bursting dawn', the 'dripping stone', the leaping fountains and the 'headlong light' embody a vitality that must continue intact as the verse ebbs masterfully over a decrescendo of d's into a sleepy cry among deepening shades.

'I like to think of that building,' Yeats wrote of the Tower, 'as a symbol of my work, permanently visible to the passer-by.' It was a symbol which looked out upon a darkening age. Yeats had thought of his home as 'a setting for my old age, a place to influence lawless youth with its severity and antiquity'. Yet out of his windows he could see that lawlessness raging, and the man writing his will could write also of the dying of civilisation:

All we can see from our windows is beautiful and quiet and has been so; yet two miles off near Coole, which is close to a main road, the Black and Tans flogged young men and then tied them to their lorries by the heels and dragged them along the road till their bodies were torn in pieces. I wonder will literature be much changed by that most momentous of events, the return of evil. (*Letters*, p. 680)

Meditations in Time of Civil War is written against the background of the coming emptiness. Juno's peacock screams, reminding us that that scream in *A Vision* is the death-cry of a civilisation. The Tower will one day become a roofless ruin with the owls building in its cracked masonry and the *primum mobile* that fashioned us inexorably decrees the night of the owl. The 'self-delighting self-appeasing' freedom of 'radical innocence' is replaced by a deadlier self-sufficiency:

> Nor self-delighting reverie,
> Nor hate of what's to come, nor pity for what's gone,
> Nothing but grip of claw, and the eye's complacency,
> The innumerable clanging wings that have put out the moon.
>
> (*CP*, p. 232)

Outside the Tower's door an 'affable Irregular' jokes about violent death and the poet is sufficiently part of the scene to admit that the link of horror is also a link of envy. The consolations of the night remain:

> No moon; only an aching heart
> Conceives a changeless work of art. (*CP*, p. 228)

Nineteen Hundred and Nineteen, the finest of Yeats' political poems, inherits the same setting. It is described oddly by Yeats as 'not philosophical but simple and passionate, a lamentation over lost peace and lost hope'. In fact, the tone is anything but elegiac. It is driven and controlled by moral indignation which both shapes it and secures it from the abyss which its vehemence skirts. The technique is evident from the first stanza, when the 'ancient image' made from the imperishable olive tree at Colonus and the 'famous ivories' of Phidias' art (to Yeats the zenith of Grecian civilisation) are made to pass away like the grasshoppers and bees of a transient summer. The theme develops further in the startling comparison of public opinion and inviolable law to the 'pretty toys' which a society discards in its maturity. Then the grim fulfilment of that maturity explodes:

> Now days are dragon-ridden, the nightmare
> Rides upon sleep: a drunken soldiery
> Can leave the mother, murdered at her door,
> To crawl in her own blood, and go scot-free;
> The night can sweat with terror as before
> We pieced our thoughts into philosophy . . . (*CP*, p. 233)

It is interesting to compare this with the later use of a similar image in *The Gyres*:

> What matter though numb nightmare ride on top,
> And blood and mire the sensitive body stain?
> What matter? Heave no sigh, let no tear drop,
> A greater, a more gracious time has gone; (*CP*, p. 337)

E

The posture of withdrawal, of visionary detachment results in a significant loss of specificity which may or may not be compensated for by the incantatory weight of the latter poem. In any case, the contrast suggests that *Nineteen Hundred and Nineteen* derives its strength (and some would add, its failings) from its angry and passionate involvement. The poet, too, is the victim of a nihilism so corrosive that even the timeless triumphs of the imagination are pitched about in the 'circle' of history. The monuments of Byzantium are no longer unageing:

> no work can stand
> Whether health, wealth, or peace of mind were spent
> On master-work of intellect or hand,
> No honour leave its mighty monument. . . . (*CP*, p. 234)

Even the dragon of art offers no escape from the dragon of reality. Men dance the measures of the Platonic year and are whirled around upon its 'furious path' with the gong's 'barbarous clangour' announcing the end of each era. In the third section even the swan, the image of the solitary soul, rides 'those winds that clamour of approaching night'. As it leaps into its 'desolate heaven' the thought of it brings not tranquillity but madness, a rage to annihilate both the past and the half-born future. The fourth section, with its single, stabbing contrast, sweeps into the fifth, a 'liturgy of scorn' as B. L. Reid terms it, which ends climactically in the scorning of scorn itself.

In the last section the forces of nihilism gather for their climax. The 'violence of horses' echoes the apocalypse. Herodias' daughters, whom Yeats associates with the Sidhe, and who according to Jeffares are taken from Arthur Symons' poem *The Dance of the Daughters of Herodias*, embody a situation in which 'evil gathers head'. The 'labyrinth of the wind' supersedes the labyrinth of meditation and the 'labyrinth of another's being' from which the poet had turned aside in *The Tower*. In the maze of anarchic violence, all sense of direction is destroyed:

> All turn with amorous cries, or angry cries,
> According to the wind, for all are blind. (*CP*, p. 237)

Then, in a master-stroke of poetic strategy, the wind drops and the

indignation settles, bringing not relief, but the image, both demonic
and moronic, of Robert Artisson, Dame Alice Kyteler's incubus.
Dame Alice had been brought before an Inquisition in 1374, and
Yeats, Jeffares tells us, had studied the proceedings in the British
Museum library. The force of the climax lies not only in the movement from acceptance to adoration of evil but in the imbecility of
the thing that is adored.

The almost torrential eloquence of *Nineteen Hundred and Nineteen*
lays it open to the charge of incoherence. Stock concludes that the
last section 'for all its energy . . . is as near to despair and to utter
loss of control as the end of any poem Yeats ever wrote'. Reid considers that 'Yeats' passion here is really frantic and compensatory.
To what he sees as the spiritual anarchy of the cosmos he tries to
oppose an equally anarchic defiance.' Actually the counter-forces,
though muted by the dominant tone of the poem, remain creative
in their total effect. Thus though men move in the dance of history,
they continue to move in it as dancers. They create the dragon and
therefore control it. The swan, however ferocious the winds of destruction that it rides, remains inviolate in its pride and beauty.
The artist's rage for destruction is balanced by an equally indestructible passion for commitment.

> Man is in love and loves what vanishes
> What more is there to say? (*CP*, p. 234)

There are times when the forces of mindless violence seem inescapably dominant in history. *Nineteen Hundred and Nineteen* conveys
this dominance unflinchingly but conveys it with a sense of desecration that unmistakably judges what it communicates.

Two Songs from a Play (the play is *The Resurrection*) sets the
images of achievement and destruction within the wheel of cyclic
re-enactment. *The Golden Bough*, Virgil's *Fourth Eclogue*, Yeats'
story *The Adoration of the Magi* and Proclus' description of Christianity as a fabulous formless darkness are among the elements which
these powerful lyrics absorb. For an account of the intricate relation-
ships between these 'sources' the reader is advised to turn to
Ellmann's *The Identity of Yeats*.

In his preface to *The Resurrection* Yeats suggests that 'the sense
of spiritual reality comes whether to the individual or to crowds

from some violent shock', and, as Vendler notes, the two songs are a systematic application of shock tactics. Yet they are something more than shock for shock's sake. If Dionysus is 'holy', and the virgin 'fierce', if the signs of Christianity are 'turbulence' and the 'odour of blood', the jolt to traditional thinking is meant to suggest that all annunciations have a common ground in mystery and terror. Indeed, the central figure of the virgin and her star which, as Ellmann demonstrates, merges Virgo and Spica, Minerva and Dionysus and Mary and Christ, acts to confirm this quasi-identity. Again, if God's death is 'but a play', it is because a play exists to be re-enacted and because a play represents the truth of the imagination which is, in the end, the most vital form of truth. Finally, if the second stanza of the first song contrasts so mordantly with Shelley's *Hellas*, it is not to oppose bitterness to optimism, but in order to reach through the apparent mockery to a fuller recognition of man's tragic stature. The cry of defiance comes fittingly in the last lines:

> Whatever flames upon the night
> Man's own resinous heart has fed. (*CP*, p. 240)

The destruction of all that man has created is an act of darkness that illuminates the darkness. The pyre which is both funeral pyre and beacon is fed by man's heart asserting both his achievement and his tragedy. The image looks back to the faith asserted ringingly in *The Tower* and forward to an even more startling reassertion:

> He knows death to the bone—
> Man has created death. (*CP*, p. 264)

Leda and the Swan, one of the most unimprovable poems ever written, is the final fusion of history, myth and vision. Using the sonnet form, which is employed traditionally for love and public issues, Yeats writes a poem which is about both and neither. Except for the daringly judged break in the eleventh line, the formal requirements are rigorously observed and the great power of compression, which can force such massive themes into so brief and tightly controlled a compass, finds its reward in the power and richness of the poem. Yeats did not come to this perfection easily. Ellmann shows that at least six stages of revision were needed and that it was not until the second published version that Yeats achieved the onslaught of the first line, the 'sudden blow', the impact of which is the poem.

Melchiori tells us that the sources of Yeats' sonnet include, besides Michaelangelo, '*the Hypnerotomachia*, Spenser, Shelley, Pater, Moreau, Blake and the Theosophists'. Other scholars have suggested alternatives and the search for pictorial origins, in particular, has been pursued with a zeal that makes one wonder whether the anatomy of Leda is truly to be found in the art galleries of Europe. It is not simply that everything that enters the poem is transformed in its creativeness so that, like all great art, it is radically unlike the elements it absorbs. The poem also lives in its immediacy so that whatever it means must be reached through its impact. Bird and woman blot out the Babylonian mathematical starlight and Yeats himself tells us that as he wrote *Leda* all politics went out of it.

From the very beginning the line of attack is plain. The 'sudden blow' (replacing the indecisive 'hoverings' of earlier drafts), the 'dark webs' with their suggestion of an irresistible, inscrutable fate (superseding the needless anatomical detail of 'webbed toes'), the 'great wings' contrasted in their power with the 'staggering', 'helpless' girl and the enfolding movement of the fourth line (reinforced by the repetition of 'breast'), all suggest a controlled and crushing violence, indifferent to everything but its apocalyptic function. Then the second stanza moves us into Leda's stunned acquiescence with 'vague', 'feathered', 'loosening' and 'white rush' progressively suggesting her collapse of identity while driving onward the basic assault of the poem. The inescapable contrast is between power and helplessness; and the recognition made violently real by the poem is that any revolutionary change in the direction of history must seem *at the point of change*, to be the product of superior and, indeed, overwhelming force. The virgin is always fierce and empires must always stand appalled whenever she calls out of the fabulous, formless darkness. The 'strange heart' which takes over Leda's being does so in the moment of death which is the quick of all crisis.

The turn into the sestet is masterfully contrived with the sound shuddering through the ninth line, out of the act and into its consequences. The movement into time reveals starkly that violence is the fruit of violence while the obvious overtones of 'broken wall' and 'burning roof' link the future firmly to the foreground. The break in the eleventh line is not so much a return to the present as a movement from embodiment to questioning; the question is asked because the poem has both created and answered it.

> Being so caught up,
> So mastered by the brute blood of the air,
> Did she put on his knowledge with his power
> Before the indifferent beak could let her drop? (*CP*, p. 241)

The repeated *so* ought not to be evaded. It is not in the abstract, but in the context of the poem's actual onslaught, that the reader's judgement is required to be made; and the forces that have 'caught up' and 'mastered' Leda have never been presented as other than irresistible, apocalyptic violence. The double savagery of 'brute blood', underlined by the alliteration and the two meanings of blood, is typical in directing our response; and the slack, detumescent monosyllables of the last line are indicative both of lust satisfied and a historical purpose fulfilled. Time and thought may make the proportions different but in the crisis, in the explosion of truth, every annunciation is revealed in power and terror.

Among School Children moves in a different element to Leda though it does deal ironically with the 'daughters of the swan'. Written after a Senate-sponsored visit to Waterford Convent (the immediate basis for the reference to the 'smiling public man'), it begins naturalistically enough with the standardised patter of the guided tour. But the fading into symbol is soon under way and a 'Ledean body' bent over a sinking fire recalls a moment of childish communion when two natures blended into a sphere, or into the yolk and white of the same shell. The alteration of Plato's parable in the *Symposium* serves to remind us that the sphere and the egg, which can turn perpetually inside out without breaking, are Yeatsian symbols of ultimate reality. It also reminds us that Yeats regards the restoration of innocence as the highest achievement of the intellect.

The remembrance of a childlike (and transient) unity of being gives way to the harsher images of age, of the 'comfortable kind of old scarecrow' and of the woman 'hollow of cheek' as though she 'drank the wind', yet still a fit subject for Quattrocento art. Recalling (as Saul notes) the second song from the opening of *At the Hawk's Well*, Yeats asks which mother would accept the decrepit shape of her son in old age as compensation for the pain of bringing him into this world. The 'honey' of generation is the drug that destroys in the newly born soul the recollection of pre-natal freedom (Yeats, taking the phrase from Porphyry, uses it, as he admits, for his own ends); but mothers, too, need their share of oblivion if the process of life is to continue.

The fluent singing movement of the sixth stanza signalises the shift into philosophy, but the consolations of wisdom are ironic. Plato suggests to us that we live among phantoms. Aristotle's more substantial knowledge is gently mocked and one is reminded that Alexander learned little from his mentor. Golden-thighed Pythagoras (Tindall quotes Plutarch for the detail and Wain, Diogenes Laertius) represents the philosophy of art in contrast to that of nature, or ideas; but even the music of the spheres is, in the last analysis, the song of a scarecrow.

The three selves of child, lover and the scarecrow and the three philosophers, give way to another triad: the 'Presences' worshipped by the passion of lovers, the piety of nuns and the affection of mothers. These are mockeries of the heart but the poem has already suggested that there are also mockeries of the mind. Nevertheless it is man who creates the ideals which he is ironically unable to attain; heavenly glory only exists as the intellect and the imagination shapes it. This is the familiar and central Yeatsian movement—out of absurdity into an affirmation of man's creative power, validated by the irony through which it has been made to live. The verse also conveys this recognition, not only in what it says but in how it moves; an intensity of irony, which can be almost derisive, is swept without hesitation into the poetry, surviving not as a tension to be exploited, but as a part of the fluent, securely singing, unity.

The last stanza raises an important difficulty of construction. It is possible to read the first sentence as 'Labour becomes blossoming or dancing, whenever the body is not bruised to pleasure soul, etc. . . .' or as 'blossoming or dancing in which the body is not bruised to pleasure soul etc. is labour'. The first reading is the one that is generally (though implicitly) accepted; but the second is grammatically possible and, radical though it may seem, perhaps has the weight of the poem behind it. The imaginative logic is surely more consistent if we argue that beauty and despair, the pleasure of the soul and the bruising of the body, the diligence of the scholar and his 'blear-eyed' wisdom are inseparably part of the life process, just as the chestnut-tree is neither leaf, blossom or bole but the creative unity of all three. The poem is not, as Yeats called it, a curse upon old age; but it is also not a justification of old age or even of life. What it offers is not a solution but a response, and the oppositions it presents between youth and age, the ideal and the actual, man's nobility and man's absurdity, are presented as roots of the blossoming conviction that without contraries there can be no life. Tree and dancer do not represent life as opposed to philosophy, or a unity of being that is beyond both life and philosophy: they represent, rather, the recognition that every condition demands its opposite, that truth as it is given to us grows out of the tension between opposites and that truth cannot be known but only lived.

All Souls' Night which ends *The Tower* is a poem written well on the way to Byzantium. The ghosts Yeats calls up are not ordinary ghosts but the ghosts of occultists—William Thomas Horton, MacGregor Mathers of the Golden Dawn and Florence Farr,who taught in Ceylon and died of cancer, but not before providing Yeats, via a 'learned Indian', with corroborative evidence of the fifteenth phase. The truths Yeats has to tell are 'mummy' truths—a witty word suggesting the wisdom of the dead and wisdom that is unageing—and the living who mock those truths remain governed by them. Over the muscatel we are informed that the 'gross palates' of the living can drink of the whole wine, while ghosts must satisfy themselves with the 'wine-breath'. By the end of the poem the mummy-cloth has been wound around sufficiently to permit a reversal of this statement. 'No living man can drink from the whole wine.' It is the fume of the eternal which is the quintessence of things.

II

When Yeats re-read *The Tower* in 1928 he found himself 'astonished at its bitterness'. He recognised that this quality gave the book its power and he was prepared to concede that if he was in better health he might be 'content to be bitter'. But, struggling against high blood pressure, spitting blood and exhausted, he had driven himself into a nervous collapse. 'I long to live out of Ireland', he wrote to Olivia Shakespeare, 'that I may find some new vintage'. Convalescing in Rapallo, 'an indescribably lovely place', he hoped to 'put off the bitterness of Irish quarrels' and to write his 'most amiable verses'. 'Once out of Irish bitterness, I can find some measure of sweetness and light, as befits old age—already new poems are floating in my head, bird songs of an old man, joy in the passing moment, emotion without the bitterness of memory.'

Sweetness and light are not the outstanding qualities of *The Winding Stair* and are probably the two moods which Yeats was least capable of evoking. But the exaggeration points to a familiar pattern drawn, as Unterecker notes, with more than usual exactness. That *The Winding Stair* is a counterpoise to *The Tower* is evident from such unlikely details as the contrast between the eleven poems of *A Man Young and Old* and the eleven of *A Woman Young and Old*, each concluded by a passage from Sophocles. More important perhaps is the manner in which *A Dialogue of Self and Soul*, with its choice of rebirth, answers *The Tower*'s choice of death. 'Images of sterility', Unterecker comments, 'dominate *The Tower*; regeneration and sexuality (the famous passions of Crazy Jane and Tom the Lunatic) act as shaping forces in *The Winding Stair*. The focus is primarily on things masculine and political in *The Tower*, on things feminine and aesthetic in *The Winding Stair*.'

All this is as it should be in the nature of Yeats' procedures, but it is important not to push the poetry too vigorously into its proffered framework. *The Winding Stair* may represent the choice of life against the artifice of eternity; but no poems in it possess the inclusive life-consciousness of *Sailing to Byzantium* or *Among School Children*. Decay is not absent from its images, though the poet looks down the stair to a tradition betrayed, rather than around him at present anarchy. The swan drifts upon the darkening flood, the pebbles on Arnold's beach rattle under the receding wave, wisdom remains the property of the dead and man must still choose between the life and the work.

Even the title of the first poem of *The Winding Stair* draws its strength from the old vein of bitterness (Eva Gore-Booth and Con

Markiewicz were still alive when the poem was written). The innocent and the beautiful ought to have no enemy but time, a truth to
which Yeats later provides the counter-truth:

> Bodily decrepitude is wisdom; young
> We loved each other and were ignorant. (*CP*, p. 301)

The poem, however, seems to suggest other enemies; the gazelle's
innocence is destroyed in the corruption of politics and those who
built the gazebo are convicted of guilt. The pun between gazelle
and gazebo ties together the grace of youth and the accomplishment
of culture. The question, which the poem cleverly leaves open, is
whether 'politics' and mob condemnation are not really part of the
time-process; and when Yeats joins the destroyers ('Bid me strike
a match and blow') the suggestion is that history is on the mob's
side.

   Death follows fittingly upon the first poem, reiterating the indes-
tructibility of man in the face of destruction. Written after the
assassination of the Minister of Justice, Kevin O'Higgins ('the one
strong intellect in Irish public life'), it suggests that man is capable
of challenging death precisely because he knows that death must
come. A 'dying animal' (the phrase remembers *Sailing to Byzantium*)
remains unaware of the imminence of death. It is the heart of man
fastened to the animal that makes death meaningful in the perspectives of dread and of hope. The significance of death, in the last
analysis, is given by the quality of man's response to death. Man
knows death to the bone (the irony should be evident) and what he
has created can also be defeated.

   A Dialogue of Self and Soul, the crucial statement of Yeats' commitment to life, was, he tells us, 'written in the spring of 1928,
indeed finished the day before a Cannes doctor told me to stop
writing'. The emblem of the self is the five-hundred-and-fifty-year-
old sword given to Yeats by Junzo Sato in Portland, Oregon, during
his 1920 American tour. Sheathed in its scabbard, still razor-keen
and unspotted by the centuries, the combination represents the
looking glass and the embroidery of art, the energies that survive
time, love and war, and the masculine and the feminine. It is worth
remembering that in *Meditations in Time of Civil War* sword and
scabbard stood for 'Soul's beauty being most adored', and that in a

later poem the blade and the gold-sewn silk which sheathes it are 'beauty and fool together laid'. These links are not made to suggest anything so simple as inconsistency; rather it is suggested that while certain symbols endure through Yeats' poetry, each individual poem must create those symbols anew.

If the 'consecrated blade' and its scabbard are emblems of the day, the tower is an emblem of 'ancestral night'. The soul's condition is darkness and the acceptance of that darkness is deliverance from the 'crime' of death and birth. It also leads to a kind of dark enlightenment in which unitive apprehension of *is, ought, knower* and *known* replaces the separations of the intellect. The 'breathless air' which is totally beyond life, the 'hidden pole' which is the pivot of truth and the starlit sky from which the moon of self is absent, all indicate the conditions of phase one, where, with the self annihilated, the plenitude of reality overflows and pours into the inert basin of the mind. But the price of revelation is the death of all personality ('man is stricken blind and deaf and dumb') and thinking of that revelation the tongue becomes a stone. The ambivalence of the symbol is exactly judged. The stone stands for death and the commitment to rebirth is a kind of dying to absolute reality; but the inherent tendency of the stone is downward into the only life that is humanly possible.

Building upon this ambivalence the self commits itself to rebirth in an impassioned outburst in which the bitterness of life is affirmed with daring intensity so that its sweetness can be vindicated. Few poets, apart from Yeats, would accept so spectacular a risk and there are some who argue that the risk was beyond him, that the conclusion is imposed on the poem, instead of developing from it. Such a conclusion underestimates the irony of the soul's claims; it also ignores the subtle but clearly intentional links between the blindness of soul and the blindness of self, the forgiveness that is bestowed upon the dead and the forgiveness achieved by a deeper living of life, the 'fullness' that overflows into the minds of the dead and the 'sweetness' that flows into the breasts of the living. What Yeats is suggesting is not the obvious point that life is worth living even at its most bitter. Rather it is his familiar proposition that what we know of ultimate reality is only known to the extent that it is lived.

Blood and the Moon remakes the symbol of the Tower. Once

emblematical of the night, it is now emblematical of a power that both utters and masters the race out of which it rises, dominating it as the actual Tower dominates the storm-tossed cottage below it. But mockery is also inscribed upon the emblem; the Tower, like tradition, is 'half dead at the top'. The passage is an instructive exercise in shock tactics with the repeated 'blessed' creating a sense of holiness which seems deliberately shattered by 'bloody' and 'arrogant'. Yet it is a kind of religion of the blood, a sanctification of history and tradition which is being urged by the symbol.

Looking back on the 'winding, gyring, spiring treadmill' of the ancestral stair that is tradition and history, Yeats looks back also on the delayed Irish Renaissance, the eighteenth-century unity of being and culture, in which Swift, Goldsmith, Burke and Berkeley contributed in various ways to the organic society and the life of the mind. The word 'blood' takes on additional connotations by being linked to the state and by being associated with *Saeva Indignatio* and with Swift's blood-sodden heart.

In the next section the moon comes to represent the reality that shines into and shapes action, while blood represents the dark, organic and propulsive power which clamours drunkenly for, distorts or simply ignores the reality which it cannot embody, but also cannot tarnish. The sense of an incorruptible radiance, involved in change yet inviolably apart from it, is strongly conveyed by a symbolism which gives due weight to the brute forces in change. The next section then moves the engaged symbols apart:

> No matter what I said,
> For wisdom is the property of the dead,
> A something incompatible with life; and power,
> Like everything that has the stain of blood,
> A property of the living; (*CP*, p. 269)

It is a conclusion charged by the force of the poem, with 'dead' suggesting both the past which the present has rejected and ruined and the world beyond life, the incorruptible moonlight. At the same time, the stain of blood is the mark of life. Power completes wisdom; but it can do so only by betraying it.

Coole Park, 1929, looks down the staircase of a more personal history. Lady Gregory had been obliged to sell the house and its lands to the Forestry Department in 1927; though she was allowed to stay on as a tenant for the remainder of her life. The poem looks back in tribute without looking forward in anger to those who would destroy the great gazebo. Assembled in the cast are Hyde, who beat the sword 'the Muses buckled on' into the ploughshare of scholarship, Yeats himself, 'ruffled in a manly pose', John Synge, 'that meditative man', and Lady Gregory's 'impetuous' nephews, John Shawe-Taylor and Hugh Lane. Coming and going like swallows, their work was given pattern and purpose by Lady Gregory's 'powerful character' while the great house preserved unity of being ('Thoughts long knitted into a single thought') and a 'dance-like glory' begotten from its walls.

Coole Park and Ballylee, 1931 is set in a stormier landscape. Nature has pulled on her 'tragic buskin' and her 'rant' (the lyric duly survives the mockery of its language) serves as a mirror of the poet's mood. Water stands for the generated soul (the symbol is taken from Porphyry) rushing past the tower in the race of life, plunging underground into the death of dark Raftery's cellar and emerging, reborn, into the lake at Coole. The swan, another emblem of the soul, sets aright through its loveliness the imperfections of both knowledge and ignorance. It rises in 'sudden thunder' from the 'flooded lake' on the banks of which the trees are 'dry sticks' under a 'wintry sun'. The difference should be noted between this landscape and that of the *Wild Swans at Coole* with its 'brimming water' and 'autumn beauty', and even the 'dry sticks' of the stripped beeches find their echo in the 'sound of a stick' in the room where Lady Gregory is dying. The glory of the past is not unlike that of the swan: it can be gone in the morning 'no man knows why' and ink in a pen can write out its destruction.

Stormily white and arrogantly pure, concentrating the heavens in its beauty, the swan rides the waters, belonging to them and yet aloofly above them, as the soul rides the stream of its own life. Respect for what the poetry accomplishes prohibits further specification of its symbols. It is necessary only to point to the final stanza where the last romantics (romantic because, committed to an irrecoverable past of sanctity and loveliness, they set their faces against the coming reality) look upon a landscape where 'all is changed', where the 'high horse' of poetry is without a rider, and where the swan, no longer in control of its destiny, drifts on the darkening and engulfing flood.

In December 1929 Yeats was close to death from Malta fever. 'I warmed myself back into life', he tells us, 'with *Byzantium* and *Veronica's Napkin*, looking for a theme that might befit my years.' A total commitment to the after-life is perhaps not the best way of warming oneself into life and *A Dialogue of Self and Soul*, which was also written out of illness, points vehemently in a different direction. In addition, *Mohini Chatterjee*, which precedes *Byzantium* in *Collected Poems*, seems to suggest that the timeless is best reached, not by repudiating time, but by pounding it away with the cannonade of birth heaped upon birth.

Interpretations of *Byzantium* are varied enough to suggest that every reader makes his own poem from the same words. What is suggested here is that *Byzantium* deals with the tensions between change and the changeless, tensions implicit in much imaginative experience and recreated memorably in the poem's language. It is because of this universality that *Byzantium* has its impact on those not deeply instructed in the Vision and on those who remain unschooled in the subtleties of Platonic mysticism. This is not to deny that the modelling of the poem may be metaphysical or religiophilosophical; but if disbelief is suspended in the presence of the poem it is largely because the modelling seems to disclose the inherent form of a generally valid experience.

The initial position in *Byzantium* is a decisive segregation of being from becoming. The 'sensual music' of an earlier poem has become the 'fury and the mire of human veins'. The starlit and moonlit domes of the first and fifteenth crescents disdain the 'mere complexities' of man's divided nature. The language, striving to express a reality that transcends language, relies heavily on techniques of definition by negation.

> Before me floats an image, man or shade,
> Shade more than man, more image than a shade;
>
> Miracle, bird or golden handiwork,
> More miracle than bird or handiwork,
>
> At midnight on the Emperor's pavement flit
> Flames that no faggot feeds, nor steel has lit, (*CP*, pp. 280–1)

The first quotation (as Wilson notes) echoes Dante's address to Virgil, with the crucial difference that Dante does not mention images. Yeats is suggesting that, in the last resort, it is the creative mind which must instruct us in transcendent reality.

When the 'great Cathedral gong' (which Yeats may have read about in W. G. Holmes' *The Age of Justinian and Theodora*) has tolled its midnight summons to eternity, 'Hades' bobbin', bound in 'mummy-cloth' which (as in *All Souls' Night*) suggests both the dead and the unageing, offers a means of unwinding the thread of time and the path of the gyres. The superhuman is totally beyond the human, a mouth without moisture and without breath. Nevertheless, it is involved in the human, as the gyres of life and death involve each other. Yeats' favourite quotation from Heraclitus, echoed in the last lines of the stanza, drives home this embattled interdependence.

In a correspondence which is by now celebrated, Yeats informed Sturge Moore that *Byzantium* 'originates from a criticism of yours. You objected to the last verse of *Sailing to Byzantium* because a bird made by a goldsmith was just as natural as anything else. That showed me that the idea needed exposition.' Perhaps this admission should be read in the same way as Milton's statement that *Paradise Regained* was written to satisfy Ellwood. The qualities of the bird are justified by the necessities of the poem, necessities which arise from its almost passionate disengagement of the supernatural from the corruptions of the natural. Ellmann points out that Yeats would have learned from Eugenie Strong's *Apotheosis and After Life* of how the cock became the herald of rebirth and was depicted as such on Roman tombstones. But, though the golden bird can crow like the cocks of Hades, the emphasis is rather on its scorning aloud the mire and blood of existence. Nevertheless the bird, even in its changeless glory, is 'embittered' and that fact keeps it tenuously but significantly linked to the 'bitter furies of complexity' which it disdains.

Byzantium in Yeats' earlier poem was a place of stillness, of unageing monuments, of fire frozen into gold mosaic, of sages standing rather than spirits dancing, of equilibrium perfected in the artifice of eternity. In the later poem the dance which is the climactic symbol of the holy city is characterised by intense and tormented energy. The writhing movement of the *f* and *l* sounds in the fourth stanza encloses a scene in which the 'blood-begotten spirits' leave 'fury' behind only to enter into 'agony'; and as the intensity of the agony is raised by the ritual repetition of the word itself and the alliterative link between 'dance' and 'dying', the climax comes in the realisation that the experience, however overwhelming, is unreal, that the flames are incapable even of singeing a sleeve. Critics, from Ure onwards, have noted that Yeats has in mind the *Noh* play *Montemezuka* in which the torments of the sufferer are essentially self-inflicted. But what is also involved is the recognition that the experience of the totally transcendental cannot be related to that which it transcends. Mystic experience is beyond words and therefore can be engaged only tangentially with poetic experience that lives finally in words. To glimpse the quality of mystic experience, a struggle of the imagination is called for which in its nature cannot be sustained. What Vendler calls the 'shuddering poise' of the fourth stanza is an enactment of the struggle and of the inevitable defeat which follows from it.

The last stanza moves the poem back into the natural world. Though the 'smithies break the flood' and the 'Marbles of the dancing floor/Break bitter furies of complexity' the very word 'break' suggests a position under assault, a defence erected against an inundation. The emphasis is on the turbulent plenitude of nature, the images that beget fresh images (echoing in creative terms the supernatural 'flames begotten of flame'), and the 'spirit after spirit' upon the backs of the dolphins which, in the run of the poem, are like an advancing army. Yeats could have learned about his dolphins from many sources, including Hermes Trismegistus and Eugenie Strong. He also writes to Sturge Moore of 'Raphael's statue of the Dolphin carrying one of the Holy Innocents to Heaven'. The common reader might remember *Lycidas* and the use of the dolphin by Elizabethan writers to symbolise that which is both in and out of its element.

The syntax of the last lines is obscure and it seems best to treat (1) the bitter furies of complexity, (2) the images that beget fresh images and (3) the dolphin-torn and gong-tormented sea as objects of the verb 'break' in the fifth line. This interpretation, which Vendler supports, seems to be borne out by the evolution of the poem in manuscript, as given to us by Bradford and Stallworthy.

In any case, as Vendler points out, 'the governing force of the verb "break" is spent long before the end of the stanza is reached, and the last three lines stand syntactically as absolutes'. The magnificent last line which guides the poem into its stormy peace suggests through the embattled force of 'torn 'and 'tormented' how man's life is split asunder by forces which he cannot evade but to which he cannot surrender without denying his nature. Man remains suspended between flesh and spirit, and cannot choose either without ceasing to be man. The conflict which rends him is the sign that he is human.

Although *Byzantium* is a powerful accomplishment it is justifiable to ask whether it is not uneasily close to being a *tour de force*. Yeats' poetic strength lies in his deep sense of continuity between the supernatural and the natural, and the correlative of that sense is a language where familiar woods and trees are given symbolic potency, where the personal blends into the legendary, and the mythical merges into the actual, where the world we inhabit is not denied but extended in significance. But when the supernatural becomes an uncompromising repudiation of the natural, when birth becomes a 'crime' and the emblem of life a bloodstain, the energy of rejection and the counter-energy of acceptance become so ferocious that even Yeats' creative strength is not always capable of holding them in a poem. In saying this, it should be remembered that Yeats' poetic practice is based, to some extent, on the deliberate strengthening of contraries—'the greater the tension, the greater my self-knowledge'—and that consciousness for him is identified with conflict. It is perhaps also true for the reader that any increase in the distance between extremities increases the excitement of having them bridged. Nevertheless, there is a line beyond which daring cannot go, though the creative power of a poet can drive the line back. When contraries are driven into too stark and determined an opposition, the effect must be to inhibit the openness and interchange which should form the basis of their poetic synthesis. There is a tendency to substitute the attitudes which formalise experience for the experience which joins them and out of which they grow. 'Either, or' is a formula for religious rather than poetic recognition. Poetry must rest upon the understanding (felt as an imaginative principle) that eternity is in love with the productions of time.

After the plunge into life of the '*Dialogue*' and the thrust into the timeless of *Byzantium*, *Vacillation* takes the position that its title indicates. Man runs his course between antinomies which the flaming brand of death or remorse can destroy. But there is an alternative—creative union rather than obliteration—and possibly this is the nature of joy.

The Mabinogion tree to which, as Stauffer notes, Yeats refers in *The Celtic Element in Literature* represents the organic union of opposites, a union strikingly conveyed by the interweaving recurrences of the language. The artist who hangs the mask of Attis between the 'staring fury and the blind lush leaf' dies into art and so experiences creatively the flaming brand that destroys the antinomies. He 'knows not grief' and, though too deeply absorbed in the experience of creation to understand completely the significance of what he creates, the implication is that he does know joy.

The third section suggests how daily life runs between practical antinomies. Man must obtain all the gold and silver that he can— the apparently gross materialism is misleading, and the point is that silver and gold stand for the lunar and solar principles, for interior as well as exterior acquisitiveness. The man of property must also be a man of insight, earning the love of women by his 'idle' thoughts and the gratitude of children by his 'rich estate'. At forty (Yeats was forty-four when he wrote *The Coming of Wisdom with Time*) he must renounce the leaves and flowers, the 'Lethean foliage' of his youth. Those works are extravagant which do not fulfil a certain idea of extravagance, the heroic gaiety of those who come 'proud, open-eyed and laughing to the tomb'.

The fourth and fifth sections define yet another vacillation. In certain moments of ordinary life the body blazes like the Mabinogion tree, remorse is cast out, as in *The Dialogue of Self and Soul*, and everything we look upon is blessed. Yeats, as Ure notes, is remembering, but also transmuting, an experience which he records in *Per Amica Silentia Lunae*. At other times the tree is seen neither in symbolic sunlight nor symbolic moonlight. The sense of responsibility for errors of action or omission creates not the tree's storm-scattered intricacy, but what Cuchulain calls 'intricacies of blind remorse'.

The sixth stanza grows out of personal regret into a powerful recognition of the transience of all things. The 'rivery field', the 'new-mown hay' and the melting snow set the scene, not for rebirth and for the stirring of life, but for the tolling in of the apocalyptic refrain: 'Let all things pass away'. But the contrast defines a crucial vacillation. If all things pass into death they also pass into life. One civilisation succeeds another and every defeat must also be a conquest. The 'gaudy moon' of permanence is hung like Attis' image on the tree of opposites, of day and night, destruction and creation, that is now seen to grow out of 'man's blood-sodden heart'. The almost melodramatic colouring of the image stiffens the shock of recognition, suggesting with stark insight the world which man makes for himself with its crude compulsions and its maimed nobility.

The transience of all things strengthens the soul's claim that we should seek the reality beyond things. In the renewed debate with the self (now the blood-sodden heart from which the tree springs), the conclusions of the *Dialogue* are reaffirmed. Isaiah's coal, while purging away sin and iniquity, brings not inspiration but dumb-foundedness. The artist's element is not the fire of salvation, the simplicity achieved when the dross of impermanence is refined away, but the complex impurity of existence, the fury and the mire of human veins. Yeats' association of fire with simplicity is an old one going back to *No Second Troy*, and the cancelled drafts of *Byzantium* contrast the simplicity and integrity of the purgatorial dance with the flood of intricacy from which it is safeguarded. Nevertheless, in rejecting what Eliot calls 'A condition of complete simplicity/ Costing not less than everything', Yeats' preference is not uncom-promising and the alternatives, neatly offered in stichomythia, are less mutually exclusive than they seem. If the state of sin is pre-ferred to that of salvation the very formulation of the preference— 'What theme had Homer but original sin?'—reminds us that original sin is also the principal theme of Christian religion.

For these reasons, Von Hügel, the Roman Catholic author of *The Mystical Element of Religion*, is substantially more than a man of straw. Although Yeats once wrote to Olivia Shakespeare that in the whole range of his lyric poetry, from *Oisin* onwards, the swords-man had throughout repudiated the saint, the repudiation is never decisive and the justice of the poetry would suffer if it were. On the

other hand, Virginia Moore's argument that Yeats was fundamentally a Christian seems to err in the opposite direction. Stauffer
is more balanced in suggesting that Yeats builds what he can make
use of into his own honeycomb: Von Hügel is dismissed with
blessings on his head, the miracles of the saints and the honouring of
sanctity are accepted on both sides and it is even admitted that the
heart might 'find relief' in Christianity. The final courtesy is the
suggestion that the artist's part is 'predestined' rather than chosen.
The final irony, however, is the quoting of scripture for the poet's
purpose. The miracle implicit in Samson's riddle—that life should
come out of death and sweetness out of strength, that the honeycomb should be built in the putrefying body—is the fundamental
paradox of the life-process of which the poet is the 'predestined'
interpreter. What is rejected is penitential Christianity, and this in
favour of something more inclusive, the tree which is inalienably
both death and life, the body and the spirit, the reconciled duality
of the artist's total vision.

In the spring of 1929, Yeats tells us, 'life returned to me as an
impression of the uncontrollable energy and daring of the great
creators. . . . I wrote *Mad as the Mist and Snow* and after that almost
all that group of poems called, in memory of those exultant weeks,
Words for Music Perhaps'. In a letter written on 9 March 1929 Yeats
informed Lady Gregory that he had written five of *Twelve Poems for
Music*. By 29 March he claimed to have written nine and by 13
September the number planned for the series had risen to thirty,
with over half of them already composed. Yet the very rate of his
progress filled Yeats with doubt: 'I am writing more easily than I
ever wrote and am happy, whereas I have always been unhappy
when I wrote and worked with great difficulty.' Yeats' dates may not
always be trustworthy, but Ellmann's chronology shows that several
of the poems on Crazy Jane were written before *Byzantium* and that
virtually all of them (as well as the poems on Tom the Lunatic) were
written before *Vacillation*. Their appearance after the latter poem
is one more reminder that the aesthetic order is not the chronological.

Crazy Jane, Yeats told Olivia Shakespeare, was founded upon an
old woman who lived in a little cottage near Gort and who had 'an
amazing power of audacious speech'. She was, he added, 'the local
satirist and a really terrible one'. Some doubts have been expressed

as to whether the origin of Crazy Jane is quite so simple as this statement suggests. In previous versions of the poems she is referred to as Cracked Mary, a creature whom Yeats mentions as early as 1904 and whom he treats as the source for the song in *The Pot of Broth* that refers to 'Poor Jack the journeyman'. In any case, having created his character, Yeats found it amusing to think himself possessed by her. 'I have begun a longish poem called "Wisdom",' he wrote to Olivia Shakespeare, 'in the attempt to shake off "Crazy Jane" and I begin to think that I shall take to religion unless you save me from it.' To his wife he was even more emphatic: 'I want to exorcise that slut, Crazy Jane, whose language has become nu-endurable.' The exorcism seems to have been ineffective and Yeats, who was probably never scandalised, eventually found himself converted. 'I approve of her,' he told Olivia Shakespeare. As for the poems themselves, he declared provocatively: 'Sexual abstinence fed their fire—I was ill and yet full of desire. They sometimes came out of the greatest mental excitement I am capable of.' Yet if intellectual excitement fed the poems it did not determine their fundamental character. 'I want them to be all emotional and all impersonal,' Yeats wrote elsewhere. He described them as 'the opposite of my recent work and all praise of joyous life'. The characteristic qualification followed: 'In the best of them it is a dry bone on the shore that sings the praise.'

Actually, satire and sluttishness are not the outstanding qualities of the series, and even the much-vaunted sexuality of the poetry needs to be accepted in its context if it is not to obscure the central meaning. It is more legitimate to regard the essence of Crazy Jane as her derelict dignity in the face of circumstance, a kind of heroic inviolability amid the humiliations of the blind man's ditch. More fundamentally, however, Crazy Jane represents the cnoviction that the truth can only be possessed in time and that to live the truth man must consent to live it whole. The validity of experience resides in its completeness and one can only mutilate that completeness by forcing it into the categories of either body or spirit. Again and again Jane expresses the sense of wholeness, the recognition that opposites need each other to complete themselves, a recognition consummated in the act of love, which remains the stubborn centre of her wisdom. Love is like the lion's tooth, eloquent also of anger and of the rage to destroy. If it stops short of total possession, if it is unable to 'take the whole/Body and soul', it remains not partially, but totally unsatisfied. Fair and foul are near of kin, flesh and spirit demand each other and 'nothing can be sole or whole/That has not been rent'. The obvious anatomical puns should not obscure the truth that Eden is known only to those who have lost it, and that only those whom conflict has divided can enter fully into the meaning of unity.

The meaning of experience can perhaps only be known outside time ('All could be known or shown/If time were but gone'), but the sense of permanence inheres in all experience that is completely lived. The great battle is fought unendingly in the narrow pass, the ruined house lights up and Wild Jack remains a lover, though other men use Jane's body for a road. The past is indestructible if it is fully possessed. The fiddlers may be 'all thumbs' and 'the fiddle-string accursed' but Jane remains inviolably of Ireland. The great lord of Chou may consider that all things pass away, but it requires a victim of the flux to be aware of the other side of reality: 'All things remain in God.'

This sense of wholeness as the union of opposites is reinforced by the dramatic convention, the contrast between protagonist and circumstances, between the inviolable insight and the repeatedly violated body. It is underlined by the ironic convention, the wisdom of those whom the world calls half-witted and the reversal of apparent values as the bishop turns into the coxcomb he condemns. Finally, it is strengthened by the linguistic convention, the deliberate contrast between the spiritual understanding and the phallic phrases. These incongruities bind the poems together, opening into and subtly validating the greater incongruity of its central recognition, the sense of permanence in the midst of change. Crazy Jane does not hunger for Byzantium, nor does she bless everything that she looks upon; but she knows that the tree and the moon that is hung upon it grow out of the apparent waste land of the heart.

In his preface to *The Words upon the Window Pane*, Yeats describes Plotinus as the first philosopher 'to establish as sole source the timeless individuality or daimon instead of the Platonic idea, to prefer Socrates to his thought. This timeless individuality contains archetypes of all possible existences whether of man or brute, and, as it traverses its circle of allotted lives, now one, now another prevails. We may fail to express an archetype or alter it by reason, but all done from nature is its unfolding into time. Some other existence may take the place of Socrates, yet Socrates can never cease to exist.' Tom the Lunatic, a more explicit Plotinian than Crazy Jane, sings aloud on Cro-Patrick, the Irish Kailas, knowing that in each species there is one perfect individual that expresses the divine archetype without distortion. All that is created acclaims, proclaims and declaims the timeless individuality and stands indestructible in the unchanging eye of God. The generative imagery of the last stanza of *Tom the Lunatic* declares vividly the sense of permanence in the vigour of change and renewal and the conviction is pressed further in *Old Tom Again*. All things sail out of perfection and life and death, 'winding-sheet and swaddling clothes' are the suppositions of 'fantastic men', accidents which cannot impair the essence.

The concluding poem in the series introduces us appropriately to Plotinus himself and the things which sailed out of perfection struggle back into it. The poem is based upon the Delphic Oracle's pronouncement on Plotinus' journey to the Elysian fields, which is preserved with a commentary in Porphyry's life. Yeats knew the translations by Taylor and Mackenna and probably also drew (as Henn notes) on the additional commentary by Henry More. The originals mention Minos, Rhadamanthus, the golden race of Zeus, stately Pythagoras and the choir of immortal love; but certain touches such as Rhadamanthus' blandness and the buffeting Plotinus receives are typically Yeatsian. The blood which blocks Plotinus' eyes comes from what Porphyry describes as the blood-drenched waves of life and the salt in the blood, according to Wilson, is the contaminating salt of material concerns. Plotinus is regarded by Yeats as from the East and Rhadamanthus in Plato's *Gorgias* is as Ellmann observes, the judge of Asian souls. The inhabitants of Elysium include a philosopher, a musician (Pythagoras) and a choir of love, because, according to Plotinus, metaphysicians, lovers and musicians are those most capable of visionary experience. Tindall describes *The Delphic Oracle on Plotinus* as gay, preposterous, full of mysterious overtones and surrealist rather than symbolist. The poem is certainly more fully organised than this judgement suggests though it perhaps does not merit Wilson's evaluation of it as 'technically one of the most perfect of Yeats' lyrics'.

III

In the preface to *The King of the Great Clock Tower* Yeats tells us that, finding that he had grown too old for poetry, he decided to 'force himself to write' and that in *Parnell's Funeral* he 'rhymed passages' from a lecture he had given in America. The poem is more than this account of its genesis suggests and scarcely deserves Stewart's description of it as 'a political and anthropological *mélange*'. Though indignation threatens to overwhelm its structure it is adequately possessed by its complex of images. Its elements had long been in Yeats' mind. As far back as 1896 he wrote to William Sharp that he had seen 'between sleep and waking, a beautiful woman firing an arrow among the stars'. 'Had some great event taken place,' Yeats then asks, 'in some world where myth is reality and had we seen some portion of it?' It is a comment that is significant in relation to *Parnell's Funeral*.

Elaborating the image in his notes, Yeats tells us that the archer is the Mother-Goddess (also Artemis) who is pictured upon certain Cretan coins of the fifth century B.C. as 'a slightly draped, beautiful woman sitting in the heart of a branching tree'. The star is the 'child whose sacrificial death symbolised the death and resurrection of the Tree-spirit or Apollo'. The image fuses in the poem with Maud Gonne's account of how a star flashed out of the heavens in broad daylight, as Parnell's body was lowered into its grave; but the point is that Parnell's death is a rite of destruction, not a rite of renewal. The 'animal blood', the 'frenzied crowd', the 'popular rage', and the '*Hysterica Passio*' are signs of mob hysteria rather than purgative frenzy. An age is the *reversal* of an age, and the requirements of Yeats' system add historical weight to political indignation. Those who destroy Parnell merely drag him down; it is a sacrifice in which the victim's heart is not eaten and from which the victim's spirit cannot be reborn.

Ribh's supernatural songs are the first fruit of the Steinach operation and, in a sense, Ribh complements Crazy Jane by representing the sexuality of spirit rather than the spirituality of sex. Yeats tells us that Ribh's Christianity, like much early Irish Christianity, comes perhaps from Egypt and 'echoes pre-Christian thought'. Elsewhere, he associates early Christian Ireland with India and mentions with implicit approval a famous philosopher's belief that 'every civilisation began, no matter what its geographical origin, with Asia'. Ribh he tells us, would be an orthodox man 'were it not for his ideas about the Trinity', a reassurance which is less solid than it seems.

Discarding the segregations of *Byzantium*, Ribh maintains strenuously that natural and supernatural are wed with the self-same ring. Perhaps the counter-truth is a little too energetically proclaimed. Even for those who are, philosophically or imaginatively, monists, who are committed to a continuity between the spirit and the senses and who look on the visible as an imperfect mirror of the invisible, there are differences between human and divine love which it is considered prudent not to obscure. There is indeed a common element in the two loves; but it is intuitive understanding, not the physical spasm. Milton, an uncompromising monist, states the relationship clearly:

> In loving thou dost well, in passion not,
> Wherein true Love consists not; love refines
> The thoughts, and heart enlarges, hath his seat
> In Reason, and is judicious, is the scale
> By which to heav'nly Love thou maist ascend,
> Not sunk in carnal pleasure, for which cause
> Among the Beasts no Mate for thee was found.
>
> (*Paradise Lost*, VIII, 588–94)

It is true that Ribh also maintains, to quote his creator, that 'we beget and bear because of the incompleteness of our love'. Perfect love is a consuming conflagration. When the mind or body damps that conflagration, the mirror-scaled serpent of multiplicity is born. But the poem does not adequately enact this distinction. Its emphasis is throughout on the generative force of the love act:

> As man, as beast, as an ephemeral fly begets,
> Godhead begets Godhead (*CP*, p. 328)

and the verse, with its proliferating rhythm, underlines the recognition submerging any refinements that may be urged against it.

The poetry of 'spasm' is therefore, as one might expect, not success-ful as a means of insight into the higher reality. It is at its most effective in *Whence had they Come?* when the shudder in the loins can become, as in *Leda*, the point of union between history and myth.

Ribh at the Tomb of Baile and Aillinn is on a different footing. The 'pitch-dark night' defines, by contrast, the light of a love purified by tragedy by which Ribh's eyes (purified by asceticism) are rendered able to read his holy book. The latent implication need not be ignored; the sacred book of the arts is also best read in the light of tragedy. At the same time the 'juncture of the apple and the yew', above the tomb of the lovers, points upwards to a higher 'juncture' where 'whole is joined to whole'.

> For the intercourse of angels is a light
> Where for its moment, both seem lost, consumed. (*CP, p.* 328)

Though Swedenborg is his immediate point of departure, Yeats is here drawing on a long tradition of angelology which includes such names as Psellus, Milton and More. On the other hand, the force of the word 'lost', its connection to the earthly tragedy and the sudden blaze of meaning into 'consumed', are Yeatsian and decis-ively creative. The subtle relationship of the two worlds is finely realised by the complex of images. The natural is best interpreted by the presence of the supernatural; but that presence, though 'some-what broken' by the leaves through which it shines, is itself a refine-ment of the natural.

Ribh considers Christian Love Insufficient is a powerful poem in the Hound of Heaven tradition, showing how the soul, in the strength of its hatred of God, strips away the deceptions and evasions that separate it from God and is brought, at the hour of its midnight, to naked and uncompromising dependence on its creator. The passionate search, whatever its initial direction, must eventually destroy all alternatives to reality. The sense of the discovery of God through the struggle against God links the poem to *The Four Ages of Man* in which man's life is seen as a hierarchy of four battles and defeats, culminating in the midnight defeat that summons him to Byzantium and the final victory of the soul over the mind.

'I think profound philosophy must come from terror,' Yeats said, in a 1936 broadcast, and *Meru* represents his sense of the abyss of thought. Much of the poem's force arises from its inversion of normal assumptions. The rule of reason and of law are normally stabilising forces in society. Here it is 'manifold illusion' which preserves the precarious 'semblance of peace', the flimsy artificiality which hoops civilisation together. The mirror-scaled serpent is multiplicity but man forces himself out of its coils into the unity which is his own destruction. His life is thought, but thought also means the death of illusion and, in a twist of the image that is both startling and startlingly just, thought is suddenly given animal characteristics, ravening and uprooting, refusing to be held back in its savage thrust towards the truth by man's instinctive terror of its consequences. Reality is the core of desolation, with the evasions and protections stripped away, the naked truth beating on the naked body. There is no suggestion here of the double knowledge of *Lapis Lazuli*—'All things fall and are built again'. Rather there is the recognition that every achievement brings on the night of its death and that, caverned in night under the blizzard of reality, man wakes into a dawning, devastated world, swept clean of the monuments and glories which are also the magnificent illusions of its past.

10

The Severed Heads

The Resurrection, Yeats' second play upon the theme of Christ's death, is a considerable advance upon *Calvary*, both in dramatic weight and in theatrical effectiveness. Christ who was surrounded by images of those he could not save is now surrounded by images of those who must accept him; the climax, as Miner observes, comes in the *Noh* tradition, when the real nature of the god is revealed and enlightenment (or the shock of understanding) follows.

Yeats tells us that when he wrote *The Resurrection* he was pre-occupied with a 'myth that was itself a reply to a myth', that in his revulsion from the idea of progress he had felt a 'sort of ecstasy at the contemplation of ruin' and that from *Rosa Alchemica* onwards he had had the sense of a civilisation 'about to reverse itself' and of a new civilisation 'about to be born from all that our age had rejected'. If the catastrophic reversals of the gyres were prefigured there were also premonitions of Yeats' other major symbol. The Fool and the Blind Man, Cuchulain and Conchubar are 'in some sense those combatants that turn the wheel of life'. *The Resurrection* likewise is based on a conflict between two principles or elemental forms of the mind that 'whirl perpetually, creating and recreating all things'.

Yin and Yang cannot be perfectly opposed without certain simpli-fications. Yeats' Greek is more Roman than Greek in his attitude to public works and to keeping the barbarian out, and is at best only half Greek in his contemptuous dismissal of Dionysiac ecstasy. But he is a subjective (in Yeats' parlance) in his insistence that the sins of men are their own property, that the gods possess themselves eternally and that man must seek to do likewise, and that there is something morbid in the 'utmost possible suffering as an object of worship'. The point of these exaggerations is that truth lies within oneself and not in submission to exterior principles. But the basis of truth is the entirety of the self; the failure of the Greek is not in locating truth internally but in finding its source in reason alone. The Hebrew, the dialectical opposite to the Greek, believes in total submission to an exterior good, but is glad that such sacrificial dedication is not necessary and that he can marry and have children instead. One is happy because Christ is dead and the other because he was never alive. Both are prepared to defend a staircase till they are run through, but neither has what may be called metaphysical courage. The Syrian, who enters the play later, is not so much a third force as a reminder that, at the moment of crisis, it is the irrational which intervenes and transforms the nature of history.

If this were all, the play would be a debating piece, neither very thoroughly nor accurately argued. It is kindled into drama by its climax and by the lyrics which give its pattern significance. The minor ironies are not absent and it is no accident that the Greek quotes Greek philosophy in the moment of truth. But more important is the Dionysiac song, outside the window from which the Greek looks, the song in which the invoking of the Virgin Astrea recalls the 'fierce virgin and her star' of the opening lyric and makes potent Yeats' observation that each new civilisation is born from all that its predecessor had excluded. The Greek ignores certain elements (and is representative in doing so) and these rise to rebuke him in the crisis of insight. His shortcoming is precisely that he regards God's death as if it were a play and the opening song is thus drawn into the dramatic structure, giving the failure of mind a lyric equivalent. Platonic tolerance and Doric discipline acquire new meanings in the argument and movement and the songs have therefore a relevance and weight beyond that which they possess in *Collected Poems*. Most important of all, the symbol of the beating heart with which the first song begins forms the substance of the play's highly effective climax and is echoed significantly in the last lines of the closing lyric. Civilisations rise and fall but, through the wounds of their death, man can reach to the 'resinous heart', the nucleus of divinity that both destroys and feeds all civilisations.

'Emer must dance, there must be severed heads,' the Old Man

says in Yeats' last play, *The Death of Cuchulain*. 'I am old, I belong to mythology' is his justification for this grisly demand. Yeats' pre-occupation with severed heads goes back to the 1897 edition of *The Secret Rose* in which the head of Aodh, hanging by its hair from a bush, sings to Queen Dectria the lyric now known as *He gives his Beloved Certain Rhymes*. Reminders of the Irish ancestry are frequent in *The King of the Great Clock Tower* which Yeats first wrote in prose, 'that I might be forced to make lyrics for its imaginary people' Later he rewrote it in verse because 'prose dialogue is as unpopular among my studious friends as dialogue in verse among actors and play-goers'. Pound pungently denounced the play as 'putrid' but Yeats, after its première on 30 July 1934, thought it 'most effective'. Pound, he said, 'may have been right to condemn it as poetry but he condemned it as drama'. Four months later, more aware of the play's faults, he was still convinced of its dramatic virtues. 'I don't like *The Clock Tower* which is theatrically coherent, spiritually incoherent.'

In his preface to the play Yeats describes the dance with the severed head as 'part of the old ritual of the year: the mother goddess and the slain God'. In a letter to Olivia Shakespeare he observes that 'the slain God, the risen God' forms the subject of both *The Resurrection* and *The King of the Great Clock Tower*. These remarks seem an invitation to a reading such as Wilson's in which the King and Queen represent 'the masculine and feminine principles in deity', the clock tower represents time, and the Stroller-Swineherd stands for the 'Victim-Saviour' and for 'the fallen condition of spirit in the material world'. The play is, however, accessible to less rarefied readings, such as those by Vendler and Kermode, in which the fundamental relationship is between the poet and his muse, or between the artist and the romantic image.

Despite Yeats' protestations the dramatic content of the play is slight. The Queen says nothing throughout, her solitary song being sung by the Second Attendant. The King, unfortunately for Wilson, is not even remotely suggestive of the masculine principle in deity and his upbraiding of his consort

> Why sit you there
> Dumb as an image made of wood or metal,
> A screen between the living and the dead? (*CPl*, p. 634)

is hardly reminiscent of Zeus addressing Cybele. Perhaps the King is like the common reader in his sustained failure to understand his queen. She walks into his house unannounced. Her name, family and country remain unknown. When her song is over he is unable to understand 'the meaning of those words'. When her dance is consummated he first prepares to strike her, but then 'kneels, laying the sword at her feet'. All this suggests, not an Olympian deity, but the unimaginative, everyday intelligence, baffled by forces which it cannot comprehend but which it is nevertheless forced to recognise as valid. It is, of course the Stroller who understands the Queen and the King in suggesting that the two may have been lovers is displaying some of the natural wisdom of jealousy.

To the Stroller all things are inferior to the image of eternity. His wife in comparison with it is 'fat, slow, thick of the limbs/In all her movements like a Michaelmas Goose' and even the Queen, to the extent that she has to exist (and the action deliberately leaves her uninvolved in existence), is 'neither so red, nor white, nor full in the breast' as the ideal. Eternity is a place of fulfilment but between it and the quasi-fulfilments of time there is an abyss which only ritual death can bridge. Mortal men are 'abstracts' of the reality beyond, and mere 'crossed fingers' in the higher paradise can exceed the pleasures of the nuptial bed; but when the hands on the Great Clock-face reach midnight, when the 'old year dies' and the bell tolls its summons to Byzantium, those who seek the truth must be prepared to perish into its ecstasy. The only head that the Queen can kiss is one that is severed from the body of change. Art sings and achieves its timelessness only out of the sacrifice of the artist.

Yeats is wise enough not to urge his moral unreservedly and the last song is an interchange between a 'rambling, shambling travelling-man' (obviously the Stroller) and a 'wicked, crooked, hawthorn tree' which prefers prudent rootedness to the perilous search for the image. For the former, the ruined house which is Yeats' symbol of permanence lights up as in *Crazy Jane upon God*. For the latter, lovely ladies and gallant men are 'blown cold dust or a bit of bone' but that does not alter the ordinary hope that man can continue to live without seeking life out of death.

> I have stood so long by a gap in the wall
> Maybe I shall not die at all (*CPl*, p. 641)

The remark must be read in conjunction with the stage direction that immediately precedes it. The Queen, after her ritual dance, 'has come down stage and now stands framed in the half-closed curtains'. She is seen, in other words, through a gap in the wall. One lives with occasional glimpses of reality. Those who seek the fuller wisdom must pay the sterner price.

'In *The King of the Great Clock Tower*', Yeats wrote, 'there are three characters, King, Queen and Stroller, and that is a character too many; reduced to the essentials, to Queen and Stroller, the fable should have greater intensity. I started afresh and called the new version *A Full Moon in March*.' This account slurs over the symbolic function which the Queen's passivity has in *The Great Clock Tower* and also fails to indicate that what emerges from the rewriting is not so much a strengthening of the essential relationship as a radical change in the direction of that relationship. The first play deals, so to speak, with the hunger of time for eternity, the second with the completion of eternity in time. Because the cleavage between the two worlds is so great the price of satisfaction in the first is death and the price of fulfilment in the second, desecration. The basic antinomy is accordingly reformulated. The Queen becomes Turandot, the implacable princess of many legends, conceived in terms of virgin cruelty. The Stroller becomes the swineherd with the foulness of his rags and flesh insisted upon, in contrast to the Queen's incorruptible beauty. He is now less concerned with the image in his head:

> What do these features matter? When I set out
> I picked a number on the roulette wheel.
> I trust the wheel, as every lover must. (*CPl*, p. 626)

than with the fulfilment that he both seeks and offers:

> A song—the night of love,
> An ignorant forest and the dung of swine. (*CPl*, p. 625)

The opening lyric in fact equates 'Crown of gold' with 'dung of swine' and in the dance with the severed head itself, the head is symbolically first enthroned and then placed on the ground. As love pitches his mansion in the place of excrement Crazy Jane's truth is given a dramatic setting. On the other side of the antagonism, the

Queen, coveting fulfilment, also abhors the force that urges her to it. Her virgin cruelty must destroy what her deeper self desires. An act of blood and indeed a baptism in blood is necessary if she is to enter the blood and mire of existence. She is sufficiently the Great Mother to address the severed head as 'Child and darling' in a song which is almost a lullaby, yet sufficiently a sensationalist to be excited by the thought of standing before a stake and hearing 'dead lips sing'. Yeats, who thought Salome's dance in Wilde's play 'a mere uncovering of nakedness', described the Queen's dance in *The Great Clock Tower* as 'a long expression of horror and fascination'. It is a description which applies better to the second play.

The perils of the symbolism employed in *A Full Moon in March* are evident and, though the Jack and Jill lyric which follows the beheading distances the symbolism and renders it more oblique, it cannot be said that these perils are wholly avoided. Fortunately, the love-hate nexus is sufficiently suggestive and sufficiently absorbed into the play's movement to enable it to be read simultaneously as a sexual, an aesthetic and a metaphysical parable. It is the co-presence of these readings that saves the play from the accusations of decadence that would probably apply to it if it were accessible on one level alone.

A Full Moon in March ends with a lyric of haunting beauty as the 'holy, haughty feet' of the Queen descend into existence from the 'emblematic niches' in which the sages of Byzantium stood. She whose emblem is the moon, whose element is the unmixed perfection of the heavens, seeks out the 'savage, sunlit heart' of the world, however terrified that heart is by her presence. The pitchers in which 'time's completed treasure' is gathered exist so that their contents can be poured again upon the soil of time. In an earlier play the Woman of the Sidhe, also a creature of the symbolic full moon, had lacked completion 'by an hour or so' because of her longing for Cuchulain. In the later play the deficiency is more radical:

Second Attendant: What can she lack whose emblem is the moon?
First Attendant: But desecration and the lover's night. (*CPl*, p. 630)

It is a conclusion both humane and disturbing. Both the lilt of the language and the shock of its meaning bring into lyric life the recognition that eternity is in love with the productions of time,

F

while the movement of the play serves as a sombre reminder that the cost of that love cannot be less than sacrifice.

The last of the four wars which man wages is against God, and *The Herne's Egg*, which Yeats described as 'the strangest, wildest thing I have ever written', is an account of how this war is lost. Congal and Aedh, who have fought a series of exactly matched, ceremonial battles, declare the customary peace after the fiftieth battle and Congal proposes to enrich the banquet which follows with a 'certain novelty or relish', namely, the sacred Herne's eggs. Attracta, the priestess of the Great Herne, will not permit the sacrilege; the eggs are taken by force and the Herne's curse is pronounced. Congal is to become a fool and to die at a fool's hands, a fate which he shrugs off as the end of every soldier and one which requires no curse to bring it about. Before the banquet Attracta replaces a Herne's egg by a hen's egg, and this egg, served to Congal, is taken as a mortal insult which leads to the killing of Aedh in a battle no longer gentlemanly. Congal, who realises that he has been the instrument of the Herne's will, in destroying a kind of pre-lapsarian equilibrium, retaliates by effecting, through the verdict of an improvised court, an earlier suggestion that seven men should melt the 'abominable snow' of Attracta's virginity. The aim is to make the Great Herne suffer 'through his betrothed' while at the same time freeing Attracta 'from all obsession' and enabling her to live 'as every woman should'. On the morning after Attracta's mystic marriage seven men maintain that they lay with her, while Attracta insists that she slept beside the Herne as his 'pure bride'. Warned by the Herne's thunder, six of the seven retract their statements and are sentenced to be reborn 'a step or two' down the ladder of being, in sundry animal shapes. Congal's shape is undecided, possibly as a tribute to his courage. While the others prostrate themselves, he half kneels in terror but will not be shaken from his version of the truth. On the 'holy mountain' of Slieve Fuadh he insists on the same story, though there is only a Fool (and perhaps the Herne) to hear him. Convinced that he has won the 'second bout' with his divine antagonist he now enters upon the final battle. The Fool wounds him with a kitchen spit, but not fatally; in the end it is Congal who kills himself with the same instrument, though not until he has had almost hysterical doubts that he himself may be the Fool who gives effect to the Herne's curse. Nevertheless, he considers that since he has died of his own will, the third bout has been won. He has held his own in life but when his life ends he is powerless and has to seek Attracta's protection. As the tethered donkey of Corney, her servant, tries to break loose, Attracta hastily attempts to lie with Corney, in an endeavour to save Congal from rebirth as an animal. But she is too late. The donkey breaks loose, couples with another donkey and it is the shape they breed which is imposed upon Congal. Perhaps he is reborn in order to carry the Herne's eggs.

'Shri Purohit Swami is with me,' Yeats wrote to Dorothy Welles-ley, 'and the play is his philosophy in a fable, or mine confirmed by him.' Wilson, in his full examination of the play's sources, has duly and strenuously stressed the Indian influence, but it is difficult to find a play less like Indian philosophy in its tone and impact. What Yeats calls the 'wildness' of the play and its grim tragi-comedy are characteristically Yeatsian. As for the marriage of the Herne and the priestess its source is surely the myth of the Swan and Leda (which the play specifically mentions), whatever may be its analogues in other mythologies. The state which Attracta enters is not the trance of *Samadhi*, because progress towards *Samadhi* depends, not on identifying Being with any shape, but on disengaging it from every possible shape. Congal's fall may demonstrate the fate of limited selfhood when it sets itself against unlimited reality, but it is easier to regard it as a progress in *hubris* begun possibly in ignorance, but persisted in with a full knowledge of what it entails. The liberal use of table-legs, candlesticks and kitchen utensils may show the pro-gressive degeneration of man when he begins to substitute his own for a higher judgement, and the trial of Attracta is of course a pointed case of judgement usurped; but what is also represented is a further evolution in Yeats' always sharp sense of the absurd. Man is not only defeated but defeated without dignity; the holy mountain lies under the 'moon of comic tradition'. In these circumstances it is hardly answer enough to reply that man's arrogance brings on his defeat. His humiliations, moreover, are now such that he can no longer respond to absurdity by nobility. All he can do is to refuse to surrender and even in fighting for himself he can no longer be sure that he is not really doing the Herne's will.

Taken in the context of Yeats' work, *The Herne's Egg* seems to represent a further and even an impetuous step forward in the segregation of the supernatural from the natural. The terms of the opposition can no longer co-exist, let alone involve each other creatively. The dialogue between self and soul has become not merely a battle but a battle that must grow progressively more sordid. The hero enters the battle in the first place because he cannot comprehend his opponent, because for him alleged possession by a transcendent reality is merely an ecstatic delusion, a protection against the responsibility of living. But having made his challenge he cannot withdraw it, however strongly knowledge may counsel prudence. The very nature of his heroism obliges him to press on to ultimate defeat. The progression achieved between these contraries is not clear; perhaps one can argue that Congal comes to recognise the reality of the Herne (though not the Herne as the only reality) and that the play's ungainly climax shows Attracta's recognition that there is some use in the 'imperfection of a man'. Yeats is also tactful enough (or possibly confused enough) to leave the crisis of the action ambiguous. 'Will I be the woman lying there?' Attracta wonders, and after the horror and terror with which Yeats likes to invest the mystic marriage, the woman who emerges is undeniably different and ironically more human. Whether the difference is the work of seven men, the Herne, or a combination of both, is a matter which the play does not settle, and the reader is permitted to conclude that the Herne is not necessarily the master of every irony. These concessions leave intact the theme of the assault upon God, the compulsive recklessness of man pitted against his fate, for which there seems to be no precedent in any mythology but Yeats' own.

In *Purgatory* the ruined house lights up again to reveal another side of the indestructible past. T. S. Eliot finds it difficult to accept a purgatory 'in which there is no hint, or at least no emphasis upon Purgation', but it is a phrase from *Little Gidding*—'the rending pain of re-enactment'—which expresses best the quality of Yeats' conception. Much can be said about the relationship of Purgatory to *A Vision*, but at the dramatic level the impact of the play lies in the spectacle of a man struggling to break free from the prison of the past, from the cycle of cause and consequence, and yet inexorably re-creating the past in the very act by which he seeks to destroy it.

The action of the play is starkly simple. The daughter of a great house marries into the stables. She dies in childbirth while her husband squanders her heritage. The son, abandoned by the father to grow up in the image of his own drunken ignorance, acquires, through the good offices of others, a haphazard education that includes Tertullian and Rossetti in addition to Book III of *A Vision*. When the house has been destroyed in all the more important senses it is finally burned down in a fit of drunkenness and the son, aged sixteen, stabs his father to death among the ruins. The play opens after a generation has passed. The son, who murdered his father, now an old man, stands before the dead house with his own son (inevitably aged sixteen) begotten 'upon a tinker's daughter in a ditch'. The house lights up for him (though not for the boy) as he watches the shade of his mother, purgatorially re-enacting the past. The act of lust in which he was conceived is lived over again and the old man is left wondering whether sensual pleasure or remorse is uppermost in its compulsive repetition. It is, however, not quite the time for philosophy. While the old man watches, the son attempts to rob him, repeating history in more degenerate terms. They struggle and the money in the old man's bag is scattered. The house lights up again for both man and boy and, as the boy looks on horrified, the father stabs him. The justification for this act is that it ends the consequences of the mother's deed upon others. Pollution will not be passed on and history cannot repeat itself. But the consequences of the mother's deed upon herself can be ended only by herself or by the 'mercy of God'. The old man had known this but had forgotten it in the moment of murder; and in any case the gratuitous violence of the second crime (insisted upon in the stage directions) resurrects the evil which it is designed to root out.

For a moment it seems as if the angry severance of the knot has succeeded. The tree before the house stands bathed in white light 'like a purified soul'. Then the hoof-beats heard on the mother's wedding night return and the old man's exclamation at the moment of murder ('My father and my son on the same jack-knife') is twisted into ironic significance. History repeats itself in the very effort to save it from repeating itself.

It is possible to interpret *Purgatory* quasi-politically, as representing the surrender of big-house culture to drunken democracy, but such a reading, though not illegitimate, can only be peripheral. Moreover, the description of the symbolical tree in its prime— 'Green leaves, ripe leaves, leaves thick as butter,/Fat, greasy life'— suggests an attitude to the past that is scarcely idyllic. To read *Purgatory* as an exercise in terms of *A Vision* is perhaps more instructive, but does not take us very far in explaining the play as a play. However, the particular device which *A Vision* suggests, the dramatisation of the 'dreaming back', does contribute to the play's nightmarish validity, distances it from ordinary probability and makes the old man's otherwise implausible motives acceptable within the scheme of suspense. For the rest, the effect of the drama surely lies in the sense that it conveys of the blindness of action, the imprisonment of people in themselves. The mother (whose 'crime' presumably is that she abandoned responsibility for sensual indulgence) cannot escape from her deed, because in reliving it she renews its pleasures. The old man, even in compassion for his mother, remains the victim of the bestiality in his blood. The boy, trapped even more deeply in violence than his father, finds it sufficient justification for murder that it is in the nature of the young to kill the old; in saying this he makes it clear that the chain will extend to infinity unless his own death breaks it. The labyrinth in which man lives is self-created; yet, precisely for that reason, the effort to escape from it only entangles him more deeply in its complexity.

When the curtain finally falls on Yeats' drama it falls appropriately on the death of a hero. It is also appropriate that the hero's death should take place at the end of a long road of irony and after the heroic convention has been dragged through many ditches. 'I make the truth!' Cuchulain cries at one point in the play, and it is true enough that he makes his death though not necessarily because the death-wish has come upon him. He cannot however control the style of his dying.

The opening dialogue of the play has been described as confused but it is in fact a web of misunderstanding. Eithne Inguba enters, urging Cuchulain to sally out and fight; yet in her hands she carries a letter from Emer advising him that to fight would be suicidal and that he is to wait until the next day for reinforcements. Eithne pleads bewitchment while Cuchulain scents betrayal. He proceeds to substantiate his illusion. When Eithne asks 'What mouth could you believe if not my mouth?' he reminds her that it was Emer who brought him back from the dead. Having convinced himself of her fickleness he forgives her for it since 'everything sublunary must change'. Even Eithne's desperate taunt that a Cuchulain who forgives treachery has ceased to be himself is interpreted as exultation in his approaching death. Her readiness to meet Congal's fate ten times over in order to demonstrate her fidelity is dismissed as the typical talk of a woman plotting deception.

The tragedy of errors is plausible enough at the dramatic level, but what gives it substance is the underlying doubt as to whether Cuchulain believes his illusion or is determined to make it real. 'The scene is set' are almost Eithne's first words and Cuchulain responds with the same ritual recognition.

You have told me nothing. I am already armed. (*CPl*, p. 695)

The drum beats, the Morrigu arranges the dance and history, as much as Eithne, is the hero's sublunary mistress. When the time of obsolescence approaches there is no real alternative to dying recklessly. It is this undertone which saves the play from what could otherwise be the operatic *cliché* of the betrayed man rushing out to face impossible odds. 'All that is written,' Cuchulain tells Eithne, and the words have a significance beyond the content of Emer's letter. When he adds: 'I much prefer/Your own unwritten words' the choice is equally significant. Both the hero and the poet choose the unwritten because it can still be their privilege to write it.

The end of a long road is honesty and Yeats does not shrink from the end. Cuchulain makes a myth whereas Deirdre only enters one; but Cuchulain, unlike Deirdre, is not permitted to die well. Aoife, Cuchulain admits, has the right to kill him and if she did she would give the legend style; but Aoife is bundled off-stage with a dramatic crudeness indicative of Yeats' anxiety to bestow his last insult on the heroic convention. With Congal pierced through by a fool's spit under a comic moon, it remains for Cuchulain to die by a blind man's knife; and the Blind Man, though not Tiresias or Thamyris, has 'good sense', which is one way of describing the wisdom of the Paudeens. 'Twelve pennies: What better reason for killing a man?' is Cuchulain's grim recognition of the rights of the Philistines.

The anti-heroic convention can be as vulnerable as the heroic but Yeats does not leave us at either extreme. Cuchulain sees the head which the Blind Man is about to decapitate as 'about to sing', and the words not only stress Yeats' obsession with the symbol but also remind us that no external circumstances can limit the authenticity with which man declares himself in death. After drum and pipe declare their martial music the harlot, the outcast of history, sings to the beggar-man, the outcast of responsibility. The lyric glances at a super-sexual paradise ('Maeve had three in an hour, they say') and then descends to a more securely established middleground. There is another reality beside the tragic dance of 'love and loathing, life and death', the passion for existence and the passion to transcend it:

> Are those things that men adore and loathe
> Their sole reality?
> What stood in the Post Office
> With Pearse and Connolly?
> What comes out of the mountain
> Where men first shed their blood?
> Who thought Cuchulain till it seemed
> He stood where they had stood? (*CPl*, p. 704)

Reality is not merely glimpsed but created in those great acts of affirmation, whether poetic or heroic, through which man penetrates to his essential nature. The Morrigu may contrive the plot and arrange the humiliations but it is William Butler Yeats who writes the poetry.

Writing to Ethel Mannin, Yeats introduces *The Death of Cuchulain* with that familiar quotation from Goethe: 'A poet needs all philosophy but must keep it out of his work.' Despite the alternatives suggested it seems best to read this statement, as Ure does, as reflecting Yeats' commitment to a theatrical rather than a symbolist strategy. It is true that the old man in the play declares that 'Where there are no words there is less to spoil', but he does so in a specific context of irascibility; it must be remembered that he also asks for an audience similar to that which attended the first performance of *Comus* and prescribes for them a course of reading no more esoteric than 'the old epics and Mr Yeats' plays about them'. The roomful of people who share one lofty emotion may be the remote descendants of Blackfriars rather than of the Globe, but they constitute a theatre, however selective.

The attempt made here has been to see Yeats' plays against the cumulative literary logic which his work and preoccupations build up, and to relate that immediate context to nothing more remote than the larger context of the human predicament. Innocence of the System is neither desirable nor possible, but fortunately for us and for Yeats, exact knowledge of the System does not loom heavily in the aesthetic result. Any serious examination of Yeats' drama on this basis can only increase respect for the variety and validity of its achievement. Yet, in the end, there are certain dissatisfactions, dissatisfactions which do not arise simply because the achievement is difficult to define. The trouble is not that the plays, in a restricted sense, are 'undramatic'. That accusation can be levelled at more than one dramatic tradition outside the West and to make the accusation at all is evidence of a certain provinciality. In any case, if the label does not fit the fact, the responsibility still is to see the fact for what it is worth. Yeats' theatre is certainly better examined as the theatre of ritual, or as the lyric illumination of the heightened and isolated moment. Yet even under those conditions the plays do little which the poems do not do better; the poet in the theatre is not quite enough of a poet. The very sparseness of the economy in Yeats' later plays increases the demands made on the language and the truth is that neither Yeats' blank verse nor the loosened rhythms of *The Herne's Egg* and *Purgatory* are equal to the requirements which this fastidiousness creates. Characteristically, it is in a poem, *Ribh at the Tomb of Baile and Aillinn*, that Yeats' blank verse achieves the accent of insight. In the plays it can be stubbornly post-Jacobean and on the occasions when it escapes from the past it is not fully able to achieve a shape of its own. If the plays succeed, notwithstanding this central inadequacy, it is partly because of the effect of the lyrics that envelop the dramatic core and extend it in significance and partly because the alignment of forces in each particular play is responsive to interpretation at more than one interlinked level. Nevertheless, when Yeats tells us that he wrote *The King of the Great Clock Tower* in order to force himself to write lyrics, and that he expected *The Herne's Egg* to give him 'a new mass of thought and feeling overflowing into lyrics', he is probably suggesting the right order of importance for himself. It is in a roomful of images rather than people that words are restored to their ancient sovereignty.

II

An Old Man's Frenzy

THE image of Yeats' last poems is many-sided, and while lust and rage may dance attention on them, they are not wholly and perhaps not even predominantly the poems of the Steinach operation. The masks of age are chosen to round off an aesthetic life that has been shaped with both care and energy; they include, beside the comforts of the second-best, the aesthetic ascent of the lapis-lazuli mountain, the visionary reading of history under the System's bleakly joyous light, the passionate recollection of friends and old companions, and the sombre fitness of a dying life as a candle with which to survey a dying culture.

Behind all is the mockery of the abyss. Plato's ghost sings 'what then?' in accents of mounting derision. The ruined house lights up but only in the night; in the morning there is crumbled and roofless reality. Nothing is left for those who have reached the time for dying to say. The circus animals desert man in the refuse mound of the heart. He perfects what he can and achieves a sense of the whole, only to dismiss what he achieves into the night; 'Lie down and die' is Echo's unyielding response to the torment of questioning. The mind moves upon silence like a long-legged fly on a stream. If the dawn breaks it is only to reveal that all but extinguished candle of life.

In this context rage and lust have something more than their normal connotations. 'I have told you all my poetry comes from rage or lust', is one of those admissions Yeats makes to Dorothy Wellesley which critics are obliged to call disturbingly frank. Nevertheless, its very frankness ought to remind one that poetry is more than the materials from which poetry is made and even if *The*

Spur were the only poem in *Last Poems and Plays* it ought to be sufficient evidence of this truth. Since there are other poems in the collection there is evidence that Yeats is making his familiar contrast between the foul rag and bone shop and the works of the imagination it makes possible; and, if the contrast becomes more provocative as the end approaches, that gaiety is the privilege of any man about to be swept away on the tide of silence.

Lust is presented as the easier remedy, the choice of the lower truth against the higher. Yet it is the inferior truth which life chooses in its nature and to which those about to die cling most strongly. The spurs of lust are meant to remind us that the sense of life is keenest when life is ebbing. The poet has only words that pierce the heart and the muses, who prefer the embraces of gay, warty lads, do so in the imagination and its second-best marriages. Yet the act of love, however imperfectly achieved, remains the centre of the sense of wholeness. Three bushes grow from inextricable roots. The soul seeks the desecration of the body and the body knows the presence of the soul. Behind each kiss a 'contrapuntal serpent' hisses. Love is divided in its manifestation yet single in its substance. It is the recognition both of tension and of unity. This is Crazy Jane's truth in a more sombre setting and the features of lust, however shocking, therefore belong to a traditional mask of insight.

Rage too is a complex and creative emotion. It is not a succession of frustrated tantrums. Its ancestors are Timon and Lear and its driving force that bitter energy of questioning through which and despite which the sense of order must discover itself. It is the apocalyptic rage of *Nineteen Hundred and Nineteen*, rage against a future in which ancestral pearls are pitched into a sty and in which even massacre becomes a form of redemption. It is the rage of disillusionment against the fruits of revolution, the beggars changing places as the lash continues. But it is also rage chastened by a sense of necessity. History may be scorned but its course cannot be altered. The wheel turns inexorably and the only consolation that it offers is the eventual return of a now unfashionable gyre.

Most characteristically, rage is an old man's frenzy. 'My temptation is quiet,' the poet cries (or, more correctly, whispers), and the recognition is man's necessary defiance of Echo's advice to lie down and die. Acquiescence and the stillness of a decaying house are the accepted and respectable postures of age; frenzy is their dynamic counter-statement. The nature of the redeeming force is defined with subtle precision. The mill of the mind consuming its rag and bone, the mechanised intellect working on an impoverished substance, can sift and pulverise but not reveal the truth. The alternative however is not 'loose imagination', and the word 'loose' is decisive in suggesting a force that is irresponsible and anarchic as well as free-ranging. Given these inadequacies, the creative choice emerges:

> Grant me an old man's frenzy,
> Myself must I remake
> Till I am Timon and Lear
> Or that William Blake
> Who beat upon the wall
> Till Truth obeyed his call; (CP, p. 347)

Imagination, for all its looseness, is insufficiently radical, tethered to the self; what is called for is a transformation of the self, and the second line conveys through its movement, the potent ambiguity of its syntax and the force of self-scrutiny derived from the inversion, the effort and inward-reaching strength of that transformation. The wall is an interior as well as an outer resistance and the man who beats on it is both prophet and victim, the descendant of all those who have achieved vision in madness. Thirty years ago it was words that obeyed the poet's call. Now it is truth and the substitution is significant just as Attracta's wish 'That I all foliage gone/May shoot into my joy' is a deliberate step forward from withering into the truth. What distinguishes 'an old man's eagle mind' is a bleak, fierce energy that can pierce clouds as well as batter walls, that can shake the dead whose property is wisdom. By implication it also shakes the living who are fundamentally dead. Instead of the mind grinding, or the imagination foraging, in processes that ebb towards extinction, there is the leap upward into impassioned and sweeping detachment, the seer's perspective that commands the truth.

These preliminaries merely underline the obvious truth, that Yeats' work, like all poetry of substance, will not yield to convenient definitions. They also suggest, not that the last poems are latent in the first, but that they bring them that sensitive and achieved relationship which aesthetic life should inherit from ordinary living. 'It is myself that I remake,' Yeats says in an earlier poem and the twist which this line receives in *An Acre of Grass* is proof of the thoroughness of this continual remaking. Equally, the other echoes in the poem ('rag and bone', and 'Truth obeyed his call') suggest how several of Yeats' poems become fully alive only in the presence of others.

A sense of the personal, poetic past, of the context which the last poems urge upon the reader, is important in assessing the objection (of which Leavis is the most formidable advocate) that they suffer from a betraying loss of tension. Up to a point this criticism is just. The impression left by several poems (including even the rich darkness of *The Statues*) is that the System has now come to provide not metaphors for poetry but an apparatus for fabricating poems. Some of the political postures are also definitely and crudely off the boiler; and the glorification of the 'indomitable Irishry' against the 'base-born', 'filthy, modern tide' arouses legitimate resistance even though Ireland is primarily being mythologically exalted and every reader of Yeats' poetry is, in an important sense, a citizen of that country. Nevertheless, the complexity of these poems can be underestimated, though to say this is not to grant that tension and complexity are infallible symptoms of poetic excellence. The subtleties of Yeats' refrains, for example, have been explored convincingly by more than one critic. It remains to be added that the refrain often serves a symbolic-structural function, as the wall of fate against which the poem rages, or as the latent core, the meaning of which is progressively revealed as the poem lives around it. Again, the concentration in *An Acre of Grass* is probably as much as the form can accommodate and the clean, stripped metrics are used with masterly skill; note, for example, how the off-beat rhymes are discarded, and how the whole structure tautens as the poem leaps to its crisis of affirmation. Most important, the cryptic or declamatory quality of some of the poetry is not because it is negligent in establishing its terms but because it is the conscious culmination of its past. That past is not merely a matter of knowing the system; the positions which the poems adopt in relation to the system are determined by the point at which they stand on the wheel of possibilities. These poems are deliberately poems of age and age is a time of withdrawal, detachment and summation. If these qualities are prominent in such poems as *The*

Gyres, Lapis Lazuli and *Under Ben Bulben* it is not simply because certain values are being preferred (though that may be part of the explanation), but also because a picture is being filled, and a life completed. There are, for example, striking similarities between *The Gyres* and the second of *Two Songs for a Play*: all that man esteems endures only for a moment, the painter's brush consumes his dreams and 'Beauty dies of beauty, worth of worth'. But the centre of recognition is radically different: one is felt in the flesh and the other seen from the mountain. The point is not that the first realisation is superior to the second but that both are designed as parts of a whole. 'Tragic joy' could legitimately be resisted as inhuman if it were not in balance with other formulations that lie outside the poem.

Beginning with an enigma as fertile as Milton's two-handed engine, *The Gyres* moves in the sixth line into a reminiscence of *Nineteen Hundred and Nineteen* and the further reminiscence in the second stanza encourages the contrast of the angry involvement of the earlier poem with the exultant disengagement of the later. Yet non-involvement is not quite the position that the poem adopts. Tragic joy is not so much detachment as the mutual cancellation of opposed attachments. The energy of the paradox rises from the balance that it creates, and the sense it is able to convey of a position both in and out of the process it contemplates. Because of its panoramic understanding, the point of view it adopts and shapes, the poem possesses the momentum of the abstract. When it approaches the concrete it seems to falter significantly. 'Lovers of horses and of women' is not the kind of phrase that gives life to the historical process and although 'dark betwixt the polecat and the owl' is considered by some an audacious discrimination it is only so in terms of a personal language. It is at this point that the right of a poet to draw on his own past approaches its boundary. A poet, within limits, can prescribe a context for his poetry, and within limits can take many things for granted; but he would be ill-advised in taking language for granted. The connections of a poem with other poems strengthen it and possibly even complete it; but they do not give it its essential life. A poem may inherit its content; but it is not a poem until it re-creates it.

Lapis Lazuli, a more fully controlled poem than *The Gyres*, is also closer to Yeats' demand for 'an act of faith and reason to make us rejoice in the midst of tragedy'. The difference between 'tragic joy' and 'Gaiety transfiguring all that dread' is the difference between the apocalyptic and the aesthetic; and disengagement is effected in art not by withdrawal but by recognition.

'I notice that you have much Lapis Lazuli', Yeats wrote to Dorothy Wellesley. Someone, he added, 'has sent me a present of a great piece carved by some Chinese sculptor into a semblance of a mountain, with temple, trees, paths and an ascetic and pupil about to climb the mountain. Ascetic, pupil, hard stone, eternal theme of the sensual east. The heroic cry in the midst of despair. But no, I am wrong, the east has its solutions always and therefore knows nothing of tragedy. It is we, not the east, that must raise the heroic cry.' These remarks are interesting, not because of their view of 'eastern' philosophy, but because of the implication that asceticism is the 'theme' of sensuality and also because of the recognition that the tragic sense can offer no 'solution', but rather the kind of response that makes reality meaningful in the absence of a solution. 'The heroic cry in the midst of despair' is the rather highly coloured outline of this response, but the poem, because it is a poem, moves wisely away from the element of hysteria in the phrase. The offhand language of the opening is meant to distance and discipline the panic at the edge of the abyss. Profound philosophy must come from terror and life begins only when it is recognised as tragedy; the confrontation that gives art its validity can only be endured when it is aesthetically controlled:

> Black out; Heaven blazing into the head:
> Tragedy wrought to its uttermost. (*CP*, p. 338)

The storm of reality is taken into the repose of art and the word 'wrought' is exact in suggesting the achieved balance of intensity and finesse. The consequences of 'uttermost' should also be noted. The point is that the dimensions of man's fate have already been compassed by art; the understanding which includes them cannot be rendered obsolete by further progress in the techniques of terror. Today we have more efficient methods of destruction than 'Aeroplane or Zeppelin' or the 'bomb-balls' employed at the battle of the Boyne; but the response of the poet and the depth of his recognition remain unalterably valid even under the sign of the mush-room.

> Though Hamlet rambles and Lear rages,
> And all the drop-scenes drop at once
> Upon a hundred thousand stages,
> It cannot grow by an inch or an ounce. (*CP*, p. 338)

As the theatre opens into the theatre of history, one is conscious of the difference in tone from *The Gyres*. The 'irrational streams of blood' which dominated the first poem are significantly absent and lines such as 'Camel-back, horse-back, ass-back, mule-back' have a quality both pictorial and remote. The repetitions suggest a procession or a pilgrimage as well as history's cyclical re-enactments. Callimachus' art is described in terms which may, as Wilson suggests, be influenced by Furtwangler's *History of Art* but the poetic purpose of the description is to blend the sense of beauty with that of evanescence in a rhythm which both absorbs and counteracts the latent tragedy of the recognition. The effect is wholly different from that of *Nineteen Hundred and Nineteen* with its superficially similar recollection of 'Phidias' famous ivories'. Thus the poem moves steadily away from the stance adopted in *The Gyres*, from an exultation in the destructive element to an aesthetic poise of the destructive and creative:

> All things fall and are built again
> And those that build them again are gay. (*CP*, p. 339)

As the poem withdraws into the work of art, the processional effect is made to surround it so that history and change become the panorama interpreted by its point of view. Nothing is left out of the symbolic absorption and everything absorbed is given significance:

> Every discoloration of the stone,
> Every accidental crack or dent,
> Seems a water-course or an avalanche (*CP*, p. 339)

Words such as 'plum', 'cherry-branch', 'sweetens' and 'delight' create the sense of a disengagement, both stylised and traditional, in its serenity. Tragedy does not cease to be tragedy; but it is seen differently from the hill of the muses:

G

One asks for mournful melodies;
Accomplished fingers begin to play.
Their eyes mid many wrinkles, their eyes,
Their ancient, glittering eyes are gay. (*CP*, p. 339)

The shock of disaster is softened by 'mournful', and 'accomplished fingers' suggest not only technical prowess but the tragic experience soothed into artistic order. The zest of performance (and history is a kind of performance) creates a certain gaiety, irrespective of the theme that is performed; but eventually one discovers that the theme itself is gaiety. The repetition of 'eyes' emphasises the changelessness of vision in the wrinkled face which itself becomes the mask of an ancient wisdom; and 'glittering' suggests both the inner life of art and the manner in which artistic vision animates and gives significance to its context. The result is not gaiety alone but gaiety in balance with the tragic recognition—the sense of life asserting itself in complete confrontation of all that seems to make life meaningless.

Lapis Lazuli is succeeded by *The Three Bushes* with its recognition of the impossibility of knowing love's completeness, except possibly in death, which draws three partial recognitions into the totality to which they all aspire. Then follows *An Acre of Grass* with its powerful definition of 'frenzy'. Plato's ghost comes next in what Yeats termed a 'melancholy biographical poem', to mock both public recognition and the unswerving effort to bring something to significance. In contrast, *Beautiful Lofty Things*, the first of those poems of passionate reminiscence which are to reach their climax in *A Bronze Head* and *The Municipal Gallery Revisited*, suggests how significance can come unsought in the heightened moment that reveals the individual:

Maud Gonne at Howth station waiting a train,
Pallas Athene in that straight back and arrogant head:
All the Olympians; a thing never known again. (*CP*, p. 348)

There is no need to emphasise the poetic confidence capable of making such a comparison ring true, the force of conviction necessary to move actual friendships so securely into legend. Athene is not known in epic convention by her straight back and arrogant head, but the description and the shift in the direction of comparison succeed because the imperiousness of the pose makes it Olympian. With no suggestion of heroic sentimentality the everyday moment in a minor railway station blazes naturally into the dimensions of myth.

To Dorothy Wellesley ends like *Beautiful Lofty Things*, with one of those resounding last lines which look back on the whole poem and reshape it, raising it to a new level of significance. 'All depends', Yeats had told Dorothy Wellesley, in discussing the quality of great drama, 'on the completeness of the holding down, the stirring of the beast underneath.' That 'stirring' is conveyed in the poem by the contrast between 'the moonless night, the dark velvet, the sensual silence, the silent room and the violent, bright Furies'. What is born in tranquillity is not content nor satisfied conscience, nor emotion recollected in the Wordsworthian manner, but the Proud Furies demonic and benign, bringing the poet their ambiguous blessings. The irrational persecutes the artist; but it is also the source of the artist's power.

The Curse of Cromwell (Yeats regarded Cromwell as the Lenin of his time) is the first of several efforts in what Yeats believed to be a popular idiom. In 1935 Yeats had wished to plunge himself into 'impersonal poetry' to 'get rid of the bitterness, irritation and hatred my work in Ireland has brought into my soul'. By 1937 he had made one of his typical reversals and, laying aside 'the pleasant patter I have built up for years', he resolved to seek instead 'the brutality, the ill breeding, the barbarism of truth'. The Roger Casement poems, *The O'Rahilly* and *Come Gather Round Me Parnellites*, are part of this process and presumably also reflect the advice (which Yeats claimed to have found in Aristotle) to think like a wise man but to write like the common people. Philosophical poetry, he told Dorothy Wellesley, in words which came interestingly from the author of *A Vision*, 'is not your road or mine, and ours is the main road, the road of naturalness and swiftness'. He believed that in his popular poetry he had recovered 'a power of moving the common man I had in my youth'. In fact, these poems are a considerable improvement on his earlier ballads, but they are by no means the height of his work and the best are those that show least evidence of the barbarism of truth or the randy laughter of porter drinkers. *The Wild Old Wicked Man* for instance moves into an area in which the thinking of the body has become thinking in a marrow-bone and in which the life celebrated is a second-best life in terms of the lower choice as well as the higher. Yet the oblivion of love, however limited and frustrated, is preferable to the oblivion of death; the life choice is the human choice; and when the old man 'mad about the hills' looks up to the 'old man in the skies' the convergence suggests not only the more urbane delusions of *The Indian Upon God* (man making the divine obstinately in his image), but also that these delusions are all we can know of reality. The truth is that man is imprisoned in life and covets his prison.

John Kinsella's Lament for Mary Moore lives in the same limitations. The paradise of the earlier poetry where the earth and the sky and the water were remade like a casket of gold has now withered to a more restricted ideal:

> No expectation fails there,
>   No pleasing habit ends,
> No man grows old, no girl grows cold,
>   But friends walk by friends.
> Who quarrels over halfpennies
>   That plucks the trees for bread? (*CP*, p. 384)

The world of old age is necessarily one of lesser satisfaction; in it the death of an 'old bawd' can mean the loss of Eden.

Side by side with the 'popular' poetry the genre of reminiscence comes to its climax. *The Municipal Gallery Revisited* is a much-admired but possibly overrated poem. The wit of such lines as 'My mediaeval knees lack health until they bend' is not particularly distinguished and the *ottava rima* has none of the subtlety of *Sailing to Byzantium*. Indeed, the movement of saying seems to be dissociated increasingly from the thing said. The stream of reverie recalls *In Memory of Major Robert Gregory* and *A Prayer for my Daughter* but the poem is not like its predecessors, possessed by a central image, or cluster of images which its unfolding progressively defines.

A Bronze Head is a more striking poem, saying its farewell to Maud in a sombre, 'mummy-dead' landscape where the *hysterica passio* of the mob has become the *hysterica passio* of inner emptiness, echoed and amplified by the emptiness of the heavens. The 'dark tomb-haunter' memorialised in the bronze head has had other and more magnanimous forms. Yet perhaps no form fully expresses the substance. Perhaps substance is composite, irreducible to a single principle, held in being between the extremes of life and death. The poem suggests this and then, before the proposition can become dominant, veers away to emphasise the unity behind apparent diversity. The end is implicit in the beginning. The terror which haunts the close of life is nascent in the 'wildness' of the filly, 'sleek and new' at the starting post. We have thus two poetic forms of that composite substance, truth, and the final subtlety is to suggest that the poet does not know the truth that exists from the truth he has created. Imagination casts out everything that is not itself and there is a wildness in the artist that answers and shapes the wildness of the subject. Then the perspective shifts again and the stern gaze of judgement expresses one more aspect of the composite, 'Human, superhuman' substance. The 'foul world' in its decline and fall is farther than ever from being a second Troy. The verse strides authoritatively through its anger, and the monstrous alliteration of 'gangling stocks grown great' shows how fully alive the movement is to the passionate contempt which it conveys. The end comes in the ferocious paradox of the final alexandrine with that climactic force of which few besides Yeats are capable.

Yeats tells us that in 1900 'everybody got down off their stilts' but Malachi Stilt-Jack has stilts that are 'fifteen foot' high. These represent a slight scaling down of the 'twenty-foot' stilts of his 'great-grandad' but 'no modern stalks upon higher'. High talk is part of the circus of poetry: amusing, shocking, and required as entertainment. But the poet is not simply a maker of high talk. He himself is part of the metaphor that he makes and the stilts move him compulsively through another world of cataclysmic forces, in which the night 'splits', the dawn 'breaks loose', the sea-horses 'bare their teeth' and the poet stalks on, hunting out reality through the violent and 'terrible novelty of light'. The blaze of illumination that makes a poem is always unprecedented, an unique blessing of the 'proud furies'; yet, even as it is created, the sea-horses laugh at it and the poet in his quest for reality leaves it behind. The poem is a 'high' declaration of the nature of poetry and is, of course, strengthened in Yeats' familiar manner, by the motley and mocking circus imagery, through which it stalks to the assertion of its true life.

The Circus Animal's Desertion uses the trappings of *High Talk* but this time the stilts and the ladders which might have replaced the stilts are gone. The circus animals, the trained performers of poetic language, had all been 'on show' till 'old age began'; now that they have departed, we are driven back from the dream to the dream's origins. The themes of the poet are themes of the 'embittered heart' or, in a more telling phrase, 'heart-mysteries'; but it is the dream itself, the shape and the life of the art work, the deed which isolates and breaks open character, to which the artist gives his 'thought and love'. The circus animals, the 'players and painted stage', are more attractive than the truths of which they are emblems.

So far, the poem has been manœuvred to suggest that the poet has been remiss in his allegiance to a transcendent reality, and even the early phrase, 'I must be satisfied with my heart', is fully compatible with such a reading. It is not till the third section that the central disclosure is made. The poet's 'masterful images' grow in 'pure mind', the shaping climate of his imagination, but the quest for reality, the stripping away of the distractions of the 'circus', only exposes the dream's disreputable origins:

> A mound of refuse or the sweepings of a street,
> Old kettles, old bottles, and a broken can,
> Old iron, old bones, old rags, that raving slut
> Who keeps the till. (*CP*, p. 392)

The five times repeated 'old' drives in the humiliated recognition, but there is a note of confidence also in the angry resignation with which the poet lies down in the heart's 'foul rag-and-bone shop'. The holy tree remains holy, irrespective of the soil from which it grows; and the greater the distance between the work and its roots the more powerful, in a sense, is the implicit testimony to the transmuting and creative power of the artist.

The Statues is an attempted fusion of cultural history with Irish nationalism. It is a poem which retains some of its stubborn darknesses despite Koch's pioneering analysis and Wilson's thorough and sensitive reading. The first line with its dramatic-oracular question projects us into an obscurity which has been variously explained; here it is suggested that Pythagoras' 'numbers' form the abstract basis of Western art, but that 'passion', the pressing of 'Live lips upon a plummet-measured face', is necessary in order to embody these abstractions. To quote an earlier poem, the 'aching heart' is the condition from which the 'changeless work of art' must be conceived. Boys and girls 'pale from the imagined love/Of solitary beds' can provide passion to complement abstraction, but it is the artist, 'Greater than Pythagoras', who blends the two elements in the fully formed, definitive spontaneity of 'calculations that look but casual flesh'. Cultural self-expressiveness is the inner voice of any civilisation and it was therefore Phidias rather than the Greek galleys which turned back the East at Salamis. That this is the 'thought' of the poem at this point is evident from a passage in *On the Boiler* to which attention was first drawn by Louis MacNeice.

Europe was not born when Greek galleys defeated the Persian hordes at Salamis, but when the Doric studios sent out those broad-backed marble statues against the multiform, vague, expressive Asiatic sea, they gave to the sexual instinct of Europe its goal, its fixed type.

Maud Gonne's beauty (alluded to also in the opening lyric of *Emer*) is clearly behind the ideal that is envisaged.

. . . her face, like the face of some Greek statue, showed little thought, as though a Scopas had measured and long calculated, consorted with Egyptian sages and mathematicians out of Babylon, that he might face even Artemisa's sepulchral image with a living norm. (*Autobiographies: The Stirring of the Bones*)

It is Phidias who provides the dream of beauty with the 'looking-glass' of art and so puts off the 'many-headed foam of Salamis'. 'Many-headed', Wilson notes, is Aeschylus' epithet for the sea but it also expresses what Yeats considers to be the 'multiform, vague' character of Asiatic civilisation.

After repelling the invasion, Western culture moves outward, an image from it crossing the many-headed ocean. In a letter to Edith Shackleton Heald, Yeats indicates that in reading the third stanza we should 'remember the influence on modern sculpture and on the great seated Buddha of the sculptors who followed Alexander'. This difficult stanza is, as Koch notes, further (and oddly) clarified by Yeats' description, in *Autobiographies* of Watts' portrait of William Morris:

Its grave wide-open eyes like the eyes of some dreaming beast, remind me of the open eyes of Titian's Ariosto, while the broad vigorous body suggests a mind that has no need of the intellect to remain sane, though it gives itself to every fantasy; the dreamer of the Middle Ages. It is the fool of Faery . . . wide and wild as a hill, the resolute European image that yet half remembers Buddha's motionless meditation, and has no trait in common with the wavering lean image of hungry speculation, that cannot because of certain famous Hamlets of our stage fill the mind's eye. (*Four Years: 1887–1891*)

The seated Buddha is thus at least partially in the tradition of Phidias and of 'those Greek proportions which carry into plastic art the Pythagorean numbers, those forces which are divine because all there is empty and measured'. Buddha's emptiness (emptied incidentally of *hysteria passio*) is the still centre of Paul Ruttledge's conviction that 'where there is nothing, there is God'. In this perfection of being, the external world is recognised as an illusion and the exploration of the many in preference to the repose of the one becomes the multiplication of essential unreality. It is to this emptiness that Grimalkin, the witch's cat, must crawl. 'Europe belongs to Dante and the witches' sabbath, not to Newton', Yeats wrote in a letter to Olivia Shakespeare, though it must be added that Newton was scarcely deficient in 'calculation, number, measurement'. Nevertheless, it is the authentic voice of Europe as Yeats conceives it (though certainly a voice both diminished and trivialised) which recognises its affinity with the Buddha's wisdom.

'Cuchulain', Yeats writes, 'is in the last stanza because Pearse and some of his followers had a cult of him. The Government has put a statue of Cuchulain in the rebuilt post office to commemorate this.' This may be the immediate justification, but when Pearse summons Cuchulain to his side he invokes an image both heroic and artistic and calls upon the Irish tradition as a means of defence against the flood. The days of Salamis return and the 'filthy, modern tide', formless like the fabulous formless darkness of an earlier historical crisis, is in designed correspondence to the 'many-headed foam' over which Phidias triumphed. It is this pattern which saves (and probably only just saves) these particular two lines from being merely abuse. The Irish who are custodians of the faith protect it from the tide of the coming dark ages by climbing into their 'proper dark' (presumably between the polecat and the owl) and by tracing again the lineaments of that plummet-measured face which first affirmed the dimensions of Western culture.

The above explanation of *The Statues* is not offered as an endorsement of Yeats' (or Furtwangler's) theories of art or as a justification
of rampant nationalism however powerfully mythologised. In fact,
the mythologising is not wholly successful, notwithstanding the
poem's oracular confidence. The imaginative logic of the poem does
not permit it to define itself and the exterior connections needed for
definition are personal rather than traditional. The Hamlet-Buddha-
Mediaeval dreamer-Grimalkin complex receives little substantiation
in anything that the verse does, while the rhyming of 'fat' and 'sat'
and the emphasis on fly-eating are scarcely successful as wit and are
(it is to be hoped) not meant to be anything more. The climax too is
a failure of language as much as of invective; the last stanza of *A
Bronze Head* is more successful with sentiments that are nearly as
reactionary.

'Thereis now overwhelming evidence', Yeats wrote to Dorothy
Wellesley, 'that man stands between two eternities, that of his
family and that of his soul.' In *Under Ben Bulben* Yeats takes up this
theme and marries it, as in *The Statues* but with greater dignity, to
the immemorial wisdom of his country:

> Many times man lives and dies
> Between his two eternities,
> That of race and that of soul,
> And ancient Ireland knew it all (*CP*, p. 398)

'Between extremities Man runs his course' were the first words of
Vacillation. The new affirmation is narrower but also deeper. It is a
truth spoken by the sages around the Mareotic lake and by that
'pale, long-visaged company' of horsemen who appeared to the
mind's eyes after Cuchulain's death. They evoke both the occult
tradition (soul) and the folk traditions of the supernatural (race);
but they suggest also the ceremonial presences behind the man
gravely and irrevocably writing the last words of the work that is his
monument.

In *The Gyres* irrational streams of blood stained the earth and the
prophet on the mountain awaited the reversal of history. *Lapis Lazuli*
saw the fall of all things from the hill of the muses so that the creative
instinct could build them again. Yeats always writes dramatically
in his poetry; the point of view, even when it is contemplative, is

shaped to the specific situation. So in *Under Ben Bulben* the poet, in his last words at the foot of the mountain, recognises not so much that life follows death, but that death itself is ultimately unreal:

> Though grave-diggers' toil is long,
> Sharp their spades, their muscles strong,
> They but thrust their buried men
> Back in the human mind again. (*CP*, p. 398)

The third section quotes from Mitchel's *Jail Journal* but also remembers Yeats' conviction, expressed many years previously, that all noble things are the result of warfare. Conflict within the mind completes the mind and it is the man who has experienced completion out of conflict who 'laughs aloud, his heart at peace', and can accomplish his task whether historic or everyday.

The next section reviews the history of culture declaring as in *The Statues* that 'Measurement began our might', dwelling on Michaelangelo and the perfection of Quattrocento art and placing Calvert, Wilson, Blake and Claude in the tradition but towards its end, as 'Gyres run on' and the 'greater dream' passes away. Confusion follows, but the responsibility of the poet and sculptor is to fill the cradles of the wheel rightly, to lift each phase to its proper aesthetic significance (or to assert firmly the values which certain phases corrupt) and thereby to bring the soul of man to God.

We live at a time when 'conduct and work grow coarse', with the 'sort now growing up', the 'base-born products of base beds' all 'out of shape from toe to top'. To preserve artistic integrity other days must be recalled: the singing of the peasantry, of country gentlemen, of monks, porter-drinkers, lords and ladies who have been beaten into the earth over seven heroic centuries. Only thus can the 'indomitable Irishry' preserve its heritage against the present. This is not an inspiring or even an acceptable conclusion, though the verse with its blend of solemnity and earthiness nearly overcomes the reader's natural resistance.

The last lines are bleakly and perfectly in character. Tragic joy is a privilege of the prophet and gaiety transfiguring dread a privilege of the artist. But these balances of emotion are in the end the result

of attachments that inhere in the human condition. The dead alone
can see with an objectivity that is emotionless:

> *Cast a cold eye*
> *On life, on death.*
> *Horseman, pass by!* (*CP*, p. 401)

The Completed Symbol

'I MUST leave my myths and images', Yeats wrote in 1899, 'to explain themselves as the years go by and one poem lights up another.' This is a remark that is important in defining both the range of his achievement and its characteristic wholeness. His poems are sufficient in themselves, able to live out of their own vitality and to create in each case the individual shapes of their particular lives; but they also form constellations of intention (to use a happy phrase which is said to be Frost's) and these constellations in their turn compose a sky. The star is its own light; but behind every star is the presence of the whole heaven. He offers both facts, the individual, differentiated life and the wholes which these lives sustain and connect to each other. The effect is not dissimilar to Yeats' conception of the relationship between the *anima mundi* and the individual mind; and the aesthetic power of the pattern, once sensed, is both arresting and deeply satisfying.

Metaphors are needed for criticism as much as for poetry, and for a good poet no single metaphor will do. This book has spoken of Yeats' development, of his growth as a poet, or alternatively of his discovery of himself, of the stripping away of those distractions that hid from him the reality of his own voice. The end is implicit in the beginning either as seed or as core and, to quote Yeats, 'our intellects at twenty contain all the truths we shall ever find'. These are metaphors of process and their disadvantage is that they suggest that what comes later is superior to what is earlier because it is more fully developed or more purely quintessential. They should be complemented by a metaphor of pattern in which different positions are seen, not as superior or inferior to one another, but as stating a collective recognition none of them could state singly. Having said this, it should be added that Yeats was enough of a poet to forget whatever patterns his poetry had created whenever he needed to do so in order to write a poem.

In the end both types of metaphors should be fitted into a cogent understanding. Yeats' conception of his own poetic growth (to use yet another metaphor) is quasi-biological as well as literary. The withering into the truth, the abandonment of youth's lethean foliage, the physical transformation from the blossoming plant to the dry bone singing its praise upon the shore and the intellectual transformation from the thinking of the body to thinking in a marrow-bone, all point to certain stern recognitions that penetrate the images of ageing. But if something is lost, something is also gained. The dawn may be wanton and ignorant but it is the twilight that brings its decrepit and poverty-stricken wisdom. The way is open to the understanding that every position in which man lives is limited by the nature of its life, that a poet must accept and translate into poetry the particular insight given him by that stage of his life at which he stands and that the whole truth is best approached, not by a single poem, but by a procession of poems, moving patiently along the curve of possibilities.

Not every poet can live with such a theory but Yeats is able not only to live with it but to make it the source of his poetic strength. It is for this reason that his work acquires its characteristic and cumulative solidity. Each individual poem is not only vividly itself but has behind it, holding it in position, the context of a considerably larger presence; and the apparent extremism of many poems is held in check by their correction elsewhere in the constellation of intention. The potential achievement of such a method lies in its capacity to create a whole which is greater than the sum of its parts and which gives every part its valid place in a universe. Its potential weakness is the danger that the parts may suffer in their individual life, that they may become not experiences but assertions, fitted into the curve instead of spontaneously proclaiming it.

The curve of Yeats' poetry is not a pure one; it is necessarily altered by the effort to find a style, as well as by the climate of his achievement, the movement from the nineteenth into the twentieth century. Nevertheless, the balance of the design can be discerned. The last poems stand in a deliberate poise against the first. Instead of withdrawal to the dream we have withdrawal to the mountain. Instead of the aesthete's loneliness there is the loneliness of the man deserted by the circus animals. Instead of life disdained we have life raged against but also eagerly accepted. Characteristically, the cry of a rabbit in *The Man and the Echo* is sufficient to distract from the confrontation with nothingness. Between these extremes (shaped both by language and the *données* of youth and age) is the poetry of the mainstream, of involvement, of responsibility, of creative tension and conflict, of the supernatural felt as a presence in the natural. This is the centre of Yeats' achievement, but a survey of the whole achievement brings recognition that even this centre is made more complete and valid because of the annotation in the margins.

The best poems cannot be written out of a closed position. Whatever the definitions that the wheel makes it must make them out of an awareness of alternatives. A poem that shuts out its contraries and bolts down its counter-truths is in danger of becoming not a poem but a rhetorical contrivance. Yeats' rhetorical self-assurance is sufficient for him to make the gesture look remarkably like the experience, but he seldom falls back on the inferior strength and seldom refuses the struggle with himself. His tactics are naturally most functional when they work on a sense of continuity between worlds, with man as the creative centre in which the recognition of that continuity is focussed. Such a recognition works with the grain of language, not denying but extending its primary significance. But even in less promising situations the alternatives are firmly and even exultantly faced; the heroic definitions, for example, are achieved and held against the assault of the absurd; and Yeats' great power emerges as the power to drive an insight through against the derisions of irony to a comprehension in which the attacking ironies are included and transcended.

As the wheel turns, it is justifiable to ask what it encircles. With Yeats the centre is man, and if his place in the tradition is more central than Eliot's it is because his primary concern is with man rather than meaning. The quest for belief and the hunger for significance are the very substance of Eliot's poetry, defining both its intense integrity and its specific narrowness. For Eliot, the vision revealed or the hints and guesses permitted constitute the end of the search. For Yeats, belief is merely the platform from which he advances into poetry or, to use a more decorative phrase employed by his father, the leafy wood out of which the nightingale sings. Yeats' interest is less in knowledge than in how man lives his knowledge. 'Man can embody truth but he cannot know it' is his closing conviction stated in the last of his letters. His poetry is the record of that embodiment.

Shaping Yeats' image of man is a basic and impregnable sense of his dignity. The onslaughts of the ironic upon that dignity are the modern expression of a tradition which goes back to man ambiguously placed in the Great Chain of Being, torn by the conflict of flesh and spirit, the centre of a universe still imaginatively that of Ptolemy, the 'glory, jest and riddle of the world'. Yeats' image is, of course, arrogant beyond its ancestry. It is scarcely tempered by the sense of awe. If man makes himself, or rather remains himself, within this hostile universe it is through heroic defiance rather than moral transformation. Man cannot sit still awaiting revelation. He must beat upon the wall till truth obeys him. Nevertheless the thread goes back clearly from 'Man has created Death' to 'I am duchess of Malfi still', and it is not merely the singing strength and the proud full sail of language that Yeats inherits from the great Elizabethans.

Eliot advanced to a traditional synthesis from the fragments he had shored against his ruins. Yeats came to a private dispensation after public and literary causes had collapsed. The thirties saw the evolution of a transient myth of the coterie, and in the forties there was much advocacy of the personal myth as the answer to the writer's dilemma. If by a myth is meant a supreme fiction which both declares and interprets the individual and which can mediate between an interior and a public language, then Yeats' system is among the most comprehensive and powerful of such myths. But what is important in the myth is not its specific dispositions but the simple fact that it fully answers the man. When the god fails it cannot be replaced by another god that explains the facts better and the failure of which is less likely. Poetic insight is born from inner commitment and, however stony may be the soil of its strength, the holy tree must always grow in man's heart.

The driving force in Yeats' poetry is the assertion of man's creative power against the attack of circumstance, embodied even in the destructive distortions of that strength. It is also a deep sense of man as the continuing battleground and of tension and combat as the springs of his being. Taken away from this background and divested of their enveloping irony the Yeatsian assertions may often seem strident and inflated. But the cry of 'Death and life were not/ Till man made up the whole' springs from the same resolute integrity as Eliot's very different 'Teach us to care and not to care/Teach us to sit still'. Yeats is far removed from Eliot's humility and also from Auden's defensive irony, from the carefully underplayed commitments, and from the mature mind sharing its knowingness with the reader. But the reward of fervour is immediacy; and in Yeats, unlike some of his contemporary colleagues, it is not merely the intellect which is at the tips of the senses but, surprisingly and excitingly, the senses also. Most important, Yeats is the supreme poet of what an earlier century would have called the passions; it is through these passions, worked upon by the organising power of poetic language, that Yeats is able to enter the centre of conflict which is man and to re-create that conflict as the substance of poetry.

A Select Reading List

(I) THE WRITER'S WORK

1. *The Collected Poems of W. B. Yeats* (2nd edn., Macmillan, London, 1950)

2. *The Variorum Edition of the Poems of W. B. Yeats*, edited by Peter Alit and Russell K. Alspach (Macmillan, New York, 1957)

3. Jeffares, A. Norman [Editor]. *W. B. Yeats. Selected Poetry* (Macmillan, London, 1962)

4. Rosenthal, M. L. [Editor]. *Selected Poems of William Butler Yeats* (Macmillan, New York, 1962)

5. *The Collected Plays of W. B. Yeats* (2nd edn., Macmillan, London, 1952)

6. Alspach, Russell K. [Editor]. *The Variorum Edition of the Plays of W. B. Yeats* (Macmillan, New York, 1966)

7. *A Vision*, 1st edn., (Werner Laurie, London, 1925). Issued on 15 Jan., 1926

8. *A Vision*, 2nd edn., (Macmillan, London, 1937)

9. *Autobiographies* (Macmillan, London, 1956)

10. *Mythologies* (Macmillan, London, 1959)

11. *Essays and Introductions* (Macmillan, London, 1961)

12. *Explorations* (Macmillan, London, 1962)

(II) LETTERS AND SPEECHES

13. *Letters to the New Island* (Harvard Univ. Press, Camb., Mass., 1934)

14. *Letters on Poetry from W. B. Yeats to Dorothy Wellesley* (Oxford Univ. Press, London, 1940)

15. *J. B. Yeats, Letters to his son W. B. Yeats and Others* (Faber and Faber, London, 1944)

16. *Florence Farr, Bernard Shaw, W. B. Yeats: Letters* [Editor] Clifford Bax (Home and Von Thal, London, 1946)

17. *W. B. Yeats and T. Sturge Moore, their Correspondence*, edited by Ursula Bridge (Routledge and Kegan Paul, London, 1953)

18. *W. B. Yeats. Letters to Katharine Tynan*, edited by Roger McHugh (McMullen Books, New York, 1953)

19. *The Letters of W. B. Yeats*, edited by Allan Wade (Rupert Hart-Davis, London, 1954)

194   A SELECT READING LIST

20. *The Senate Speeches of W. B. Yeats*, edited by Donald R. Pearce (Faber and Faber, London, 1961)

(III) BIBLIOGRAPHIES,ETC.

21. *A Bibliography of the Writings of W. B. Yeats* by Allan Wade (2nd edn., revised, Rupert Hart-Davis, London, 1958)
22. *Prolegomena to the Study of Yeats's Poems* by George Brandon Saul (Univ. of Pennsylvania Press, Philadelphia, 1958)
23. *Prolegomena to the Study of Yeats's Plays* by George Brandon Saul (Univ. of Pennsylvania Press, Philadelphia, 1958)
24. *A Concordance to the Poems of W. B. Yeats*, edited by Stephen M. Parrish (Cornell Univ. Press, Ithaca, 1963)

(IV) BOOKS AND PAMPHLETS ABOUT YEATS

25. Adams, Hazard. *Blake and Yeats: The Contrary Vision* (Cornell Univ. Press, Ithaca, 1955)
26. Alspach, Russell K. *Yeats and Innisfree* (Dolmen Press, Dublin, 1965)
27. Berryman, Charles. *W. B. Yeats: Design of Opposites* (Exposition Press, New York, 1967)
28. Bjersby, Birgit. *The Interpretation of the Cuchulain Legend in the Works of W. B. Yeats* (Upsala, 1950)
29. Bradford, Curtis B. *Yeats at Work* (Southern Illinois Univ. Press, Carbondale, 1965)
30. Bushrui, S. B. *Yeats's Verse Plays. The Revisions, 1900–1910* (Clarendon Press, Oxford, 1966)
31. Chatterjee, Bhabatosh. *The Poetry of W. B. Yeats* (Orient Longmans, Calcutta, 1962)
32. Clark, David R. *W. B. Yeats and the Theatre of Desolate Reality* (Dolmen Press, Dublin, 1965)
33. Donoghue, Denis and J. R. Mulryne [Editors]. *An Honoured Guest* (Arnold, London, 1965)
34. Ellmann, Richard. *Yeats, The Man and the Masks* (Macmillan, London, 1949)
35. Ellmann, Richard. *The Identity of Yeats* (Macmillan, London, 1954)
36. Ellmann, Richard, *Eminent Domain* (Oxford University Press, New York, 1967)
37. Engelberg, Edward. *The Vast Design. Pattern in W. B. Yeats's Aesthetic* (The University of Toronto Press, Toronto, 1964)
38. Fraser, G. S. *W. B. Yeats* (Writers and their Work, no. 50, 1954; new edn., 1962)
39. Gibbon, Monk. *The Masterpiece and the Man: Yeats as I knew Him* (London, 1959)
40. Gordon, D. J. and others. *W. B. Yeats, Images of a Poet* (Manchester Univ. Press, Manchester, 1961)

41. Gurd, Patty. *The Early Poetry of W. B. Yeats* (Press of the New Era Printing Co., Lancaster, Pa., 1916)

42. Gwynn, S. L. [Editor]. *Scattering Branches* (Macmillan, London, 1940)

43. Hall, James and Steinemann, Martin [Editors]. *The Permanence of Yeats* (Macmillan, New York, 1950)

44. Harper, George M. *Yeats's Quest for Eden* (Dolmen Press, Dublin, 1966)

45. Henn, T. R. *The Lonely Tower* (Methuen, London, 1950, revised 1965)

46. Henn, T. R. *W. B. Yeats and the Poetry of War* [Warton Lecture, 1965]. (Oxford University Press, London, 1967)

47. Hoare, D. M. *The Work of Morris and Yeats in Relation to Early Saga Literature* (Cambridge Univ. Press, 1937)

48. Hone, J. M. *William Butler Yeats. The Poet in Contemporary Ireland* (Maunsel and Co., Dublin and London, 1916)

49. Hone, Joseph. *W. B. Yeats, 1865–1939* (Macmillan, London, 1942)

50. Hütteman, Gerta. *Wesen der Dichtung und Aufgabe des Dichters bei William Butler Yeats* (Bonn, 1929)

51. Ishibashi, Hiro. *Yeats and the Noh* (Dolmen Press, Dublin, 1965)

52. Jackson, Grace Emily. *Mysticism in A. E. and W. B. Yeats in Relation to Oriental and American Thought* (Ohio State University, 1932)

53. Jeffares, A. Norman. *W. B. Yeats. Man and Poet* (Routledge and Kegan Paul, London, 1949)

54. Jeffares, A. Norman. *W. B. Yeats. The Poems* (Edward Arnold, London, 1961)

55. Jeffares, Norman and K. G. W. Cross [Editors]. *In Excited Reverie: A Centenary Tribute to William Butler Yeats 1865–1939* (Macmillan, London and New York, 1965)

56. Jeffares, A. Norman. *A Commentary on the Collected Poems of W. B. Yeats* (Macmillan, London, 1968)

57. Kirby, Sheelah. *The Yeats Country* (Dolmen Press, Dublin, 1962)

58. Koch, Vivienne. *W. B. Yeats. The Tragic Phase* (Routledge and Kegan Paul, London, 1951). Reissued by Faber and Faber, London, 1967, with a foreword by Richard Ellmann

59. Krans, Horatio. *William Butler Yeats* (Heinemann, London)

60. Lister, Raymond. *Beulah to Byzantium* (Dolman Press, Dublin, 1965)

61. MacNeice, Louis. *The Poetry of W. B. Yeats* (Oxford Univ. Press, London, 1941)

62. Malins, Edward. *Yeats and the Easter Rising* (Dolmen Press, Dublin, 1965)

63. Malone, A. E. *The Irish Theatre* (Constable, London, 1929)

64. Masefield, John. *Some Memories of W. B. Yeats* (Cuala Press, Dublin, 1940)

196 A SELECT READING LIST

65. Maxwell, D. E. S. and S. B. Bushrui [Editors]. *W. B. Yeats, 1865–1965; Centenary Essays on the Art of W. B. Yeats* (Ibadan Univ. Press, Ibadan, 1965)

66. Melchiori, Giorgio. *The Whole Mystery of Art* (Routledge and Kegan Paul, London, 1960)

67. Menon, V. K. Narayana. *The Development of William Butler Yeats.* (Oliver and Boyd, Edinburgh, 1942)

68. Moore, Virginia. *The Unicorn* (Macmillan, New York, 1954)

69. Nathan, Leonard E. *The Tragic Drama of William Butler Yeats: Figures in a Dance.* (Columbia Univ. Press, New York and London, 1965)

70. O'Donnell, J. P. *Sailing to Byzantium. A Study in the Development of the Later Style and Symbolism in the Poetry of W. B. Yeats* (Harvard Univ. Press, Camb., Mass., 1939)

71. Oshima, Shotaro. *W. B. Yeats: A Study* (Taibunsha, Tokyo, 1927)

72. Oshima, Shotaro. *William Butler Yeats* (Kenkyusha, Tokyo, 1934)

73. Oshima, Shotaro. *W. B. Yeats and Japan* (Hokuseido Press, Tokyo, 1965)

74. Parkinson, T. *W. B. Yeats, Self-Critic* (Univ. of California Press, Berkeley, 1951)

75. Parkinson, T. *W. B. Yeats: the Later Poetry* (University of California Press, Berkeley, 1964)

76. Pollock, John L. *William Butler Yeats* (Duckworth, London, 1935)

77. Reid, B. L. *William Butler Yeats. The Lyric of Tragedy* (Univ. of Oklahoma Press, Norman, 1961)

78. Reid, Forrest. *W. B. Yeats: a Critical Study* (Secker, London, 1915)

79. Ronsley, Joseph. *Yeats's Autobiography* (Harvard University Press, Camb. Mass., 1968)

80. Rudd, M. *Divided Image* (Routledge and Kegan Paul, London, 1953)

81. Salvadori, Corinna. *Yeats and Castiglione* (A. Figgis, Dublin, 1965)

82. Saul, George B. *In —— Luminous Wind* (Dolmen Press, Dublin, 1966)

83. Seiden, Morton Irving. *William Butler Yeats. The Poet as Mythmaker* (Michigan State University Press, 1963)

84. Skelton, Robin and Ann Saddlemyer [Editors]. *The World of W. B. Yeats* (Adelphi Bookshop for the University of Victoria, 1965)

85. Smith, Arthur J. M. *Poet Young and Old—W. B. Yeats* (Univ. of Toronto Press, 1939)

86. Stallworthy, Jon. *Between the Lines* (The Clarendon Press, Oxford, 1963)

87. Stallworthy, Jon. [Editor]. *Yeats's 'Last Poems'* (Macmillan, London, 1968)

88. Stauffer, Donald A. *The Golden Nightingale* (Macmillan, New York, 1949)

89. Stock, A. G. *W. B. Yeats. His Poetry and Thought* (Cambridge University Press, Cambridge, 1961)

90. Strong, L. A. G. *A Letter to W. B. Yeats* (Leonard and Virginia Woolf, London, 1937)

91. Telfer, Giles W. L. *Yeats's Idea of the Gael* (Dolmen Press, Dublin, 1965)

92. Tindall, William Y. *W. B. Yeats* (Columbia University Press, New York, 1966)

93. Torchiana, Donald. *Yeats and Georgian England* (Northwestern University Press, Evanston, 1966)

94. Unterecker, John. *A Reader's Guide to W. B. Yeats* (Thames and Hudson, London, 1959)

95. Unterecker, John [Editor]. *Yeats. A Collection of Critical Essays* (Prentice Hall, New Jersey, 1963)

96. Ure, Peter. *Towards a Mythology* (University Press of Liverpool; Hodder and Stoughton, London, 1946)

97. Ure, Peter. *Yeats the Playwright* (Routledge and Kegan Paul, London, 1963)

98. Ure, Peter. *Yeats* (Writers and Critics, Oliver and Boyd, Edinburgh, 1963)

99. Vendler, Helen Hennessy. *Yeats's Vision and the Later Plays* (Harvard Univ. Press, Camb., Mass., 1963)

100. Whitaker, Thomas R. *Swan and Shadow: Yeats's Dialogue with History* (University of North Carolina Press, Chapel Hill, 1964)

101. Wilson, F. A. C. *W. B. Yeats and Tradition* (Gollancz, London, 1958)

102. Wilson, F. A. C. *Yeats's Iconography* (Gollancz, London, 1960)

103. Winters, Yvor. *The Poetry of W. B. Yeats* (Allan Swallow, Denver, n.d.)

104. Wrenn, C. L. *W. B. Yeats: a Literary Study* (T. Murby and Co., London, 1920)

105. Zwerdling, Alex. *Yeats and the Heroic Ideal* (New York Univ. Press, New York, 1965)
  [See also the Yeats memorial number of *The Southern Review* and the Yeats Centenary numbers of *The Dublin Magazine, Hermathena* and *Tri-Quarterly*]

(v) BOOKS PARTIALLY ABOUT YEATS

106. Alvarez, A. *The Shaping Spirit* (Chatto and Windus, London, 1958)

107. Barnes, T. R. *English Verse: Voice and Movement from Wyatt to Yeats* (Cambridge University Press, Cambridge, 1967)

108. Bayley, John. *The Romantic Survival* (Constable, London, 1957)

109. Blackmur, R. P. *Language as Gesture* (Harcourt Brace, New York, 1952)

110. Bowra, C. M. *The Heritage of Symbolism* (Macmillan, London, 1943)

111. Bronowski, J. *The Poet's Defence* (Cambridge University Press, Cambridge 1939)

112. Brooks, Cleanth. *Modern Poetry and the Tradition* (Univ. of North Carolina Press, Chapel Hill, 1939)

113. Brooks, Cleanth. *The Well Wrought Urn* (Reynal and Hitchcock, New York, 1947)

114. Brooks, Cleanth. *The Hidden God* (Yale Univ. Press, New Haven, 1963)

115. Bullough, Geoffrey. *The Trend of Modern Poetry* (Oliver and Boyd, London, 2nd edn., 1941)

116. Cornwell, Ethel F. *The Still Point* (Rutgers Univ. Press, New Brunswick, 1963)

117. Daiches, David. *Poetry and the Modern World* (Univ. of Chicago Press, Chicago, 1939)

118. Deutsch, Babette. *This Modern Poetry* (Faber and Faber, London, 1936)

119. Donoghue, Denis. *The Third Voice* (Princeton Univ. Press, Princeton, 1959)

120. Ellis-Fermor, Una. *The Irish Dramatic Movement* (Methuen, London, 1939)

121. Ford, Boris [Editor]. *The Modern Age* (Penguin Books, Harmondsworth, 1961)

122. Fraser, G. S. *Vision and Rhetoric in Modern Poetry* (Faber and Faber, London, 1959)

123. Frye, Northrop. *Fables of Identity* (Harcourt Brace, New York, 1963)

124. Goodwin, K. L. *The Influence of Ezra Pound* (Oxford University Press, New York, 1967)

125. Gowda, H. H. Anniah. *The Revival of English Poetic Drama* (Bangalore, 1963)

126. Harrison, John. *The Reactionaries: Yeats, Lewis, Pound, Eliot, Lawrence* (Schocken, New York, 1967)

127. Henn, T. R. *The Harvest of Tragedy* (Methuen, London, 1956)

128. Hoffman, Daniel. *Barbarous Knowledge—Myth in the Poetry of Yeats, Graves and Muir* (Oxford University Press, New York, 1967)

129. Hough, Graham. *The Last Romantics* (Duckworth, London, 1947)

130. Kermode, Frank. *Romantic Image* (Routledge and Kegan Paul, London, 1957)

131. Knights, L. C. *Explorations* (Chatto and Windus, London, 1946)

132. Leavis, F. R. *New Bearings in English Poetry* (Chatto and Windus, London, 1932, new edn. 1950)

133. Lentricchia, Frank. *The Gaiety of Language. An Essay on the Radical Poetics of W. B. Yeats and Wallace Stevens* (University of California Press, 1968)

134. Loftus, Richard J. *Nationalism in Modern Anglo-Irish Poetry* (University of Wisconsin Press, Madison and Milwaukee, 1964)

135. Lucas, F. L. *The Drama of Chekhov, Synge, Yeats and Pirandello* (Cassell, London, 1963)

136. Macleish, Archibald. *Poetry and Experience* (The Bodley Head, London, 1961)

137. Marreco, Ann. *The Rebel Countess: The Life and Times of Constance Markievicz* (Weidenfeld and Nicolson, London, 1967)

138. Miller, J. Hillis. *Poets of Reality: Six Twentieth Century Writers* (Harvard University Press, Camb., Mass., 1966)

139. Miner, Earl. *The Japanese Tradition in British and American Literature* (Princeton Univ. Press, Princeton, 1938)

140. Muir, Edwin. *The Estate of Poetry* (Hogarth Press, London, 1962)

141. Peacock, Ronald. *The Poet in the Theatre* (Routledge and Kegan Paul, London, 1946)

142. Read, Herbert. *A Coat of Many Colours* (Routledge and Kegan Paul, London, 1945)

143. Rosenthal, M. L. *The Modern Poets* (Oxford University Press, New York, 1960)

144. Shapiro, Karl. *In Defence of Ignorance* (Random House, New York, 1960)

145. Shaw, Priscilla W. *Valery, Yeats and Rilke* (Rutgers Univ. Press, New Brunswick, 1964)

146. Skelton, R. *The Poetic Pattern* (Routledge, London, 1956)

147. Stead, C. K. *The New Poetic* (Hutchinson, London, 1964)

148. Stewart, J. I. M. *Eight Modern Writers* (Oxford History of English Lit., Vol. XII; Clarendon Press, Oxford, 1963)

149. Tindall, William Y. *Forces in Modern Literature* (Knopf, New York, 1947)

150. Tindall, William Y. *The Literary Symbol* (Indiana Univ. Press, Bloomington, 1960)

151. Tschumi, Raymond. *Thought in Twentieth Century Poetry* (Routledge, London, 1951)

152. Ueda, Makoto. *Zeami, Basho, Yeats, Pound: A Study in Japanese and English Poetics* (Mouton, The Hague, 1965)

153. Ussher, Arland. *Three Great Irishmen* (Gollancz, London, 1952)

154. Wain, John [Editor]. *Interpretations* (Routledge, London, 1955)

155. Wilson, Edmund. *Axel's Castle* (Scribner, New York)

156. Williams, Raymond. *Drama from Ibsen to Eliot* (Chatto and Windus, London, 1954)

157. Wright, George T. *The Poet in the Poem* (Univ. of California Press, Berkeley, 1961)

General Index

201

O'Higgins, Kevin, 138
O'Leary, John, 28, 72, 73
O'Neill, Maire, 50

Parkinson, Thomas F., 39, 41, 58
Parnell, Charles Stewart, 71, 73, 152
Pater, Walter, 94, 133
Patrick, St., 17, 26
Pearse, Padraic, 77
Phidias, 86, 129, 177, 183
Plato, 127, 128, 134
Plotinus, 127, 128, 150, 151
Plutarch, 135
Pollexfen, George, 70, 109
Porphyry, 141, 151
Pound, Ezra, 70, 89, 92, 105, 158
Proclus, 131
Purohit Swami, Shri, 163
Pythagoras, 135

Racine, Jean, 60
Reid, B. L., 111, 130, 131
Robartes, Michael, 19, 38, 114–16
Ronsard, Pierre de, 30
Rossetti, Dante Gabriel, 166
Russell, George (*alias* AE), 40, 45, 47, 50

Sartre, Jean-Paul, 110
Sato, Junzo, 12, 138
Saul, George Brandon, 134–5
Savage, D. S., 18
Shakespeare, Olivia, 74, 90, 137, 147, 148, 149, 158
Shakespeare, William, 14, 60, 89, 94, 105, 184
Sharp, William, 152
Shawe-Taylor, John, 141
Shelley, Percy Bysshe, 21, 29, 39, 132, 133
Sidney, Sir Philip, 14, 109
Spengler, Oswald, 89

Spenser, Edmund, 21, 29, 133
Stallworthy, Jon, 31, 66, 121, 144
Stauffer, Donald, 146, 148
Stevens, Wallace, 43
Stewart, J. I. M., 152
Strong, Eugenie, 143, 144
Strong, L. A. G., 89
Swedenborg, Emmanuel, 82, 154
Swift, Jonathan, 140
Symons, Arthur, 41, 130
Synge, John, 50, 60, 67, 71, 109, 141

Tate, Allen, 92
Tertullian, 166
Thomas, Dylan, 124
Tindall, William Y., 135, 151
Tone, Wolfe Theobald, 72, 77
Tynan, Katherine, 19, 20, 21, 23

Unterecker, John, 18, 70, 137
Ure, Peter, 12, 24, 61, 104, 144, 166, 168

Vendler, Helen, 132, 144, 145, 158
Virgil, 131
Von Hügel, Baron Friedrich, 147

Wain, John, 135
Waste Land, The, 96, 105
Wellesley, Dorothy, 163, 171, 176, 185
Wilde, Oscar, 103, 161
Wilson, F. A. C., 97, 99, 103, 105, 152, 158, 163, 177, 182, 183

Yeats, Jervis, 70
Yeats, John, 70
Yeats, W. B.:
    Absurd, sense of, 128, 135, 163

Index to Yeats' Work